AN OPEN BOOK
THE PAUL LAWRIE STORY

PAUL LAWRIE WITH JOHN HUGGAN

AN OPEN BOOK
THE PAUL LAWRIE STORY

PAUL LAWRIE WITH JOHN HUGGAN

First published in Great Britain in 2012 by The Derby Books Publishing Company Limited,
3 The Parker Centre, Derby, DE21 4SZ.

Printed and bound by Gomer Press, Llandysul Ceredigion.

ISBN 978-1-7809-103-45

This book is dedicated to my wife Marian

And to the memory of my dear friend and coach, Adam Hunter

Contents

Acknowledgements & Thanks

So many people have helped me along the way, but no one more than Stewart Spence. In fact, these few words can only begin to convey the depth of the gratitude I feel for a man who has been by my side for all of my adult life. I've never had to worry about where to go for the sound advice we all need at various times in our careers. Thank you Stewart.

To my parents, Jim and Margaret, go my thanks for the kind of sound and sensible upbringing every child deserves. I never wanted for anything important when I was young.

To my older brother, Stephen. Thanks for those two lifts to the airport. I guess we will never know now if Dad was right about how, if you had only stuck in a little more at the golf, you would have been even better than me!

To my parents in-law, Bert and Lottie, who live with us and look after us so well. Thank you for doing all the jobs you want to do – and all the ones I don't – especially on and around the chipping green and the garden.

To Colin Fraser, my first ever sponsor and still today my best friend. Thanks for always telling me what I need to hear and not what I want to, thanks pal.

To Martin Gilbert, my great friend and business advisor for many years. Thank you for all the laughs we have shared as long-time partners at the Dunhill Links Championship (especially when you are chipping – ha ha). Seriously, you have been magic for me in so many ways.

To the late Doug Smart, my first boss at Banchory Golf Club. No one ever had a better employer, one who gave me the benefit of his experience and knowledge and, most of all, his friendship.

To the guys, Marcus Day (LT1) and Jamie Evans (LT2) at 4Sports, my management group, thanks for your time and continuing efforts guys.

To Philip Barker, my accountant for a number of years I long ago lost track of. Thank you for your expertise and advice, even when I didn't want to hear it!

To Peter and Anne Lloyd go my grateful thanks for all the help you gave a young man trying to make his way in professional golf.

To Davie Wilson, thanks for being first my taxi-driver and second my first companion on the road.

To all and every sponsor of myself and the Paul Lawrie Foundation, my eternal thanks for all you have done to help us along the way. We couldn't have achieved anything without you.

And finally, to John Huggan, my ghostwriter on this book, thanks pal, even if you weren't my first choice. Or even my second, come to think of it.

Foreword

by Sir Alex Ferguson

Everyone remembers that incredible Open Championship at Carnoustie in 1999 when Paul Lawrie took advantage of Jean Van de Velde's late mistake to win the four-hole play-off against the Frenchman and Justin Leonard of the United States. Well, maybe not 'everyone', but without question every Scotsman celebrated Paul's victory. His was a fantastic performance, one that realised the ultimate dream for every professional and made him the 'champion golfer of the year'.

I have known Paul since he was a young lad, through his progress through the golfing ranks in his native Aberdeenshire and also for his life-long love of my old team, Aberdeen FC. I've got to know him even better over the last few years, when he has come down to Old Trafford with his two sons. It always refreshes my hopes for young people when I see that Paul is a down-to-earth, feet-on-the-ground, well-mannered individual. It is sometimes difficult to cope with success, but Paul has handled all that comes with winning the biggest prize in his sport with a great deal of humility. He is a credit to both his family and the game of golf.

Of course, after Carnoustie he had to deal with the great expectations that come with victory in a major championship. And, although he hasn't won another since, he still plays his golf at an incredibly high standard. His wins at the Qatar Masters in February 2012 and the Johnnie Walker Championship in August 2012 – and his subsequent qualification for the European Ryder Cup squad – testify to not only his skill but his persistence.

When I think about it, 1999 was actually a pretty special time for we Scots. Paul lifted his first Open title and I won my first European Champions League Final in Barcelona against Bayern Munich. So it was a not-to-be forgotten few months for both of us. We will surely be the answer to a sports-quiz question in coming years!

It is a pleasure to pen the foreword to this book, one that will take you through the wide range of emotions felt by a golfer at the top end of the game. Finding out how he prepares for tournaments, copes with all the travel, misses his family for long periods and deals with the never-ending pressure to win makes for a great read. That, in fact, is the area I am most interested in. For me, it is always fascinating to hear how other sportsmen go about their jobs.

It is a privilege to have known the friendship of Paul and his family. I wish him every success with this autobiography.

Sir Alex Ferguson CBE

How I Won The Open

The weird thing is, I can't even remember the line.

Standing over the putt every wee boy hits millions of times on practice greens all over the world – 'this for the Open' – my mind was on technique, not the fact that my world was about to change forever.

Or that I was going to win the biggest event in the game to which I have dedicated my life.

Or that I was a few minutes away from lifting the most famous trophy in golf, the Old Claret Jug.

Or that millions of people across the globe had, at that very moment, their eyes trained on me.

Or even what my wife, Marian, and two boys must have been feeling as they watched me, Paul Lawrie, a wee laddie from Kemnay near Aberdeen, instantly transformed from European Tour journeyman into major champion.

No. Nothing like that was going on between my ears, even when a wasp or a bee or a fly – whatever it was – buzzing around my head made me briefly back away from the ball.

'Low and hold,' was all I was thinking; 'low' on the way back, 'hold' at the finish. Looking back now, I'm proud of that. Along with my coach, Adam Hunter, I had spent many long hours working on those two simple keys and when the time came – when it really mattered on the 18th green at Carnoustie, 18th July 1999 – I was ready.

As the ball dropped into the cup – dead centre incidentally – I raised my arms in the air and said, not loud enough for anyone else to hear: 'Yes, ya fucker.' Which is so strange. Profanity is not something I'm in the habit of using in the immediate aftermath of a tournament victory. I had certainly never said anything like that before – and I haven't since.

Of course, in my defence, it was the end of a very long and highly stressful week, one that, whatever else I go on to achieve on a golf course, will forever define my life and career. And yes, for the record, I know as well as everyone else that I got lucky. There is no question in my mind that Jean Van de Velde should have won. No question at all. But the facts are the facts: however unfortunate he may have been, Jean did make a triple-bogey on the 72nd hole. And I did win the play-off – comfortably, as it turned out.

So before you ask: No, I didn't think I was going to win the Open either. How could I? You don't start the final day of any tournament, never mind a major championship, 10 shots off the lead and tee-off with any great level of expectation. To be honest, my main aim setting out was to do enough to make the following year's Masters – a top-four finish – and consolidate my position in the upcoming European Ryder Cup team.

Only a few days earlier, of course, even that relatively modest level of ambition seemed unlikely at best. Although I was having a pretty successful season and had won the Qatar Masters a few months previously, not even my closest pals or family members would have picked me out as the next Open champion. Besides, I wasn't even in the event until three days before the off. What people often forget is that I wasn't exempt for the '99 Open; I had to pre-qualify along the road from Carnoustie at Downfield in Dundee (where I had won the Scottish PGA Masters in 1995) on the Sunday and Monday before the championship.

My qualifying performance is one more thing that has passed into the realm of myth and legend. I've heard it said that I holed out a 9-iron on the final hole to make it through with nothing to spare. Or that I birdied the last five holes to squeeze in. But the fact is, after playing the last eight holes in two under par, I qualified with a couple of shots to spare.

Which left me with an immediate problem. Where to stay? I tried the Carnoustie hotel but that was full, as were all the bed and breakfast places I called. In the end, I decided to commute every day from Aberdeen. So it was back up the road for me on the Monday evening and a day off on Tuesday.

I've told people that before and they are always surprised. I didn't go to the golf course with only two full days of practice available? No, I didn't. I knew Carnoustie well from my days on the Tartan Tour and had played it many times. So there was no need to rush down there, a fact that I feel actually worked in my favour.

Like everyone else, I had never seen Carnoustie set up the way it was that week. There was rough almost everywhere and not much fairway to be found. I could almost hear the moans and groans from the players from my house 60 miles up the coast. And, to be honest, when I got there on the Wednesday morning, I felt pretty much the same way. My opinion was that the course – one of the most difficult in the world even with no rough –

didn't need any 'tricking up'. It's a wonderful test of golf but that week it was definitely 'over the top'.

So, as it turned out, one day of on-site preparation was ample. Had I gone down there 24 hours earlier than I did, I would have run the risk of letting the way the links was presented get into my head, as it surely did for so many other players. As all golfers know, once you get into a negative frame of mind about a course it is hard to shake that notion, but I never had a problem at any time during the week.

A huge amount of the credit for that, as for so much of my success over the years, must go to Adam. He was with me every step of the way during my practice round and it was he who cultivated my philosophy for the week. Mostly, I did what I always do; I worked out which club to hit from every tee and came up with a general game plan for all 18-holes.

There was one big difference though. To this day I can hear Adam saying this over and over: 'If you do go into the rough, which will happen, you must get the ball back in play as soon as possible. If there is a choice to be made – go for something ambitious or chip it out to the fairway – you need to take the safe option. If you don't make a double-bogey this week, you're going to have a chance to win.'

That's exactly what he told me. And you know what? Only two players, Justin Leonard and myself, didn't make a double all week. It is amazing how accurate and prescient Adam was. Over and over, he kept drumming into me that everyone would be getting pissed off and how I must stay calm no matter what happened. He wasn't just a coach; he was a psychologist too.

In fact, back then, many people felt that Adam was over-coaching me. But that was never the case. Yes, he had travelled with me a lot since we started working together late in 1998, but he never did much coaching at tournaments. He was there as much to keep me company as anything else. I liked having him there in the evenings for dinner and maybe a beer.

Which is not to say that he and I hadn't done a power of work together over the previous nine months or so. In fact, almost from the moment he first wrote to me saying he was going to retire from playing – he had won on the European Tour at the Portuguese Open – Adam had transformed my practice habits. I had gone from struggling to see a way ahead with my swing to having a structured and disciplined plan about what I was trying to achieve on the course.

Adam's view was that I had always had the short game to compete on the tour – hence my nickname 'Chippy'. And length was not really a problem either; I've always been long enough off the tee. But I really didn't have a clear picture of my swing in a technical sense. Which was the biggest reason why I had always struggled with a driver in my hands. Way too often I was hitting my second shot from somewhere other than the fairway.

Straight away, Adam made my practice more regimented. Suddenly, I was doing drills to instill the correct feeling in my action. I wasn't just aimlessly hitting 60-70 balls then heading off to play. I would be hitting balls yes, but now those balls would be split into groups of six. Four would be hit with technique in mind; the other two as if I was on the course. And as I got nearer to a tournament, that split would be one technical, five as if on the course. I had never experienced anything like that before, where my practice was geared to playing rather than just hitting.

Anyway, all of that had an almost immediate impact on me. I say 'almost' for a reason. After having a knee operation at the end of 1998 I returned to the tour in Dubai early in '99 and straight away missed the cut with two poor scores, 76 and 78. Then the following week I won in Qatar, breaking 70 in all four rounds.

That was unbelievable to me. How could I go from not playing or practising, to playing two awful rounds, to winning, just like that? And the reason was simple: Adam.

That conclusion was to become even clearer to me at Carnoustie. Over the course of the week, Adam was brilliant. Every day he would say something that struck a chord in me. It's no coincidence that the one poor round I had en route to winning the Open was the 76 I shot on day three – when he wasn't with me.

Nowhere, however, did Adam get 'into' my head more effectively than when we were sitting on a buggy being driven out to the 15th tee to start the play-off with Van de Velde and Leonard. He could tell that I was a bit edgy; who wouldn't be in that situation? So he looked me in the eye and said: 'I want you to do one thing for me when you get to the tee. I want you to look at Jean and I want you to look at Justin. Have a good look at them. Have a good look at their faces.'

So I did. And right away I could see that Leonard was 'gone'. His face was pure white. Which made sense. On paper, he was the best player on that tee and so had the most to lose. He was supposed to win and clearly that knowledge was not helping him one little bit.

As for Van de Velde, he had lost his cap in the recording area and was walking around with a policeman's hat on. He was laughing and joking. But I could see right away that he was 'hiding' from what must have been a traumatic last hole. He gave me a bit of a nod when I arrived and I thought, 'you're gone'. All because of Adam's clear thinking.

Still, a lot happened between my practice round on Wednesday morning and the play-off on Sunday evening. As you can imagine, I've been asked about it all a million times, so it makes sense to run you through what I can recall from those amazing few days.

Okay, don't laugh at this point. As far as the first three rounds are concerned – 73-74-76 – my only real memory is of getting really hacked off over the back nine on Saturday afternoon. I know I played with Luke Donald over the first 36-holes but the third member of the group is a mystery to me. In fact, I had to look up my first two rounds to see what I had shot. A good memory is not part of the Lawrie make-up!

I had started that third day five over par and in good shape, I thought, to kick on over the next 18 holes. But it didn't happen. Playing with Korean K.J. Choi – I remember him – I stumbled around and finished up 10 over for the tournament.

That was bad enough, but what was really annoying me was the thought I had blown my chance of making the two-man Scotland World Cup side. It was going to be picked right after the Open and, as things stood after three rounds, Andrew Coltart was going to be joining Colin Montgomerie on the team. I can remember turning to my caddie, Paddy Byrne, on the 16th hole and saying, 'well, that's the World Cup gone then'.

At that moment, I wasn't thinking about winning the Open. The World Cup had been my second biggest goal for the week after the Ryder Cup and, as I saw it, I had blown my chances. To say I wasn't happy when I arrived back in Aberdeen on the Saturday evening would be an understatement.

The next morning, however, I wasn't thinking about anything in particular as I sat with Marian and the boys at breakfast. It was just like any other day really, as I jumped in the car after kissing them all goodbye. On the way down the road – after picking up my brother-in-law, Gary – my thoughts did wander though. I still wasn't considering victory from 10 shots back, but I was in something like 13th place, close enough to fourth and a guaranteed spot in the 2000 Masters. That was definitely on my mind when we arrived in Carnoustie.

As you can imagine, my pre-round warm-up was pretty much routine.

And again, my memory for detail is not great. My fellow European Tour pro Dean Robertson says he came out of the recording area as I was standing on the first tee. He shook my hand apparently and wished me good luck. But I remember none of that!

What I do recall is that I putted really well that day. You have to if you are going to shoot 67 on that golf course. But I can still remember only maybe four or five of the 18 holes. On the short eighth I know I holed a good putt for birdie to go two under for the day. The pin was back-left and I hit the green front-right, holing from maybe 35 feet for the two.

At the 12th I hit an awesome 4-iron from the edge of the left rough to about three feet from the flag. That was a huge birdie and a real bonus on one of the toughest holes on the course. I gave that shot back immediately though, pulling my tee-shot at the short 13th into sand and failing to get up and down.

Another birdie came along at the long 14th, the famous 'Spectacles' hole. Again I pulled my approach, but this time I got down in two off the bank to the left of the green. And at that point I was seven over for the championship. Good, but still not what I thought was a winning score.

I knew I was doing well though. You always do in a tournament, even when you can't see a scoreboard. Suddenly, the crowd gets bigger and cameramen start appearing. So you know you are in with a shout. It's not hard to work it out.

The birdie I needed over the last four holes came at the 17th. I holed a really good putt there, from maybe 20 feet. Then, off the last tee, I pulled my drive just enough that it made the left rough, where it found a poor lie.

Standing at the ball, Paddy and I were going back and forth on what to do. At first, we were going to lay-up short of the Barry Burn and try to make par with a pitch and a putt. The lie really was pretty poor. I felt like I could get maybe one ball in 10 on the green from where I was. Not great odds.

But I decided to go for it. 'We might not have this chance again,' I said to Paddy. 'I can't see seven over par or even six having a shot to win. We really need to make a birdie.'

That made sense at the time. Van de Velde was something like two or three over par with only a few holes to go. I could see him coming back to five over, maybe six, but no more than that.

So I hit a 5-iron. I gave it a good clatter too. But it didn't come out too well and didn't even make it to the burn on the fly. What it did do, however, was land short of the water and bounce over it – an enormous piece of good luck – before finishing in a greenside bunker. The ball was up against the front lip and it was a reasonably long way to the hole, but I knocked it out to maybe four feet – a lovely shot – and made the putt for par. I was in at 290, six over par, and if I'm honest, thinking that's not quite good enough. Along with, I suspect, the rest of the golfing world, I really thought Jean would get in at better than six over.

In passing, not too many people remember that fortunate part of my final-day story. But I know one who does. At a tournament in China maybe eight years later, I had shot a decent score and was being driven past the practice green en route to the clubhouse. I was leading and the wind, much to my glee, was getting up. On the green waiting to go out were my fellow Scots, Stephen Gallacher and Colin Montgomerie, and, as you do, I made a smart, jokey comment about the rising breeze as I passed by.

'Huh,' said Monty. 'He jumped the burn you know. He jumped the burn when he won.' So he had not forgotten!

Back in 1999, I signed my card and headed to the player's lounge with Adam for something to eat. We sat in the tent and watched on television. When we saw Jean bogey the 12th to go to, I think, three over par, Adam told me to go to the range and hit some balls. 'There's bogeys out there,' he said. 'You need to be ready just in case.'

So I went and hit some balls. Paddy was in the hut by the range where there was a wee television so that he could keep an eye on what was happening. I wandered over to the chipping green and spent maybe half an hour there. At this point Adam and I were just chatting, normal stuff. Certainly, we weren't working on anything technical. It was just shooting the breeze.

Looking back, of course, Adam was actually taking my mind off the situation and keeping me occupied. Now and again, he would check on what was happening and he told Paddy to let us know when Jean teed off on the 18th. 'Then we'll go in,' he said.

Paddy gave us a shout and we watched Jean drive off at the last. He was three over par on the tee. He hit it well right but the ball landed on dry land. At that point we headed back to the clubhouse on a buggy. The BBC compound was on the left of the first tee and you had to walk through it to get to the clubhouse. As we arrived, the broadcaster Dougie Donnelly motioned us over. 'You'll want to have a look at this,' he said.

As we were driving back, Jean hit his second shot, the ball rebounding off the grandstand back over the water and into very heavy rough. From there, he pitched it into the burn. Immediately, Adam said, 'Right, let's go. Let's go and do some putting. He's not going to be involved in this. It's going to be the two of you in a play-off.' Which was the one thing Adam got wrong all day.

At this point I wasn't thinking nearly so clearly. 'Bloody hell, it's the play-off for the Open.' That's what was actually going through my head. At first anyway. That this was going to be a great opportunity to win the biggest tournament in the world was the next thing in there. I know this sounds odd and maybe a bit bigheaded, but I had always thought that, given the way I play and the type of golf I like, I would have at least one chance to win an Open in my life. And this was going to be the first of those.

Eventually, Jean made what was a great triple-bogey, getting up and down from a bunker and holing from maybe eight feet, to get into the play-off. So there were three of us. On the buggy on the way out – before Adam got talking – I was nervous. Not panicking, but nervous. I wasn't bothered about how I would play, but I didn't want to make double-bogey on every hole either. I would have hated that; in Scottish parlance I would have been left totally 'scunnered'.

As soon as Adam gave me his advice about looking at the faces of the other guys, I was fine. 'You know what,' I said to myself. 'I'm going to win this.' It was amazing how calm I became. And it was a masterstroke by Adam. It was what won it for me. I got to the tee and, as I said earlier, Leonard was in a terrible state and Van de Velde was all over the place.

Not surprisingly, I was the only one who hit a decent drive off that 15th tee. Leonard was behind me and Van de Velde was in the bushes on the left. He took forever to drop after declaring his ball unplayable. I was standing in the fairway with a television camera in my face. They panned right in on me. But I was perfectly calm. I just stood there. I wasn't agitated by anything that was going on. In fact, I was dead calm. It was an amazing feeling; almost knowing I was going to win.

The 15th was actually playing a lot more difficult than it had earlier. The wind had switched completely, so what had been a 5-iron off the tee short of the fairway bunker was now a driver. Van de Velde took six and Leonard and I both made five.

At the 16th I found the right-hand bunker with a 3-iron from the tee. The other two went left of the green on what is an incredibly hard hole. And we all made four in the end. I missed from six feet after a lovely bunker shot. I still don't know how that ball didn't go in. But it didn't.

So it was still all to play for. And, with the 17th now downwind, I hit a 2-iron down the right side, which is the preferred spot. Leonard went left near the burn. And Van de Velde followed me. He then hit a nice approach to maybe 25-feet. I was maybe a yard inside him after an equally good shot. Leonard hit his ball onto the front edge from the bank of the burn.

After Justin two-putted for par, Jean made his putt for a three. At which point he looked over at me and made a fist-pump type gesture. I then followed him in and gave him some of his own medicine. I wasn't sure if he was serious at first, but we both had a bit of a giggle as we went to the next tee. So it was fine and, more importantly, I was one shot ahead of both my opponents.

The 18th hole, into the wind, was playing really long by the time we got there. It was also raining heavily. A typical summer's evening in Scotland in other words! I hit my driver because I had to. I was actually shaking a little. Not nervous, more excited. It was a bit like going to the dentist; I just wanted it over with. And when it was, my ball was right down the middle of the fairway. I ripped it.

Van de Velde pulled his tee-shot left and, rather ironically, chipped his ball down the fairway. If he had done that earlier, he would probably have won. But we will never know for sure. Leonard's drive was fine, but short of mine. I didn't think he could carry the burn from where he was, in fact. I was 221-yards from the hole and he must have been 25 yards behind me.

Justin had to have a go though. He was one behind and he knew I could reach in two. When he hit it, I didn't see his ball finish. But both Paddy and I saw it bounce. We actually thought it had hopped into the bunker, but we really had no idea where it had gone.

For all that, there wasn't a moment when I thought I should play safe with my second shot. Even if Justin was in the bunker, he could still make four. So I felt like I had to make a par to be sure of winning. Using a 4-iron, I aimed at the right edge of the Rolex clock on the hotel. My only swing thought was the one I've used practically all my career: 'Slow away.'

I absolutely flushed the shot. It pitched maybe halfway between the burn and the green and ran up to about four feet. When Paddy and I got to the green the rain was even heavier. And because I had been under the brolly the whole way, I hadn't actually looked to see where Justin had finished. It wasn't until he shouted to me to get out of the way that I realised he had been in the burn and had taken a drop. He probably thought I was taking the piss but I wasn't. Honest mate.

After Justin pitched up and Jean made five, I knew I had won. In fact, I had that thought walking to the green. Even if Justin had been in the bunker and had then holed out for a three, I still had a short putt to win. Paddy was revving up the crowd by that time. He was doing the cheerleader thing. But it still felt like an eternity waiting for the other two to play. I just wanted it over with. I wanted to hole the putt and get out of there, back to Marian.

Eventually, it was my turn. Just a four-footer. Then came the buzzing insect. On the tape you can hear a guy saying, 'Get on with it!' So I did. Once I was back in my routine, I got on with it, the same way I did in practice. And in it went.

Just wish I could remember the line. Next time I will.

And Being Open Champion

Becoming the 'champion golfer of the year' – which is what the R&A like to call the winner of the Open – was obviously the highlight of my career at the time. It still is. But there is more to holding that title than just going out and playing away as you did before. A lot more. So, while I was ready to take on that sort of mantle in a golfing sense, everything else about my new and elevated status in the game came as a bit of a shock to the system. While I knew that I was going to have to cope with a bit more of the 'celebrity' stuff that comes with being a major champion, the sheer extent of it all did knock me back a bit.

It didn't take long to get going either. In fact, as soon as I made that four-foot putt to win, my life changed as if by magic.

The first few moments of my reign are, as you can imagine, a bit of a blur. I can recall shaking hands with Jean and Justin. And I'm sure they must have said something along the lines of 'well done'. But I never really took any of it in. I certainly didn't say much to them. Had it happened now, when I'm a bit more experienced, I think I would have found something appropriate to say, especially to Jean. But back then I didn't. To be honest, how they were feeling was the last thing on my mind.

I know that sounds terrible. But that is the way it was. And in my defence it's a tricky situation, one where it is difficult to say and do exactly the right things at exactly the right moments. Months later, for example, I was on a television show, McCoist and Macaulay, where Ally McCoist asked me, 'Did you feel sorry for Van de Velde?' My response was a mildly sarcastic and drawn out, 'Yeah.' People laughed. And on the outside I did too. But I was never really comfortable making fun of what went on. And I'm still not. Like every other golfer, I have some sympathy for Jean and what he went through on that last hole.

To be fair though, I wasn't rude to either of the guys I had just beaten. I didn't shout and scream and celebrate right in their faces. I would never be that unprofessional, unlike a certain English player I could mention.

In the Italian Open of 2002 I played the last round with Ian Poulter. I was one ahead playing the 18th but drove way right out-of-bounds. I had driven it great all week. So who knows where that shot came from? But the ball went off on a weird tangent, 50 yards from where I was aiming. I eventually made a six and Ian made a three. So he won by two. That's fine. I can handle that. Golf is a hard game to play sometimes. As I'm sure you have heard a million times, we lose a lot more often than we win. So you do get used to it. But I did think his fist pumping and shouting and bawling on the green was disrespectful to me as an opponent.

Speaking of which, various levels of disrespect were things I was going to have to get used to during my time as Open champion – of which much more later. Of course, I hadn't helped myself during the play-off. Coming up the 18th hole I had scratched at a wee spot on my forehead and it had started to bleed. I dabbed at it with a towel but it wouldn't stop. On the telly Peter Alliss thought I was either crying or wiping sweat away. But it was neither of those things. How embarrassing!

Anyway, the prize giving was next. I wish now that my speech had been better than it was. It wasn't bad exactly, but I'd make a better job of it today, put it that way. I remember listening to Padraig Harrington when he won at Birkdale in 2008. His speech was much slicker than the one he made the year before. So you learn as you go. You are smarter 12 months on, a better person. But I didn't have that advantage. I wish I had said more than I did and I wish I had mentioned Jean and Justin. But my head was spinning at that point.

Next stop was the media centre. That went well enough apart from one thing I wished I could have taken back as soon as the words left my mouth. When someone asked me what I was going to do with the money, I said: 'I'm going to have me a Ferrari.' That was a mistake. I should never have said that. It sounded arrogant and not like me at all.

Again though, it is easy for me – and others – to be harsh in retrospect. At that stage of my career I had not spent a lot of time with the media. I was a decent player, but winning a major was as much a surprise to me as it was to anyone else. I wasn't a Rory McIlroy or a Tiger Woods, someone who had been groomed his whole life for success at the highest level. I just wasn't like that and didn't have that experience. So I was a little naïve.

Still my obligations were not over. From the media centre I was ushered into the R&A Tent, where I had to mingle with the members and their gin and tonics for about an hour or so. I remember saying to my manager at the time, Adrian Mitchell, that I needed to get out of there. I needed to go home. It wasn't that I hated being in there; I had just had enough. It was simply one thing too many.

Eventually, we were set free. I went back to the locker room and cleaned out my stuff. We had some pictures taken in there too. Adam was there and so was Paddy. They were both enjoying themselves.

That was not the funniest moment of the day, however. Walking back to the car along the main road we passed Simpson's Golf Shop. I've got the jug. Paddy has the bag over his shoulders and the flagstick from the 18th hole in his hands. (I still have it at home.) Adam has his camera and the box that usually carries the jug. Gary has my shoes and spare balls and anything else that was in my locker.

So we are walking along. And two old guys appear out of the darkness coming towards us. They're obviously a wee bit worse for wear. One was wearing a hat that was a bit skew-whiff. As we get nearer, they see us. So they stop, look at each other, go, 'Nah, it cannae be' and just keep walking! It was brilliant. I was pissing myself. It was just so funny.

After that, the drive home wasn't a lot of fun. The rain was torrential. I don't think I got over 35mph all the way up the road. Gary was with me and the jug was back in its box on the back seat. I had spoken to Marian briefly when I came off after the play-off and before the prize giving. Then again when she called much later, when I was between the media and R&A tents. She was getting a bit worried because, like me, she had no idea of all the things I would have to do before I left.

Anyway, about 10 minutes from the house, Marian rang Gary – who was going to stay with us overnight – to say that there were photographers and press all over the street. So I told her we would ring back when we were literally turning the corner. She could then open the garage door and close it behind us when we drove in. And that is what we did.

Of course, that didn't go down well with the snappers. The doorbell was going within minutes, so I let two or three of them into the house, the guy from the *Press & Journal* (my local paper in Aberdeen) and a couple of others. They got their pictures and off they went. Which was fine. There was no issue. I understand they had a job to do.

Once everyone had gone, I sat down with Marian and Gary to watch the play-off on television. There might have been a couple of beers involved too. What struck me was how calm I looked. I'd felt as if I was in control and that was how it looked too. And that, as I said, was down to Adam. I told the others how great he had been and what he had told me. It must have been about 1.30 in the morning when we eventually went to bed.

I was still there, fast asleep, when Marian shook me awake. Andrew Castle from *GMTV* was on the phone wanting to interview me live on the breakfast programme. So I spoke with him for a few minutes.

That was only the start of a very busy few days. Adrian had scheduled a press conference for 10 o'clock that morning at the Marcliffe hotel in Aberdeen. So it was hectic right away. Adrian actually stayed in town for three or four days. It was just manic. The phone was ringing constantly and every call came with some sort of request, although many were from friends offering words of congratulation, which were obviously welcome and nice. But all of it was exhausting. It really was amazing how many people wanted to speak to me, or wanted a bit of me, or wanted me to do something, or wanted me to sign something.

By the Wednesday, in fact, we had had enough. It was all too much, especially with a toddler and an infant to look after in the middle of everything. So we decamped to Marian's parents home in Kildrummy, where we stayed until the weekend. It was there that my new Porsche was delivered. And, on a more down-to-earth note, we have a great picture of the Claret Jug sitting on the breakfast table at my in-laws. Beside it are a bottle of ketchup and a tub of margarine. That always makes me smile.

Anyway, back in the world of golf, I tried so hard not to say 'no' to anything. But it was hard going, in a good way. I was running on adrenaline alone, I think. I have never felt so knackered as I did over those few days. It was just so tiring. I was constantly tired for a while too, even when I was away at tournaments.

My weekly routine at events had to change. Getting to the range from the clubhouse took longer, because I had more autographs to sign. I needed as much as two hours to warm up before a round as opposed to one, all because I had so many people wanting me to do things. They were never big things, but those 'just five minutes' add up when you do enough of them.

A lot of players started calling me 'Champ'. I remember Philip Walton and Paul Eales doing that often. Which was nice. But weird too. Don't get me wrong though. In the midst of it all, Marian and I did find time for some fun. Expensive fun.

I have never seen myself as overly materialistic, but I must admit to being driven when it comes to providing for my family. Right from the start of my career I wanted a big house and a nice car and enough money to give Marian and the boys the best of everything. I didn't want to be struggling.

Which was why I've always been prepared to work as hard as it took to get the things I wanted for those closest to me.

Anyway, at the time of my Open victory, we were arranging to buy a new house in the Kingswells area of Aberdeen, not far from where we were already living. We had not stopped looking at the 'homes for sale' notices in the *Press & Journal* though. One house in particular had always captured our attention. But at 'offers over £750,000' it was way out of our price range.

Things change though, especially when you win the Open! So following my press conference at the Marcliffe I went for a drive to see exactly what this house looked like. Marian stayed at home with the boys but I wasn't away long. In fact, I almost broke the front door down on the way back in.

'It's George and Barbara's house,' I yelled at the top of my voice. It was fate. Some background: In 1999 Brackenhill (where we now live) was owned by George Lumsden, one of my early sponsors. Marian and I had been to parties at the house on more than one occasion. And every time we left, I would say, 'one day we are going to own that house. We're going to buy that house. I'm telling you now, we are going to have that house.' It was perfect for us. But at that time it was just a dream.

The strangest thing is that neither Marian nor I made the connection, even though there was a picture of the house in the newspaper. Of course, every time we had been there it had been dark – and we had never known the name of the house either – so maybe that is not so surprising.

I called George straight away. He was happy to show us round a couple of days later, with one proviso: 'Bring the Jug,' he said. 'You must bring the Jug.' So I did. He showed us round but there was really no need. We knew we wanted to buy the house before we even got there.

Eventually we sat down in the kitchen. I asked him how much he wanted for the place. I don't recall his exact response, but I offered him £925,000. 'I'll buy it right now,' I said. He put out his hand and we shook on the deal then and there.

Lots of other good things came my way, too. Suddenly, I was in the field for the World Golf Championships. I was in all the majors for at least five years. I was invited to the Million Dollar Challenge in South Africa and the World Match Play at Wentworth, events I had always wanted to play in. And we had a great trip to Hawaii at the end of the year for the Grand Slam of Golf. My schedule was amazing, to be honest.

Biggest of all, however, was that my Open victory confirmed beyond any doubt that I would be part of the European Ryder Cup team that would defend the trophy against the Americans at Brookline near Boston (I would have made the team even without winning the Open incidentally). As I'm sure most of you know, that turned out to be quite an eventful and exciting week. Which is why it has a chapter to itself later in this book.

Speaking of the Ryder Cup, in my first event after the Open I was – not coincidentally – drawn to play with then European skipper Mark 'Jesse' James and his assistant, my fellow-Scot Sam Torrance. Clearly they wanted to see for themselves if this guy could really play.

On the first day, it turned out that I could. I was five under par after 10 holes when we were held up on the 11th tee. Standing there – I'll never forget this – Sam turned to Jesse and said, 'I think our boy is okay to play.'

Then, walking up the fairway, Sam asked me if I had spent any of my dough yet. I had, of course. Not only had £925,000 gone on the house, I'd bought a Porsche for £75,000. So I told him I had, 'a million quid in the first two days'.

'Oohhhh, I love that,' said Sam, a huge smile on his face. 'Good lad. Quite right. Way to go.'

I thought that was really funny.

Other perks came my way, stuff I could never have imagined growing up. One, in fact, has had a lasting impact on my life – the night I attended the BBC Sports Personality of the Year Show in London. I was sitting between Nick Faldo and Colin Montgomerie when the Manchester United team that had won the treble that year came into the room. Their manager, Alex Ferguson, was with them, of course. He is a huge hero of mine from his time at Aberdeen. I was – and still am – a regular at Pittodrie and I had been in Gothenburg to cheer on the lads when they won the European Cup Winners' Cup in 1983. So Fergie was a big deal to me.

'You'll know Alex really well of course,' says Monty. 'He's Aberdeen like you.'

When I said I'd never met the great man, Monty hauled me over to be introduced. 'Come with me,' he said.

As soon as we got over there, it was like we were old pals.

'Paul!' says Fergie. 'How are you doing? Good to meet you at last.'

Straight away I thanked him for the awesome letter he had sent me right after the Open. It was the nicest one I got – and I received hundreds. He had been on the edge of his seat watching with his wife, Cathy, and we chatted for ages. And the last thing he said was, 'you must come down to Old Trafford'.

That wasn't an invitation I was about to turn down and since then we have been there four or five times. I don't like to go too often, but Alex is very generous with his time. He always invites us into his office for a chat and we have some great pictures of him with the boys.

An even bigger gesture on his part was donating a 'Carrington visit' to my junior foundation. Carrington is the Manchester United training ground and every year Alex gives three trips there to charities. Only three. So to receive one is a big deal. You get to watch the team train on the Friday, then on the day of the match you have lunch in the Red Café, watch the game and have a wee visit with Alex in his office afterwards.

We put the prize up for auction at one of our foundation dinners. But I knew beforehand who was going to buy it. Me. I think I paid £7,000 for it.

When we turned up at Carrington we were shown into Alex's office. When he appeared he immediately started chatting with the boys. It was a blether I'll never forget. First he asked me if this was the trip he had given me for the foundation. I told him yes and that I had bought it.

'You daft bugger,' he said. 'You can come here any time. Any time you want to come, you just come.'

Then he turned to the boys.

'Are you proud of your dad?' he says to Craig and Michael. 'You should be proud of him and what he has achieved.'

I had to laugh. There we were in the office of the man who is probably the greatest manager in the history of British football – we were surrounded by awards and trophies – and he's talking about me. I'm not the most outwardly emotional soul, but stuff like that does get to me. And if I hadn't won the Open, I'm sure none of it would ever have happened.

Other things have come along over time. I have an honorary doctorate of law from Robert Gordon University. And, of course, I have an MBE, although that wasn't the most memorable experience of my life if I'm honest. I'm of the opinion that all honours are for people who do heroic things, like soldiers fighting for our country and those who do great things for charity. They are not for sportsmen who earn vast sums of money playing games. Plus, I'm not a big royalist, but I didn't want to be rude and not go. So I accepted the award and Marian and I went down to London.

We had hired a driver to take us to Buckingham Palace from the airport.

That was fine. We got there on time and were ushered into a big room. This guy appeared and took Marian away with him. I didn't see much of her all day actually. Then the whole rigmarole and protocol is explained to everyone. There isn't much you can do and quite a lot you can't!

So I'm in the queue to get my MBE from Prince Charles. Neil Jenkins the Welsh rugby player is in front of me and Lonnie Donegan the singer is behind me. I had a great chat with both of them as we waited our turn. These things take a while apparently.

It came to my turn and the announcer says, 'For services to golf, Peter Lawrie.' That made me stop. Peter Lawrie? They couldn't even get my name right! And to make it worse – at least in retrospect – Irishman Peter Lawrie wasn't even on the European Tour at that time. So there was no confusion; they just got my name wrong.

Now, I don't have much of an ego ordinarily, but I was pretty upset. I had been proud to be getting such an honour, then they go and get my name wrong. Marian was sitting with the other family members and I looked across at her. She caught my eye and rolled hers. I think she was worried I might walk out. But I just had to get on with it. The guy doing the announcing gave me a wee push, in fact. I thought he might correct himself, but he didn't.

When I got to Prince Charles, he said, 'Well done. Many congratulations. I'm not a golfer myself, but 'Mumsy' watched you win.' Then he extended his hand. That, I knew, was my signal to get the hell out of there. So I did.

Outside I was really pissed off at them getting my name wrong. It was just one more thing on top of all the disrespect I was getting generally after Jean Van de Velde 'lost' the Open rather than me winning it. That seemed to be the prevailing view. Anyway, we had to queue up again to get our picture taken. And that was too much for me. 'Let's go,' I said.

Marian tried to persuade me to stay, although she understood exactly why I was so upset. But I was having none of it. We got in the car, went straight to the airport and flew home. I understand how mistakes can happen, but that was insulting to me, I thought. It should never have happened. And, as I said, it was just one more log on the fire for me.

Looking back now, I should have stayed, at least to get the picture taken. I felt bad about that, so I offered to get dressed up in the kilt again so that Marian and I could get a portrait done in Aberdeen. I should have known better. She wouldn't do it. 'No, no,' she said. 'If you wouldn't do it at the time, if you wouldn't wait at the palace, you're nae getting it now.' She can be tough, my wife. But she was right, of course.

That story never made it into the press – thank goodness – but more attention in the media and speaking in public were two things I had to get used to as Open champion. And, to be honest, I didn't react too well to much of the coverage in the papers in the weeks and months after Carnoustie.

Understandably, the immediate focus post-Open was on Van de Velde. I didn't have a problem with that. What happened was extraordinary. So it had to be covered. But in the midst of all that, I did feel quite strongly that I should get at least some acclaim for playing so well on the last day and winning the play-off in, I felt, some style.

I kept saying to reporters, 'Look, I understand why you guys wrote what you wrote; I understand why it happened. I know as well as you do that I got lucky and that he should have won. But come on, give me some credit.'

So it was more what I wasn't reading that was bothering me. It wasn't that anyone was calling me a scumbag or anything. But it was hard for me to read things that didn't reflect what happened, or how well I had played, at least in my mind.

On the other hand, I had people telling me that it didn't really matter. My name was on the trophy. Who cares what they write? That sort of stuff. But it mattered to me. I did care. And for a long time it really annoyed me. There was no escape either. Like the poor putter who is continually faced with a series of left-to-right four-footers, I couldn't get away from Jean's image. Every time I picked up a magazine, there he was on the cover; every time I turned a page, there he was again, standing in the Barry Burn. It was amazing how many pictures there were.

Looking back, in the midst of all that I could have done with more help from my agents, International Management Group. My manager, Adrian, was a good guy. I liked him and got on well with him. And I think he did a good job. But it felt like the people behind him weren't doing much to support him or me. I certainly could have done with some media training. Maybe they thought I was better than I was, I'm not sure. But after a while it should have been obvious that I was struggling.

Then again, I don't want to give the impression I was walking round in a constant rage at any or all of this. I wasn't. And I never really fell out with anyone in the media. I didn't have a problem with them at all. Far more annoying was my loss of privacy. I wanted to go home and have my home life be like it had always been. And I didn't really want to tell the world what I did with Marian and the kids. But that was impossible. I found that very difficult to deal with.

I was – and am – a private person living a public life. I was that way before the Open win and I'm that way now, albeit I've learned how to cope with all that comes with having a reasonably well-known face. I still don't get the fame thing though. I'm not bothered what Sean Connery does or what he gets up to after dark. I'm just not. That stuff just doesn't interest me. So I struggle with the notion that anyone out there would have a vicarious interest in me.

I don't live the life of a celebrity either. Not even close. My dearest friends are just normal people. My best mate is a fish merchant. I would never dream of getting 'pally' with someone just because he's a celebrity. That would be sad. And that's the sort of thing I couldn't get my head round. I was new to the sort of attention I was getting and it was all very strange to me. People were asking me questions on politics for example. Because I won a golf tournament! That's ridiculous, or should be. Any number of times, I answered with a laugh and the line, 'Listen, I'm a golfer.'

The trouble was, my attitude and demeanour meant that a lot of people misunderstood me in the weeks and months after Carnoustie. Which was my fault. But I wasn't being rude. I just wanted to be normal. I didn't want my life to change. I wanted to stay the way I was.

Now, looking back again, I can see how unrealistic that was. Maybe I'm just not normal. Or wasn't back then. And, to be clear, winning the Open didn't make me that way. I was like that long before I won. I was just someone who didn't have a clue how to handle all the fuss and bother that comes with being the champion golfer of the year.

Happily, I'm a lot better than I used to be. I'm much more sociable. My junior foundation has a lot to do with that, too. I'm out and about a lot more now than I was back in 1999/2000. I'm a lot better at public speaking as well. But only if you give me time to prepare and make some notes. I'm still not that great at thinking on my feet. If, for example, I'm asked to say a few words at something like a school prize-giving, I'm never that keen. I'm happier just shaking hands and saying 'well done'.

But I'm nothing like I was. I remember back in 2001 when we first launched our Junior Golf Programme in the North East of Scotland. There was a press conference at Hazlehead Golf Club and I had to make a speech. There was no lectern and I stood there gripping my piece of paper. I read that speech word-for-word and never looked up once. It was an awful experience for me and, I'm sure, for those who were forced to listen.

Stewart Spence, one of my dearest friends and the owner of the Marcliffe hotel, drove me home after that. There was silence the whole way. When we stopped, all he said was, 'Right'.

But that was all I needed. 'You don't have to say anything,' I said.

'I know. I know. I know,' was his response. As he drove away I knew I had to get better at this. And I have. I can't tell you how many compliments I get these days about my public speaking. 'You should go on the circuit,' people often say. No thanks. One tour is enough for me.

And yes, before anyone asks, Prince Charles really did say, 'Mumsy'.

The Road to Medinah

For most players, the qualifying period for the 2012 European Ryder Cup side lasted exactly 12 months. Not for me though. For me, it was twice as long; starting with a moment of realisation during the 2010 matches at Celtic Manor, where I was working as a commentator for *Sky Sports*.

Don't get me wrong when I say this – I've made every effort to get into every Ryder Cup team over the course of my career – but sitting there talking about other guys hitting shots it struck me I just hadn't been trying hard enough on tour. I realised that here was an event I should be playing in, not commentating on. Which wasn't a unique conclusion, of course. Graeme McDowell, who worked in the media during the 2006 matches at the K Club said pretty much the same thing. Watching isn't nearly as good as competing.

Besides, although I heard plenty of nice compliments about my performance in front of the cameras and behind a microphone, I didn't actually think I was very good in the role. I never felt like it was for me. All week, right from the moment I arrived, I felt like I should be playing. Which is not to say that I was unlucky not to be in the team. Far from it.

At the time, in fact, I was a good way from the required standard. My final Order of Merit position was 69th that year and in the four previous seasons I had finished 61st, 72nd, 40th and 82nd. Only once in that time had I made it into the season ending 'Race to Dubai.' And that event is open to the top-60 players on the money list. So I had been consistently mediocre for a wee while by then. It was ridiculous. And that knowledge just made me feel even worse, even if, as I said, my golf wasn't exactly shocking and I was still living a comfortable enough life. But that wasn't enough. For me it has always been 'get to the top or don't bother.'

I've never been one for hitting a lot of balls at tournaments; I do the vast majority of my preparations for events when I'm at home. But back then I wasn't even doing that. I wasn't on the range or around the chipping green. I was lazy, overweight and hadn't been in the gym for goodness knows how long. Not for the first time in my life, I'd lost my spark and the desire to do what I needed to do to play as well as I can.

It didn't help that Adam wasn't really around to give me the kick up the backside that he was sometimes wont to do. But that is no excuse. Quite simply, I had let myself go a bit. Although I was plodding along making a nice enough living, I wasn't playing at anything like my full potential and my stint in the commentary box only underlined that fact. It wasn't a nice feeling.

Indeed, the contrast between now and then makes me smile. The day after I won the Johnnie Walker Championship at Gleneagles in August 2012 – my eighth European Tour victory – I was back on the practice ground hitting balls. That's the real me, someone who is keen to get out there, play golf, hit balls and keep my recent run of good form going as long as possible. I'm back to putting in the hours of practice at home and resting at tournaments. And it seems to be working.

It wasn't just the commentary, of course. Looking back, that was just the final piece of evidence I needed to convince myself I wasn't trying hard enough. There was my son Craig beating me in practice for one thing and Marian telling me I had, 'let myself go a bit', for another. That isn't what you want to hear from your wife, even if she did it for all the right reasons. But I needed to hear it. I will never forget the sinking feeling I had in my stomach at Celtic Manor – a combination of knowing I hadn't tried hard enough to be there as a player and watching guys I think I can compete with on any given week. It was awful.

So I went back to work and, quite quickly, lost about 20 pounds in weight. Which wasn't difficult given how many hours I was putting in on my game. I'm the sort of guy who, when playing poorly, practices really hard for as long as it takes to make things better. Padraig Harrington is like that too; he has to put the work in. Then there are those who like to leave things alone in the hope that it will all work out in time. And others, like my fellow Scot and European Tour pro, Stephen Gallacher, can make the necessary changes almost immediately. I envy him his talent for almost immediate correction. But I can never do that. Ingraining a swing change takes me a while.

Over the winter of 2010/11 I hit an unbelievable number of balls – probably at least 500-600 every day – mostly at Deeside Golf Club near my home. The pros there, Frank Coutts and Peter Smith, both noticed the difference. 'We hadn't seen you out there much lately,' they said. Which confirmed to me that I was just drifting along aimlessly.

I had a chat with Adam – who was in hospital at the time – and he told me to work mostly on my rhythm and that there was no need to make drastic changes. Basically, I just had to get my timing back, especially in the changeover between backswing and downswing. Once I had that, he felt, my confidence would return. And he was right. I did work a bit on my leg action – they tend to get a bit too active during my swing – and hit lots of balls with a beach ball between my knees, as well as many, many slow motion swings. Combined with a lot of work on the practice green, I could soon feel improvement in all areas of my game.

My putting, in fact, had long been a bit of an issue. All my life I had aimed the face of the club to the left of my target, then 'pushed' the putt down the proper line. I had always done that. But as long as it was working, Adam and I left it alone. I still smile at the time I was on the putting machine at Callaway. The lad there turned to Adam and asked, 'Does Paul know he is...' Adam 'wheesht' him quiet so that I wouldn't hear. 'Don't go there,' he said. 'Don't tell him that.'

But eventually I had to tackle my address position, specifically my alignment. And I did that winter. I had a line drawn on the top of my putter so that I could see exactly where I was aimed. I must have hit thousands of putts over the course of those few months.

Also driving me on was the horrible thought that Adam might not be with us that much longer. He really was very ill at that time. And the last thing I wanted was for him to die while I was playing no better than average. I wanted to give him a boost, as well as myself.

So, all in all, I didn't lack for motivation. I had that awful sensation sitting in the commentary box. I had my son beating me at golf. I had my wife telling me I was fat and lazy. And there was Adam. I would have hated for him to see me playing rubbish over the last few months of his life. Throw in my own sense of frustration and I had a lot of factors pushing me to improve.

As I say elsewhere, I made another important change around that time, when I hired Davy Kenny to be my new caddie and within six weeks we had won a tournament together. Changing everything at once – swing, caddie, attitude – really helped me, although I hadn't realised, when I won in Malaga, that it had been nine long years since my previous victory. I'd had a few close things during that period, but for whatever reason it hadn't actually dawned on me that I had gone so long without winning.

It was nice to get it done though, especially with Adam watching on television. I was two shots ahead playing the last hole, but hit a poor approach to the green with an 8-iron, the ball finishing in a bunker. A bad shot. But I won anyway. Of course, that fact didn't matter to Adam. When I called him that night, the first thing he said was, 'What were you thinking over that 8-iron?'

'Come on man, give me a break,' was my response.

At which point we both started to cry. I think we both knew just how ill he was and how important my winning was to both of us. But it had been coming, if I'm honest. I had been playing well enough without holing anything ever since the start of the year. So I could see something good happening if only I could make a few on the greens. And when I had a few weeks at home just before I won in Spain I worked hard on my stroke, as well as playing a lot of golf. Clearly, it was time well spent.

The rest of that season was a bit of a mixed bag. I spent most of the summer plodding along, playing okay but not really achieving much. But when the weather turned a bit cooler my golf warmed up. And when I finished off the season by finishing runner-up behind Spain's Alvaro Quiros in the 'Dubai World Championship' – yes, I qualified this time – I was suddenly in with a real chance of making the 2012 Ryder Cup team. The money in Dubai was huge; I won €615,094, which is more than you get for winning most tournaments, and ended up 18th on the Order of Merit, my highest finish since 2002.

All of that was nice, of course. But for me it was incidental. Pretty much all I'd been thinking about since the start of the qualification period three months earlier was the Ryder Cup. I saw it as my last chance to play for a second time really. At my age, I figured, if I didn't make it this time I was done. To make the 2014 side at the age of 45 would have been a huge ask, a full 15 years on from my last appearance. So it was 'shit or bust' as far as I saw it. I had to make Jose Maria Olazabal's team.

Also spurring me on was the fact that, at the time, there was some talk of me being captain at Gleneagles in '14. But, even if that were true, I reckoned there wasn't much chance of me being offered such a prestigious and responsible position if I had played only once against the Americans. So if I wanted to be captain – a job that would be almost impossible to turn down – I simply had to be part of the squad for Medinah.

Now, of course, my feelings have changed on that subject. Having made the 2012 team I don't want to be captain, even if the matches are in Scotland. I want to play.

Anyway, back in Dubai, that week gave me the impetus I was looking for. That was the week where I convinced myself it could be done. Because I still wasn't ranked in the world's top-50 (I was actually 87th after that week) I wasn't eligible for most of the World Golf Championships in 2012. To be honest, it is almost impossible for anyone to make the Ryder Cup side from outside the top-50. Those WGC's carry huge prize-money and there is no cut, so once you are in you are guaranteed a substantial cheque even if you play poorly. That's a huge advantage when it comes to qualifying – or not. So I left the Middle East a much more assured golfer. In fact, I look back now with a few regrets. It's easy to say now, but I really should have won that tournament. Alvaro played well, obviously, but I felt like I should have beaten him. Overall though, I was reasonably satisfied. To finish second in a field of that quality was a huge boost to my confidence and my chances of making it into a second Ryder Cup. Suddenly, it was looking very possible.

My 2012 season started in South Africa, at the Volvo Champions event, a perk for my winning in Spain. Then I was back in the Middle East for the usual three-week run through Abu Dhabi, Qatar and Dubai. Happily, my form was just as good as it had been back in December. After top-ten finishes in my first two starts, I won in Qatar. One shot ahead with 18 holes to play, I shot 65 and won going away. Even I thought that was a fair effort.

Again, that was a big shot-in-the-arm for my Ryder Cup hopes. Not only did I pocket another nice cheque, I was back in the world's top-50, at number 47. For any professional golfer, that is huge. The difference between 50 and 51 in the world is vast. Now I could start thinking about trips to Arizona for the Accenture Match Play Championship, Florida for the second WGC and, for the first time since 2004, the Masters at Augusta National. Whatever else, I had given myself every chance to make the Ryder Cup.

Everything was going well at that point. I was playing well and swinging nicely. I was holing putts. My attitude was good too. When I'm not playing well, that is rarely the case. Everything gets complicated and little things bother me. Sometimes I can't even get my glove on properly. And, me being me, I started to get in my own way a little, at least mentally.

Because I was now into all of the big events in at least the first half of 2012, I looked at my Ryder Cup chances a bit differently. Suddenly, I thought to myself, not making it would be a bit of a cock-up. So, although I wasn't saying so publicly, I was feeling some pressure.

Happily, however, my form stayed good. And at the Masters I played really well. In fact, I should have finished in the top-ten there. I shot 76 on the last day and fell back a bit after a great start. Still, I was really enjoying playing in events I hadn't been to in nearly a decade. For example, Marian, Michael and some friends came to Augusta – where we rented a house for the week – and had a great time.

It was at the Masters that I had my first exposure to Bubba Watson. He and I played together on the third day, 24 hours before he would go on to hit that amazing shot from the trees right of the 10th hole and win the play-off against Louis Oosthuizen.

It was quite an experience. Bubba, as every golf fan knows, is a bit different. He's a golfing freak in the nicest possible way. He does stuff that other people just don't do. He hits hooks and slices when he doesn't have to. He hooks wedge shots, which isn't easy to do. He's almost too talented.

Here's an example of what Bubba is like. For the first 12 holes of our round he hit a big cut (right-to-left for him, a left-hander) off every tee, other than the par-3s. Even at the first hole, which bends slightly left-to-right, he did that. Fair enough. But when we got to the short 4th, where the hole was cut front-left on the green, he hit a hook. Then, if that wasn't weird enough, at the famous par-5 13th hole, a sharp right-to-left dogleg, he suddenly decided to hit a draw off the tee, up and over the trees on the left.

I couldn't believe it, to be honest. Why would he do that? But he did. None of what Bubba did made much sense, yet he played beautifully. His putting was a bit dodgy mind, but I loved watching him hit. And he is so long. That shot he hit off the 13th tee, is the second-best shot I've ever seen a professional hit, after the putter I saw Sandy Lyle use to hit a green 100 yards away in Hawaii during a skills test.

I was standing there wondering what the hell was Bubba doing. I'm not sure I could hit a 9-iron over those trees. Off a tee-peg. But he whacked a driver right over the corner. It was a 315-yard carry to the fairway. Then he hit a 9-iron into the back bunker. So he should have hit a wedge. I, meanwhile, hit a lovely draw off the tee and a rescue club onto the green. A different game, right enough. And a nice lad, too. Other than on the first tee, where he didn't seem too keen to introduce himself, he was a pleasure to play with.

Maybe the only disappointment of Masters week was the abandonment of the par-3 tournament on the eve of the event. Michael was going to caddie for me and had his white boiler suit and green hat on when the heavens opened and they called it all off. But we'll be back in 2013, so he'll get another chance.

The course was a lot different than it had been on my last visit in 2004. I remember standing on the 7th tee and not recognising the hole, it was so much longer. Which is disappointing actually. The green there is so shallow it can't accept much more than a 9-iron shot. But one day I was going in there with a 4-iron, off a good drive. Having said that, it was cool to be back.

When I came back from Augusta it seemed like everyone was assuming I was all but certain to make the Ryder Cup. I, of course, was having none of that, at least publicly. At the back of my mind though, I was thinking, 'man, I'm in'. Which is dangerous. I had to keep going, taking one week at a time and do the best I could in every event.

It did look as if one more good week's play would all but see me on the plane to Chicago. I always knew exactly where I stood. I've always paid attention to the world rankings and the money list. I like to know what is going on. The only time I didn't look was when I was shit. I wasn't booting up the computer to see where I was when I was about 390th.

That good week actually came along at Wentworth, where I was runner-up in the BMW PGA Championship. But I should have had it all sewn up a week earlier, when I made it to the semi-final of the Volvo World Match Play Championship. That sounds okay and is, I suppose. But it should have been better. After beating Thomas Bjorn 5&4 and Retief Goosen 6&5, I was four up after seven holes against Nicolas Colsaerts. I was playing beautifully and cruising along. Then, in the middle of the eighth fairway, just as I was about to hit my approach, a photographer appeared and clicked on my backswing. It went way right into the bushes and I lost a hole I looked like winning.

Worse followed when, after Nicolas had lost his ball off the 10th tee, I snap-hooked my own drive into the rubbish. I reacted with a naughty word that was picked up on television – and earned me a good talking to from a tour official – and eventually halved the hole in seven. So I was three up instead of four.

Gradually, my lead drifted away and I lost on the 18th. I came off the course in a foul mood and stomped past the press without saying a word. In the locker room – in front of Nicolas and his coach – I booted the locker and threw my shoes against the wall. I couldn't believe what I had done. I had given it away. And I was raging, especially as the forecast for the afternoon final was awful. I'd have fancied my chances of winning in those conditions.

Anyway, all was back to normal at Wentworth. I played okay the first three days without holing much. But on the Sunday I played just about as well as I can, shooting six under par. More importantly, I proved to myself just how sound my swing was. At the last hole – a par-5 with water to the front and left of the green – I was in the fairway and having to decide whether or not to go for it. I was two shots back, so the only way I was going to win was to be aggressive.

I was 217-yards out and the pin was tucked away back-left near the water. In other words, this was a very risky shot. But it was a perfect yardage for my 4-iron and I told Davy I was going to hit a draw into the flag. He wanted me to play safe, but I was sure I could do it. And I did. It was a beautiful shot, just as I pictured it. The ball finished 10 feet away (I missed the putt) but I knew then I was a proper player again.

The good news was that I was gutted at finishing second. That told me I was ready to be a really good player. But, even though I was by then pretty sure of my Ryder spot, I persisted in telling the press that I had a bit to go and nothing was certain. I mean, what else could I say? If I'd announced to the world I was in and then didn't make it, I was going to look pretty silly. Peter Hanson – who would eventually make the team – was second in the qualifying before the PGA, missed the cut and dropped to fifth. Having said that, in the position I was after Wentworth – second – it would have almost been harder not to make it.

Still, I did find time to cause a wee bit of controversy in certain quarters when I decided not to go to the US Open in San Francisco three weeks later. It would have been easier for me to go than not, but I feel that I made the right decision. Which is not to say that I maybe should have gone. For one thing, it only added to the pressure I was feeling in the subsequent events, those I had told the world were my biggest priority. I didn't play that well in the run-up to the Open as a result, culminating in missing the cut at the Scottish Open, where I putted horrendously.

I've always been that way, of course. I'm headstrong and tend to do what I consider is best for me, no matter what anyone else thinks. There has only ever been two people in my life who can make me change my mind about anything: my wife and Adam. And the one I listen to about golf is gone. Marian is my life coach.

The other thing that made me reluctant to go to the US Open is the way they tend to set up the courses for that event. This may sound a little ironic given how Carnoustie was when I won the Open, but I hate it when the rough is grown to the point where par is going to win. That's why I enjoy the Masters so much. It is huge fun playing a course where there is little or no rough. I love that we can hit recovery shots when we stray off-line.

One last thing about long grass on courses: Around the greens it actually makes things easier. It is the poor chipper who benefits from having a wee bit of 'fluff' under his ball. The 'tighter' the lie is, the more difficult chipping becomes.

Besides, at the end of the day, I'm betting no one was that bothered about my absence. To my knowledge, no one was walking around the Olympic Club saying how much better the event would have been if only Paul Lawrie had come over from Scotland.

By the time I got to Lytham for the Open I was still pretty confident regarding the Ryder Cup. I may have dropped from second to fourth in the European standings, but I was still well ahead of the guy in sixth spot (the top-five qualified automatically), something like £600,000. So I was comfortable with that. And I played decently in the Open, at least at first. Unfortunately, the putting still wasn't so good and, despite opening with a 65, I finished well down the field. Which was disappointing. I had fancied my chances going in there.

One thing I will say about the Open though, is that I will have another chance to win it before I'm done. Why wouldn't I think that? I'm in the top-30 in the world. I love links golf. And I'm well used to the bad weather we sometimes get by the seaside in July. So it's not unreasonable to suppose I'll be in contention at least once more. I like to think so anyway.

The last wee run to the final counting event for the Ryder Cup included a World Golf Championship at Firestone and the US PGA Championship. I was guaranteed money from the first and I almost played well in the second. So, by the time I arrived at Gleneagles for the Johnnie Walker, I was definitely in the team. Which was a great feeling – and relief – one that contributed to how well I played on home turf. What made it even more special was that we had our last fitting for the team uniforms on the Tuesday afternoon that week. Everything fit, which was nice.

Right from the first hole, I played well. I was just so confident about everything I was doing. Not for one moment, especially on the last day, did I think I wasn't going to win. That feeling doesn't come along too often, so you have to make the most of it when it does. I flushed it all day on the

Sunday. It was maybe the best ball-striking day of my year. I shot four under par without even putting that well.

Coming up the final fairway was a great thrill. Both sides were lined with people shouting out to me. I loved it, especially as I was at home. It was special. And, looking back, I can't believe how relaxed I was. I know I have a reputation for sometimes looking a bit dour on the course, but if you watch the tape you can see me laughing my head off on the 18th green. Here's why.

The lad I was playing with, Romain Wattel, had hit his second shot just right of the green. He needed a ruling and it was taking forever. As we stood there, I turned to Davy and said: 'hey, get over there and tell him this is not about him; it's all about me'. That set us both off. So if you were wondering, that's why we were laughing.

A few minutes later, I was the Johnnie Walker Champion and, more importantly, a Ryder Cup player for the second time. I was nearly emotional.

Medinah

Welcome to the second greatest week of my professional career, the 39th Ryder Cup matches at the Medinah Country Club, just outside Chicago.

Sunday, 23 September 2012

Marian and I flew down to Heathrow this evening, just in case the following morning's shuttle was delayed. We stayed in the Sofitel hotel at the airport, where we bumped into a lot of familiar faces like former Ryder Cup skipper Bernard Gallacher and my former teammate, Miguel Angel Jimenez, who is one of the assistant captains this year.

I was feeling good about the week to come, having kept reasonably busy – but not overly so – in the fortnight leading up to Medinah. I made sure not to play too much because I needed some time off. A week away from the game is never enough for me. I need two to feel rested and ready to play again.

The only competitive golf I played since winning the Johnnie Walker Championship at Gleneagles was in my own Tartan Tour event at Deeside the week before – where I finished third – and was pleased that I had played better each day. I had been a bit rusty in the pro-am then played poorly on the first day. But by the finish, I felt ready for the Ryder Cup. Then I had a couple of days off, which was the plan.

Mostly, however, I had focused on the foundation. Although we have someone working part-time on all the various activities, Marian and I play pretty active roles in the day-to-day running of all that goes on. There's always something to do. Plus, we recently purchased what is now the 'Paul Lawrie Golf Centre,' on the outskirts of Aberdeen. So that had kept us busy too. And will do so in the future too.

Monday, 24 September

We checked in for the charter flight and met more 'weel kent' faces in the departure lounge, guys like Sam Torrance and Ken Schofield. Lord Macfarlane and his wife were there too.

The flight itself was very different from the one we had been on in 1999, the last time I made the European team. Back then the whole 12-man side was on the plane – apart from Jesper Parnevik, who lived in Florida. This time, there were only three of us travelling: myself, Francesco Molinari and Nicolas Colsaerts. But Jose Maria was there – he insisted everyone call him 'Ollie' for the week – along with his four assistants: Thomas Bjørn, Darren Clarke, Paul McGinley and Jimenez. There were also quite a few of the European Tour and PGA officials. And some family members; Darren's parents were there, for example. So was Jose's mum, who I hadn't met before. It was a full flight and, apart from one 'incident' pretty uneventful.

Halfway across the Atlantic, Miguel decided that he was too warm. We had been told to wear a white T-shirt, over which we all had cream cashmere jumpers and a jacket. So Miguel decided he needed to get rid of the white shirt. That, of course, involved him having to take everything off. Which was bad enough. But he then proceeded to rub his belly in a slightly suggestive manner in front of all the women. Yes, it was funny, but a little bit disturbing too, if I'm honest. There is clearly a bit of the exhibitionist in old Miguel; who isn't thin by the way.

Anyway, I was asked at the airport if the team concept was in any way diminished by the fact that most of the side was already in the States. I didn't really think so then and I still don't. Ollie made a great speech over the intercom just before we landed, thanking everyone for coming and sharing just what the week meant to him. He's brilliant at that sort of thing. Besides, we were all together by the Monday evening and the atmosphere was just as good. We ate together and caught up with all the news.

There was some official stuff to do as soon as we arrived at the team hotel. We posed with the Ryder Cup, did a quick interview – I'm not sure who it was for – and posed for more pictures, those we would be given at the end of the week. There was one with Marian and me with the trophy for example.

One of the highlights of the week was actually arriving in our hotel room; it was like Aladdin's cave. There was so much gear for both of us. But it wasn't like 1999, when all the clothing was laid out on the bed. This time there was a rail with each day's clothing in order, separated by bits of plastic saying 'Tuesday,' then 'Wednesday' and so on. That made things a lot easier for us. Then again, maybe it was done only for me. I'm not the most organised when it comes to what I'm supposed to be wearing.

But I'm not as awkward as a friend of mine, who came with me to the Masters years ago. I happened to look into his room and there was his case. In it, his wife had pinned together the clothes he was to wear each day, with a note on each indicating the day in question. So I'm bad, but I'm not that bad.

To be serious though, it's a great thrill to walk into the hotel room for the first time at a Ryder Cup. It really hits home when you see all the stuff you are given and have to try on. I know Marian and I were both excited. It's a short-lived excitement though. Like last time – when I kept only one shirt in a frame – I'll be giving a lot of the clothing away to various charities and auctioning the rest for the foundation. The only difference this time was that I asked for a couple of extra sweaters and the like for the boys.

Another nice change became clear when we went down to the team room for the first time. Every day – laid out on a big table – there were maybe a dozen things to sign, all of which was then sent to our home in a box. This time there were things like Baxter prints, large photographs, frames, flags, golf bags, all kinds of stuff, all signed by everyone as they arrived. Which was so much more straightforward than it had been in 1999. Back then, we were all running around like idiots getting everyone to sign everything. Little things like that make a difference.

The team room was a lot different too. This time we had a pool table and table tennis, neither of which was there in '99. Back then, there was just places to eat, sit and drink. Now we had stuff to do. There was a bar with sofas to sit on. There was a dance floor – I kid you not – with a big screen showing motivational videos. Then there was a section for eating, with food laid out for us. Then there was an area where we did all the signing. It was all pretty amazing – and all bigger and better than 1999.

Tuesday, 25 September
In my first practice round I played with Sergio Garcia, Rory McIlroy and Graeme McDowell. It was Sergio and I against the Irish lads and we were whipped pretty soundly, 5&4. Which cost us $400.

I was pretty tired out on the course. A six-hour practice round the day after you arrive jet-lagged is not the best. In hindsight, I wish I had spoken up the night before when Ollie asked us to play 18 holes the next day. At a normal event I wouldn't have done that; nine holes would have been enough for me. But I didn't want to be causing any bother. I didn't want to be different from everyone else. And I didn't want to upset the captain. So I played 18, albeit I was ready to stop after about seven holes.

The first match out ahead of us was Lee Westwood, Ian Poulter, Luke Donald and Justin Rose. On every green they all seemed to hit four or five pitch shots and four or five bunker shots. All of which took time. My feeling was that we had three full days to prepare so there was no need to overdo it first time out.

After we played and had a bite to eat, I had some television and media stuff to do. All of which was fine.

Back at the hotel we all ate together in the steakhouse, before 'Strictly Ryder' was set up on the dance floor. We split into three teams, competing for a trophy. Marian and I were with Justin Rose and his wife Kate, plus Miguel and his girlfriend, Suzanne. Each team had two instructors, who had 10 minutes to teach us the steps for each dance. Every group did a different dance, but within each group we all did the same thing.

Needless to say, I was hopeless, as were most of the others. Paul McGinley was pretty poor. Even I was better than him. But what was disappointing in what was supposed to be a team building and bonding exercise was that some of the guys opted out. Thomas Bjørn refused to take part, which upset his wife. She was up for it. Darren went to bed before it even started – I think he knew what was coming – claiming he was tired.

Anyway, the whole point of the thing as far as I was concerned was to have some fun. No one cared how bad anyone else was; the plan was to get everyone laughing together. Which is not to say I was looking forward to it exactly. The first thing I did when they announced what was happening was to go and have a beer. At least I could claim I was a wee bit tipsy if I turned out to be hopeless (which I suspected I would be).

Marian was better than me, but not by much. Westwood was pretty good though (I learned subsequently that his grandparents had run a dance studio and school, so he had some prior experience) and so was Justin. Funniest was Poulter. But the best of all was Miguel. I remembered him from 1999, when he and his now ex-wife did a sort of flamenco dance at one of the dinners. They knew what they were doing.

Amazingly, we won. But not because of me, or Marian for that matter. When – surprise, surprise – all three teams were tied on the same number of points, we had a 'dance-off'. One couple from each team. I was petrified it would be us. You can hide a wee bit when eight people are dancing, but not when there's only you and your partner.

Our instructor actually looked at me as a possible participant. But I was having none of that. 'Don't even think about it,' I said. So she chose Justin and Kate. They were up against the Westwoods – Lee was seen practising at the back of the room the poser – and the Poulters. Ian was hilarious. He had a 'hoodie' top on. So he put the hood up and tied the string beneath his chin.

Then he did a 'worm' across the floor. He was brilliant. And the whole thing was great fun. I loved it, even though, as I said, my dancing is about as good as Len Goodman's golf.

Wednesday, 26 September

In our second practice round I played with Colsaerts against Westwood and Molinari. We played only nine holes and lost 2&1, along with another $200. I played better though, which was encouraging. Not so good was the moment when Ollie appeared. He asked me to jump in his buggy for a chat then told me I wouldn't be playing on Friday morning in the first series of foursomes. That was disappointing, but we were there as a team so I had no problem with his decision.

Ollie told me he felt like he had to split the boys into two groups; foursomes players and four-ball players. There were a few players who fit into both categories – I suspect I was one of those – but everyone had to go into one or the other. So he put me into the four-ball group. Which meant I wouldn't play in the foursomes.

It had come down to me or Molinari to play with Lee and Ollie felt that Francesco is more of a foursomes player than a four-ball guy. So he got the nod because, as Ollie said, I could be both. That was fine by me, until we got to the Saturday and Francesco played in the four-balls. That seemed odd given Ollie's original thinking.

I told Ollie I didn't have a problem. Which was the truth. He was the captain and he should play me as often as he felt was right. I knew he was in a tough position and I didn't want to make any waves that early in the week. So all was fine. He gave me a slap on the knee and off I went to play the rest of my round.

As for the golf course, I thought the set-up was really good and really interesting. I could see the way Davis Love was thinking. On paper, they had more long-hitters than we did, so no rough made sense from his point of view. But we also had a few guys who like to hit out from the tee, so it suited us too. Had I been the American captain, I would have gone the other way, in fact. I would have gone with rough, if only because they play more of that type of golf than we do. But the way it was fitted our games as much as it did theirs.

What was great about it was how much fun the course was to play. I have to imagine the golf was more fun to watch too. There were a lot of birdies to be had and the recovery shot from the trees was nearly always an option. We were never going to be chipping out sideways, which has to be the most boring thing in the world for both players and spectators. I know I hate that sort of golf.

The greens were really good and really fast. I understood why Davis did that too. The average green speed on the European Tour is 10 on the 'Stimpmeter'. In America it is 12 and a bit.

The putting surfaces weren't what I remembered from the USPGA Championship in 1999. They had been re-done and had a lot more slope to them. I'd like to have seen them a little slower. There were a couple of places where it all got a little bit silly. So maybe 10-and-a-half on the 'Stimp' would have been enough. All in all though, I liked the course well enough.

That afternoon we had a rules meeting with John Paramor and Andy McFee of the European Tour. During that, the captain's agreement was reviewed. We were allowed to change balls during team matches, which was a change from '99. The biggest difference for me though was that, upon the completion of a hole, we weren't allowed to practise putting. Back in '99 we had been able to do that. But it made sense. Play was quicker this time, albeit still pretty slow.

After that, I headed back to the hotel for a quick nap before the gala dinner that evening. Before we left, Ollie spoke to the team to tell us his thoughts for Friday. He got a bit emotional. We were all dressed in our dinner suits and he went through every player, telling stories about him playing alongside each of us and what we all meant to him.

For example, he spoke of playing with Darren at the 2006 Ryder Cup, just after his wife had died. Then he told the story of playing with Sergio that same week. When he got to me he recalled us being paired at the Irish Open this year. He told me how great it was to see the resurgence in my career and how much work I had obviously put in to make a second team 13 years after my first. It was moving stuff. By the end, everyone was greetin' (crying). We were all in tears.

Ollie spoke non-stop for 15 minutes. When he finished, Poulter spoke up on behalf of the troops. He did that a couple of times to great effect. And when he was done, Ollie told us there was a motivational video for us all to watch. At which point I piped up. 'For goodness sake Ollie, I can't take any more! I'm too old for this! I need some Kleenex.' Which made Luke Donald throw me a box of tissues and raised a laugh.

There were, of course, lots of photographs taken. All the ladies were dressed to the nines and looking gorgeous. The lads from Getty were doing the pictures and when it came to Marian and me the power failed. We had to stand there for 10 minutes until it was restored. Typical.

On the bus on the way to the dinner – we had a police escort – there was another surprise. Miguel sang the European anthem word for word and almost in tune. I was impressed. He belted it out, every verse. He's some banana.

At the welcome dinner we sat with the Westwoods, the Hansons, the Bubba Watsons and the Strickers. There was a little bit of chat. Steve Stricker is a nice lad. And Lee knows Bubba well because they are both Ping players. So it was a nice occasion.

Both captains made speeches. Davis went first and his was unbelievably short. I don't think he was up there more than 45 seconds, a minute absolute tops. Then Ollie got up there. He was different class. I don't know if Davis forgot or not, but he neglected to mention Joe Steranka, the chief executive of the PGA of America, who was retiring after the matches. Ollie didn't forget though and over the course of the week his speeches were consistently better than Davis'. It wasn't that Davis was poor, just that Ollie was so much more memorable.

At both the opening and closing ceremonies, Davis spoke too quickly and didn't wait at the appropriate moments for people to clap. Ollie was great at pausing when he had to. Davis obviously wanted to get it done asap. Ollie at least three up.

Back in the buses, we were taken to the Gala dinner, where we were all introduced on stage by Justin Timberlake. We went down there one-by-one in alphabetical order. Which meant Colsaerts was first. He was bricking it in case he messed up. We'd had the procedure explained to us but clearly Nicolas hadn't really been listening. 'Whoa dude,' he said. 'You better run me through all that again.' But he needn't have worried. All we had to do was wave at the correct moment, then answer one quick question from Justin. Not exactly taxing.

The band 'Chicago' was playing at the Gala dinner. I've never heard of them, which only shows how little I am into music. I'm not sure exactly what time they were supposed to finish, but they went on about an hour too long. Then they played the last song twice for the audience. We should have been leaving just after 10 o'clock but it was 11.15 before we did get out of there. I'm sure I speak for both teams when I say we could all have done without that. We should have been on before the band.

At this stage in the week, I must say too that there was a definite dynamic emerging within the European team. I don't mean to imply that this was a problem – far from it – but it was one I was increasingly aware of. There was a group of our players, those who play most of their golf in the United States, who were obviously very comfortable in each other's company – guys like Rory, GMac, Sergio, Lee, Luke and Justin. They are really friendly. Which is fine. And I don't mean to imply they sat separately at meals or anything silly like that. But they were clearly 'pally' and spent a lot of time together.

I wasn't part of all that – I don't see someone like Luke Donald that often, to be honest – and I felt a wee bit older than them, which I am. So I never felt like one of them, albeit not to the point where it became a problem. It was more of an awareness. And I'm not saying it is anyone's fault. But it is what it is, to quote one of Tiger's favourite sayings. And I do think it all definitely had an effect on Ollie's pairings.

I'm not saying this phenomenon was a good or bad thing, but it was definitely there. And it made the whole experience a bit different for me. In 1999 I had arrived in Boston as the Open champion, so I could reasonably have expected to play every match. This time I wasn't sure I was going to be played an awful lot. I had said as much to Thomas Bjørn when we played together in Switzerland a few weeks before the matches and he had reassured me that I would be a big part of the plans. But I wasn't so sure then and my feeling was confirmed when I got to Chicago.

As things turned out, I feel quite strongly that I should have played four times rather then three. When Peter Hanson and I lost 5&4 to Bubba Watson and Webb Simpson in the opening four-balls I actually played quite well. I was four under par on my own ball.

But I'm getting ahead of myself. That night I went to bed feeling very proud of my wife. She looked beautiful in her ball gown, a million dollars you might say.

Thursday, 27 September
In the final practice round I played with Hanson against Westwood and Colsaerts. Again, we played only nine holes, this time the back nine. And again I lost, this time $100. So I was $700 down for the week. Thank goodness the matches were about to start.

I wasn't surprised to be playing with Peter. At the team meeting the night before, Ollie had asked us to stay behind for a chat. He told us that the prevailing feeling amongst him and his assistants was that Peter and I should play together. While I didn't have a huge problem with that plan, the fact that Peter was there with me meant that I didn't feel like I could say 'no' if I had wanted to. That meeting should have been split into two. Then both Peter and I would have been free to express our views without the other knowing what was being said.

At the start of the week, Ollie had asked us for the names of the three players we would have been happy to line up alongside. Fair enough. But I didn't do it. When he asked why, I told him I really didn't mind who I played with. And at that time he intimated that he was thinking of pairing me with Colsaerts. He was a rookie and he thought my experience would help him.

To be honest, I liked that idea. I like Nicolas as a bloke and he and I had played a fair bit of golf together in the preceding months because our world rankings were similar. I thought we had the potential to be good together.

So the meeting with Ollie and Hanson took me a little bit by surprise. But the whole thing had started with Peter's caddie, 'Woody'. He had said out loud that Paul and Peter would do well as a team. And Peter had put me down as one of his three.

Anyway, that whole exchange was apparently overheard by Thomas Bjørn, who was the assistant captain – along with Darren – I spoke with most. I think that was part of a plan – each assistant assigned to three or four players. Thomas had told me that I was in nearly everyone's top-three, because it was widely felt that I could play both formats. Which meant that Ollie had a problem with me. In short, he didn't really know what to do with me.

Of course, I'll never know if Thomas was telling me the truth or just trying to boost my confidence. I'm sure the former, knowing him. But the bottom line is that I feel like Ollie should have talked with Peter and I separately. I'd have been a lot more comfortable with that scenario. And I'd have asked what happened to the 'Nicolas and me' pairing. But I never got the chance.

What was said in that meeting was that Ollie was leaning towards pairing Peter and I in the Friday afternoon four-balls. It wasn't certain, but that was his thinking at that stage. Then, of course, we went out and lost to Colsaerts and Westwood the next morning, a match Ollie never asked me about afterwards. Yet we still ended up together on the Friday. All very odd, if you ask me.

At this point, I don't want all of this to sound as if I am having a go at either Ollie or Peter Hanson. I like both men and Peter is obviously a fine player.

Again, I'm getting ahead of myself, but on the Friday morning I had asked Jamie Spence from the European Tour what was happening in the afternoon. He immediately got Thomas on the radio. Thomas appeared in the clubhouse at about 11.20, five minutes before the pairings were announced to the world.

'Okay,' I said. 'I don't want to be seen to be having a go. But I do think we need to know what is going on.' In fact, Thomas is going to suggest that, in future Ryder Cups, there is a fifth assistant captain. While the other four are on the course with each group, he will stay in the clubhouse and pass on information to the four guys not playing, so that they know what is happening before anyone else. I like that idea.

Back to Thursday afternoon and the opening ceremony. Ollie gave another fantastic speech and managed to keep his emotions in check when talking about Seve. That must have been tough for him. I enjoyed the feeling of being introduced on stage. That sort of recognition makes all the effort to make the team worthwhile. Adam would have been proud of me.

I even thought Justin Timberlake and his poetry wasn't too bad. He asked me what it was like to be back in the team after a 13-year absence. I said, 'For an old guy it is pretty cool.' And off I went.

Friday, 28 September
Marian and I headed to the course in time to see the lads tee off. The atmosphere was awesome and made me wish I were playing. Once everyone was away, I went to the range and hit a few balls. Then I played a few holes before lunch.

At 12.05 I teed off alongside Peter against Watson and Simpson. On the first tee, Bubba got the crowd going and, while they were still whooping and hollering, he drove off. I've never seen anyone do anything like that before. But I have to admit it was pretty cool.

We got off to the worst possible start. Simpson birdied the first to go one up, then both Peter and I bogied the short second. I three-putted and suddenly we were two down and in an uphill battle.

Things only got worse from there. By the turn we were five down to what turned out to be a Ryder Cup record outward nine. And we lost 5&4, by which time they were eleven under par. As I said, I was four under on my own ball and happy with the way I played. But there wasn't much we could have done against scoring like that. Sometimes, you just have to acknowledge the fact that the other side was better. And they were.

At the end of the day we were trailing five-three. At the evening team meeting Ollie was a bit upset. He told us we needed a big day tomorrow if we were to keep the cup. He was definitely angry and let us know in no uncertain terms that we needed to make more birdies and try a bit harder. His face was set in an expression I had never seen before. We got the message.

Having said that, I'm not sure I would have done things the way he did. When you have 12 people in a room like that, you will get maybe three or four to react positively to a message conveyed the way that one was. I wasn't one of that three or four. I play better when someone puts his arm round me and gives me encouragement. I do not play better when someone starts shouting at me.

Now, someone like Poulter – who had been surprisingly left out that afternoon – probably loved what was said. He has that sort of personality. But I don't.

We had all tried as hard as we could. I know I did. I wanted to win a point so badly. But the other side played better than we did.

I was disappointed not to be selected for the following morning. As I said, I played very well despite the lop-sided defeat we suffered. Apart from Nicolas Colsaerts, I made more birdies than anyone else in the side. That should have got me into the side for the next series of matches, especially when some of our guys made no birdies yet were still playing the next morning.

I must finish with a word about young Colsaerts, who played some phenomenal golf. He made eight birdies and an eagle alongside Lee and they beat Woods and Stricker on the last green. That's impressive enough, but I was told later that, had Nicolas been playing against all of the other seven Euros on the course this afternoon – me included – we would have struggled to beat him 2&1. That's how well he played.

Saturday, 29 September

Marian and I watched the early matches tee-off from our bed back at the hotel. Then we headed to the course at about 9am.

I was playing in the afternoon with Nicolas, against Matt Kuchar and Dustin Johnson and we ended up losing on the last. It was one of those frustrating matches where we hit the ball significantly better than they did, but made nothing on the greens. They, of course, putted beautifully. And that, at this level, makes all the difference.

My mood was summed up after I missed a short putt on the 11th green. On the way to the next tee I booted some dirt beside a tree and all but covered Dustin. I was mortified and apologised more than once. Definitely not cool.

The overall score today was the same as yesterday and we are now 10-6 down. It could have been worse though. Poulter made an amazing five birdies on the last five holes to win his match. He has huge bollocks that boy.

That night, as you can imagine, Ian was on a high. He was just wild. He came into the team room and announced that he needed a 'stiff drink'. He was clearly still running on adrenaline even at that stage. But he was entitled – what a performance. And it wasn't as if the putts he holed were short either. All five were at least 10 feet long and most were significantly longer. And they all went in the middle. Unbelievable.

As for me, I've played twice and hit the ball well twice. But my putting has let me down, especially today. I was awful on the greens today. It is so disappointing. I've been looking forward so much to this week, only to putt like a complete knob.

A word too for the spectators. Some of them have been nothing short of vile this week, which is not that surprising. We knew that sort of thing was likely before we got here. When Marian and I went out to watch Westwood and Colsaerts yesterday afternoon we met them at the 14th tee. Just as they got there, someone shouted from the crowd, 'Westwood you're a wanker.'

I got 'Lawrie you're a loser.' Or variations on 'top it', 'duff it', 'lose it', or 'hit it in the water'. There was a lot of niggly stuff. But I got nothing like what happened to Justin Rose. He was apparently asked, 'Where's your Dad?' Justin's father, Ken, for those who don't know, died of cancer a few years ago. Words fail me in the face of such despicable behaviour.

I actually had a chat with Darren about the crowd. He just shook his head. He had spoken with Jeff Sluman, one of the American assistants. His verdict was that the same thing happens to the US players when they play in Europe. But I just don't believe that. I certainly have never heard anything approaching some of the stuff we were subjected to. Besides, contrast what we were experiencing with the way in which America's best are treated when they come to Scotland. Guys like Jack Nicklaus and Tom Watson are almost God-like where I come from. I just can't imagine anyone abusing them.

On a happier note, the mood in the team room was transformed by the fact that we won the last two matches. The feeling was that we had a chance from 10-6. Anything more than that would have been a lost cause though.

Ollie was in better fettle too. He told us we could do it and to focus only on our own games. He also had some nice things to say about how Nicolas and I had fought so hard in our match.

'Ian has given us hope,' he continued. 'And now we have some momentum. But the first five matches must win tomorrow. If one or two lose, I must be honest and say it isn't possible.'

I doubt if he has ever spoken truer words.

Sunday, 30 September
I teed off at 11.47 in the fifth match against Brandt Snedeker, oblivious to the fact that there had already been some controversy. Rory McIlroy had been confused as to which time zone we were in and so had miscalculated his tee-off time. When he emerged from his room he thought he had an hour and 25 minutes to go until he was to play Keegan Bradley. But he didn't. He had an hour less than that. Had it not been for a state trooper driving him to the course – way over the speed limit I'm sure – he wouldn't have made it.

All that happened without me knowing anything though. I was on the range as Rory was arriving then teeing off minutes later. It wasn't until I finished that Marian told me. I did get a laugh watching the Golf Channel the next morning before we left though. They had a thing asking 'who's to blame?' and one of the reasons was 'state trooper'.

Anyway, back on the course, I played beautifully. Maybe the only bad shot I hit all day was my approach to the first. Between clubs, I pushed it into the right hand bunker. But I got up and down for par and a half, so no harm done.

For me, the key holes were the fourth and fifth. At the former I chipped in from over the green for a birdie to go one up. I'm not normally one for fist pumping and the like but I must admit I had a wee bit of a jump and a shout to myself when the ball dropped. Which was understandable. It was a classic two-hole swing as I could easily have lost the hole had I not holed out. Then I made an eagle at the next; holing from about 10 feet after a great drive and approach. Walking to the sixth tee I was feeling pretty good, as you can imagine.

Part of that feeling is down to Colin Montgomerie. Back in 1999, he had impressed on me the need to assume that my opponent will always hole his putt. So when Brandt made it from 15 feet or so for birdie I wasn't disappointed. I felt ready to make my own putt; which I did.

Thereafter, I was never really in much trouble. By the turn I was three up. I lost only two holes, the second at the 14th, by which time I was five up. So the damage was minimal. One hole later it was all over. Brandt was a real sport about it, as was his caddie. Both were very complimentary about my play – I was six under par for the 15 holes – at the end, which was nice.

I was very emotional straight after I finished. Which is not like me. But I had been thinking of Adam all day. I was nearly in tears on the 14th tee when I was dormie five up. Marian came over to see me as soon as the match was over, which only made the day more special for me, as good as it gets outside of winning a major.

I had felt a lot of responsibility to win and produce a point. Ollie had highlighted the need for the top five matches to win – and I was number five. And that feeling was enhanced by the fact that, for a long time, Poulter was losing up ahead. He won in the end, of course.

When I finished, I waited on the 15th green for Nicolas in the game behind. He was two down with three to play but I made sure to give him a pat on the back and tell him he could still get a half. Unfortunately, he lost on the 16th, so maybe my motivational skills need a bit of work.

From there, we headed forward to watch Justin and Phil Mickelson. I arrived just as they got to the 18th tee, so I missed the huge putt Justin holed on the previous green. But I stayed to watch him make another great putt for birdie and the match on the last green.

Phil took it well though. In fact, his behaviour was impeccable I thought. He is a great example of how a true sportsman should acknowledge excellence in an opponent. What he did was very classy. I hope a lot of young golfers were watching and learning from him. It was significant that Justin, who was about to go ballistic after holing the winning putt, stopped immediately when he turned to find Phil right in his face. That was a nice mark of respect from our man.

I actually walked into both the opening and closing ceremonies opposite Phil. At the latter he shook my hand and congratulated me on our victory and 'your play today. I heard you were six under. Great playing'. That was nice to hear from such a terrific player.

While Phil's reaction to defeat was unusual in a Ryder Cup, I wasn't too surprised. One of the biggest differences between the 1999 matches and 2012 is how well the two teams get on off the course. Back in '99 in fact, I arrived not really talking to one of my teammates, Jarmo Sandelin. He and I had never really got on and we had another falling out at the Lancôme Trophy only two weeks before the matches. But we managed to get through the week for the sake of the team, even if, once the matches were over, normal service was soon resumed. He blanked me at the airport coming home, in fact.

A lot of how friendly things are now is down to how many more Europeans play in the States, but I found it refreshing to say the least. When Peter Hanson and I played Bubba and Webb Simpson they were both friendly. We chatted to them all the way round. There was plenty of 'good shot' and 'good putt'.

The same was true when Nicolas and I took on Kuchar and Johnson. There was lots of chat, none of it of any consequence, but that's not the point. And, as I said, Brandt Snedeker could not have been nicer during what must have been a difficult match for him.

None of that happened at Brookline in '99. There was hardly any interaction between the players back then. And what there was could sometimes be a bit bitchy and contentious. But not this time. Which is not to say that anyone was trying less hard to win.

After watching Justin win, Marian and I went back to the 17th tee to find Sergio. I couldn't get my head round how long it takes Jim Furyk to hit a shot. He must have backed off at least four times in the bunker at the 17th green. Even the home crowd was getting a bit restless at his antics. And he did the same with the putt and again on the 18th tee. It was amazing. I was screaming, 'hit the ball man' to myself. I know it's important. But you don't get longer because it's important.

Of course, I'm not the best spectator. I always think the worst when I'm watching. I couldn't see Justin holing his put at 18. I thought Furyk would hole his putts at both 17 and 18. I can't help it. I'm a 'glass half empty' spectator.

After Sergio won, we went back out again to see Graeme McDowell play the 17th. Once he had gone, we stayed on the tee to see Martin Kaymer. He holed a great putt there from four feet to go one up on Stricker. Then, at the last, he made another great one from seven feet or so to clinch at least a draw for the team.

Marian and I were back in the fairway when he was over the putt. Wayne Riley from Sky was standing next to us. 'What do you think?' I asked. 'No bother mate. He's German, Hell knock it right in the middle.' And he was right. Martin's hands were up in the air when the ball was only halfway to the hole.

At that, the celebrations kicked off. Ollie was up the fairway with us. I didn't hear what he said to Molinari, but they had to wait until the green cleared to hit. It took a while, which is bad. As is the fact that Kaymer took a long time to shake Stricker's hand. I hate to see that. The first thing you should do at the end of a match is acknowledge your opponent. In the excitement, Martin forgot that. Which is understandable, but not acceptable. Stricker had to stand there and wait, which is wrong.

When Francesco reached the green I couldn't see Tiger miss his putt. Then someone shouted, 'we've won', and it all kicked off again. I saw Tiger's putt later on television and I was shocked. I've never seen him miss a putt that badly before. I have no idea what was going through his head, but it certainly looked careless at best. I wonder if he cares about the difference between a draw and a loss. I know I do. But I'm not sure if he did in that situation. Who knows?

The rest of the day is a bit of a blur if I'm honest. To come from 10-6 down and win was incredible. Afterwards we were all on the bridge between the putting green and the first tee, each with a bottle of champagne. There's a great picture of me drinking from a bottle with Marian looking up at me. It was great fun, as you can imagine. As were the various interviews I did wrapped in a Saltire flag that had appeared as if by magic.

I'm not the biggest or most demonstrative celebrator though. Kaymer was going nuts high-fiving everyone in the crowd. Garcia, Rose and a few others were up on the buggies giving it 'Ole, ole, ole, ole'. I was just standing there, taking it all in. I wasn't getting up there. I'm just not like that. Don't get me wrong; I was loving it all. But I'm a wee bit older.

I wasn't alone in feeling that way either. By the putting green I came across Darren Clarke, who was enjoying a wee glass with a journalist who shall remain nameless. I asked Darren why he wasn't up on the bridge. His response was interesting. 'It's just not the same is it?' he said. 'You're the guys who have won. I'm proud of you, but it's not for me to be up there.'

After all that there was the closing ceremony. That's fun when you win, hellish when you lose. As are the press conferences both teams attend after the official part of the day is done. Ours was particularly funny as some of the lads had already been on the champers – on empty stomachs – for longer than was good for them. Sitting next to me, Graeme McDowell actually nodded off more than once.

Back at the hotel, the party really got going. I had a quick bite to eat, which was much needed on top of a fair few slugs of champagne and three or four beers. I'm not much of a drinker, so I was feeling the effects.

Before we went downstairs, Marian and I were having a wee chat about it all in our room. Outside, there was a bit of a commotion. In the corridor we found the Westwoods and two state troopers, who were escorting Mrs W to her room. They were holding her up actually. They propped her up against the wall as Lee opened the door. But not for long. When they turned round, she was on the floor. Lee told me later they left her on the bed, where she slept for eight solid hours and missed the party. Oh well.

We actually ate with Darren and his wife. Ollie sat with us too. The place was jumping by 10 o'clock. More glasses of wine disappeared, as did a few more beers. By 1am Darren had had enough. I made it to 1.30 before I had to give up. I needed my bed. I staggered back to the room and had a very sore head in the morning.

Just as we were leaving our room to go down to breakfast at 7am, we passed a member of the European team in the corridor. He was heading to his room from the party. I won't say who it was. But he's German. I'll say no more other than he was on our flight at 9am.

At breakfast we found Davy, my caddie. He looked awful. And eating something didn't seem to be helping much.

After all the cheerios we finished our packing and headed to the airport. Johann Rupert had kindly laid on a charter for all those playing in the Dunhill Links Championship, so we flew privately to Edinburgh in six hours 30 minutes. Which was very nice. We were back in Aberdeen by the early hours of Tuesday morning. No bother.

It was a great experience. Winning over there is special, especially as you have to take it in the neck from the spectators. Had it been a regular tournament, I would have been into the crowd four or five times. But at the Ryder Cup you have to take it. You can't do anything. And I think the crowds know that. They know you can't confront them.

Overall though. I loved every minute, even when I was hacked off at not playing. And yes, I'd love to do it all over again. In Scotland, too. What could be better than that?

Monday, 1 October
Home. Knackered. Happy.

Getting Started

It is safe to say that, on the morning of 1 April 1986, my 17-year-old mind was not on winning the Open or a Tartan Tour event, or even a local alliance. And playing in the Ryder Cup? That was for superstars, not five-handicappers like me. My first day as an assistant golf professional – there is a big difference between that and 'professional golfer' – was a bit more down-to-earth. I can still see my new boss, head professional Douglas Smart, emerging from the back shop at Banchory Golf Club just outside Aberdeen brandishing what he called my 'new best friends' for the next few years – a Hoover and a duster.

He was right too. My first-thing-every-morning routine consisted of vacuuming the shop floor then dusting everywhere. And I mean everywhere. I had to make sure every wooden club was spotlessly clean – and in those days they really were made of wood.

The senior assistant back then was Dean Vannet from Carnoustie. He was promoted to that position when Fraser Mann (another Carnoustie man) left to get the head pro job at Ballater and I was hired as junior assistant on £36 per week. Dean actually lived on site, in accommodation next to the club car park. I stayed there with him one night – but never again. There was no heating and no hot water. It was horrific. To this day I don't know how he managed to cope in the winter. The price must have been right, I guess.

Dean was a good lad and someone I felt could have been a really good player. But he was more interested in teaching. We had our ups and downs but overall we had a good time working together, with him as my immediate boss. I was just happy to be there, to be honest. I got the job when Doug saw me teeing off at Banchory one day. I used to play there occasionally with my dad and his taxi-driver mates. My handicap was five, which was the limit for turning pro, so when Doug asked my dad if I was interested he also arranged to play with me. Understandably, he wanted to give me the once-over.

As you can imagine, I was more than a little nervous before that game. I had no amateur record to speak of. Unlike so many of my contemporaries on tour I never played in the Scottish Boys Championship or represented my country at any of the three levels – Boys, Youths and Full International. But I needn't have worried about letting myself down. I quickly relaxed when Doug topped a 4-iron off the first tee. To be fair, he didn't play much golf. But it was still a bad one!

Another awkward moment for the youthful me came when I was at a dinner in the Marcliffe hotel and found myself sitting next to Douglas Connon. At that time he was the head of sponsorship and corporate affairs at Aberdeen Asset Management. When the first course was served I had no idea which fork or knife to use. So I guessed and went with those closest to the plate. As soon as I did that though, Douglas leaned over and whispered in my ear, 'start from the outside you peasant'.

Ever since then, I must add, Douglas has been a great friend to me. I have asked for and followed his advice many times over the years. He was always very professional and helpful. Although never again did he have to tell me which piece of cutlery to use.

My sporting 'career' to that point was more about football than golf really. I had caddied for my dad, Jim, a bit and I was, like him, a member at Kemnay. But it was football that dominated most of my time in my early and mid-teens. I was a decent player – nothing great – and I played on the right wing. What I wasn't good at was tackling. Never had the heart for that. So, while I could play and had a bit of skill, as soon as there was any roughness I was at the back of the queue.

Funnily enough, our younger son Michael is exactly the same when it comes to the physical stuff. He was in the Aberdeen FC youth set-up for a while. He has loads of ability but he is timid. Didn't know when to tackle and when to mix it up. So now, just as I did, he has stopped playing.

It was that attitude that got me playing more golf and less football. And when I made that decision, I started teeing up a bit more regularly and got my handicap down. Although I still had no thoughts of turning pro. When I first left school I was doing nothing more than mucking about at my dad's garage (he ran a taxi firm), washing the cars and helping the mechanics as much as I could.

Looking back, that day Doug saw me drive off the first at Banchory is one of the luckiest of my life. People think I was fortunate the day Jean Van de Velde went for a paddle? That was nothing to the break in life I got from Doug. I have to say he was a fantastic boss. It would have been easy for him to take advantage of me and leave me serving in the shop all day every day. But he didn't do that. Most days he would give me time to go and hit balls. And in the evenings we would play a few holes together with the other assistants.

In fact, I got into quite a tough school right off the bat when it came to playing for money. Fraser was still there for a bit when I arrived. And Dean's younger brother Lee – who was a brilliant player as a teenager – was Fraser's assistant at Ballater. Either we would go up there to play or they would come to Banchory. I would lose my shirt every time. Almost every week I lost my wages.

Long-term though, all of that was good for me; it toughened me up. I certainly learned more on the course than in the shop during the first six to eight months of my new life. Losing every night was good for me in the long run. Indeed, it was quickly obvious that I just wasn't good enough as a player. Doug and Dean especially weren't playing much so not playing that well, yet still they beat me regularly.

Things changed though. Eventually, all the work I was doing – I must have hit 600 balls a day every day at that time – started to make a difference. Eventually, I was holding my own with those guys. And eventually, I started winning more than losing.

One thing I always struggled with was giving lessons. I tried my best to avoid them if I could. In fact, I really only coached enough so that I knew enough to get through the exam. I didn't see it as a moneymaking thing. Which wasn't a problem most of the time; Dean was the senior assistant so he inevitably got most of the teaching assignments. I only ever wanted to play. The irony is that I love giving lessons now. When I take the young lads from the foundation out for a round I enjoy helping them with some aspect of their games. I'm happy to pass on whatever knowledge I've gained over the years. But when I was 17 I didn't have that attitude; I just wanted to work on my own faults.

There were times when I had to suck it up and give a lesson of course. And on my very first one Doug set me up good and proper.

I was in the shop one afternoon when this guy came in. He was struggling with his game and looking for a lesson. 'Perfect,' says Doug. 'Young Paul here will sort you out. Let him have a look at you and you'll be fine.'

At this point I'm looking at Doug as if he is mad. But off we went, down to the range, where I tell the guy to warm up by hitting a few. The plan was for me to watch and offer some advice along the way.

So he is hitting away. I'm saying nothing. But someone else is. At that time the range at Banchory was down by the river, where there was a public path. And we had a spectator. 'He's coming over the top,' he shouts out. 'Over the top.'

I was cringing, as you can imagine. 'Never mind him,' I said. 'You just keep hitting.'

After a few more shots, I say to my pupil – I thought quietly – 'You're coming over the top. You just need to wait a little on the downswing. Feel as though you're waiting for it and then try to get the club down your chest a bit more.'

Of course, the guy on the path overheard me. 'I told you,' he bellowed. 'I told you he was coming over the top.' I was so embarrassed.

The good thing was my pupil started to hit the ball a bit better. The bad thing was my heckler noticed that fact. 'I told you,' he shouted again as he walked off. 'I was right. I could be a pro. I could be a pro.'

Back at the shop, Doug asked how it had gone after my pupil had paid for the lesson. So I told him the story about the guy over the fence. He just smiled. 'Oh yes,' he said. 'That's my mate Jim. We windsurf together.'

That was all he said. All these years later, I'm still not sure if it was all a set up or not. But I have my suspicions!

All of which is not to say I didn't work hard to pass the PGA exams. I did, because I wanted something to fall back on if I didn't make it as a player. I still reap the benefits of my PGA training today, in fact. Unlike the vast majority of players on the European Tour, I work on my own clubs. I do all my own grips and lofts and lies. I don't use the wagons on the tour much. I like doing it myself. I enjoy disappearing into the garage at home and pottering about. I can even replace the old whipping that was used to secure the old woodenheads to the shafts – although I can't remember the last time I had to.

Being on the bottom rung on the professional ladder was not all fun, of course. There were plenty of aspects I didn't enjoy, like putting my hand inside someone else's sweaty shoe so that I could change the spikes. But, as I said, I worked hard. Doug was a huge help in that regard. I had left school with no qualifications – I was out the door before even sitting any exams – so the bookkeeping side of the job never came easy. But like so many other highly respected club professionals, Doug had been trained at Turnberry under the legendary Bob Jamieson, so he was great to work for and learn from. I will always be grateful to him for all that he did for me. And I'm very proud of the effort I put into getting my qualifications. As Marian says, I've got plenty of commonsense but nae brains.

As I said though, once I got started all I ever wanted to do was play golf for a living. If I'm honest, I would never have gone down the route I did if

I hadn't had to. If I'd been a good enough player I would have gone straight to tour school like everyone else. But I wasn't even close to that standard when I turned professional.

It did me no harm though. And looking back, I certainly gave it everything I had. I was living at home in Kemnay – 25 minutes from Banchory – to save money but almost every morning I would arrive at 7am so that I could hit balls before I opened up the shop an hour later. Then I would be on the range during my lunch – normally a quick sandwich – hour and again after work. So I wasn't spending a lot of time at home.

All of that hard work soon paid off too. It didn't take long for me to make my competitive mark. Only seven weeks after turning professional I won the first event I ever played in, the Moray Seafoods Open at Buckpool. I shot a 71, one over par, to win by one shot and collect the £300 first prize. I thought I was a millionaire with that cheque in my pocket, even if, because I was so shy, Peter Smith – who was then on the Scottish PGA committee – had to make my winner's speech for me.

Most of my 'tournament' golf during my first couple of years at Banchory, however, was in the form of local alliances (one of which I had won as a 16-year-old amateur, shooting 72 at Royal Tarlair). I really enjoyed those – I was very competitive and wanted to win every week – and they gave me something to look forward to amidst the day-to-day routine. Again, Doug was brilliant, letting me play most weeks. But not every week. I still smile when I think of the rare occasions when I wasn't allowed off to play; I would sulk all day.

I look back on those early days at Banchory with a lot of fondness though. I can't believe how much I practised, especially on my short game. The club actually had two ranges and I spent most of my time on the shorter of the two. There was a green down there and a bunker. I spent hours working on distance control with my wedges, something that has stood me in good stead ever since. But the clubs I used most were my 7-iron and my 9-iron. I regularly wore out the grooves on those. And I still practice mostly with those two clubs. They are always the ones I wear out first.

In recognition of how much time I used to spend down there, the club renamed the 14th hole 'Paul Lawrie' when the course was redesigned and 'my' range became the fairway for that hole. I thought that was a nice touch and one I still appreciate very much.

It was around that time too, that I got my nickname, 'Chippy'. My best mate today, Colin Fraser, was actually one of my first sponsors and he came up with it. I'm not sure if it was a compliment or an insult, mind. Back then my ball striking wasn't too hot, but my short game was. So one day, after watching me get up and down for the umpteenth time, he said to me, 'All you do is chip. You're just a Chippy.'

I was improving fast though. And winning at the levels I was playing at. Although, as I said earlier, I didn't really have a choice in the matter – I was playing in the events open to me – I was still aware that I didn't want to move upwards and onwards until I was successful in whatever arena I was in at the time. So it was that I won quite a few of those one-day alliance events, then I started winning assistants' tournaments (in 1990 I was Scottish Assistants' champion, Scottish under-25 champion and won the Assistants' Order of Merit), then it was onto the Tartan Tour, where I won the Daily Express National Pro-am (at Carnoustie) and the tour money list in 1991, then the Scottish PGA Championship in 1992. Then it was onto the European Tour, where I won the European under-25s championship. So I never moved up until I was really ready.

That's a mistake I see a lot of young lads making these days: they expect to go straight onto the European Tour from the amateur ranks. But I would argue that is too big a jump in one go unless you are a Rory McIlroy or Tom Lewis level player. For most lads, two or three years learning their trade at a lower level is a good thing.

Take David Law, who is one of the players we sponsor through the foundation. David was hugely successful as an amateur, winning the Scottish title twice and the Scottish Boys once. His original idea was not to turn pro unless he got a full European Tour card through the qualifying school. I told him I wasn't sure that was the way to go. Chipping over a bunker with your mortgage on the line is a bit different from playing for fun. So I recommended he should turn pro whatever happened at Q-school and go from there.

Happily, David took my advice and turned pro even though he failed at the first stage of the Q-school. And early in 2012 he won his first event as a pro in Morocco on the EPD circuit. So he's learning – and getting better – at just the right speed. He probably isn't quite at tour level yet, but he is getting there.

I can relate to where David is now, of course. I went to the first stage of the Q-school at the end of 1990 and failed twice. So I went back to the Tartan Tour in 1991, which was the best thing for me. Had I got my card a year before I did, I'm not sure I would have been ready for all that life on tour is about. Even dominating the Tartan Tour – which is populated mostly by club pros who don't play a huge amount of competitive golf – isn't going to have you ready for tour school. Not really. Not when you are suddenly on a range where everyone around you can really play.

So initial failure was the best thing for me – and for most people, I think. By the time I got my card I was ready. I was used to being in contention and I was used to the feeling of winning. That is a key ingredient. Winning is winning, no matter what level you win at. You still have to beat the guy next to you. And when you do, that is a big boost to your confidence. I arrived on tour a confident player.

All of which success in my early years as a pro begs the obvious question: why was I 'only' a five-handicapper when I turned professional? I've been asked that a lot over the years. The truth is that, while I played golf at Kemnay, where I was a member, my football was a bigger priority. My golf was restricted to club events. So although I played a fair bit I never thought of entering anything outside my home area. I did compete in a few junior opens at other clubs but that was about it. I certainly never considered playing in a national event, never mind winning one. I just wasn't good enough. Besides, most of them were played down in the Central Belt, a long way from my home in the North East.

It was on the Tartan Tour that I got my first taste of playing against other professionals on a regular basis. These days, the tour is made up mostly of one-day Pro-Ams – which have limited value to anyone looking to step up onto the main tour – but 20 years ago there were a number of 72-hole events. So it was a really good place to learn how to play proper tournament golf.

That was always my plan: be competitive in Scotland before I went to tour school. Which is why I played two full seasons on the Tartan Tour before I even tried the European Tour. I think too many guys try to step up too early. We all need to learn the game at lower levels before stepping up. Maybe I was just lucky in that regard. Within a year of turning pro, I could play. It all happened pretty quickly.

I passed my PGA exams in 1990. Well, most of them. I failed the rules section first time round, had to go back a year later to do it again. Which was not that surprising. I didn't know any of the rules back then. In fact, like many of my fellow tour pros, I'm not great on them now. I'm ashamed to say I still call for a referee whenever even a straightforward problem comes up. I take the view that it is just too much of a risk to assume I know what I'm doing. Too many players have been disqualified over the years when they thought they knew a particular rule but actually didn't.

That we pros are not always the best source of rules information does come as a surprise to most people though. A couple of years ago, I was watching the final of a foundation match play tournament at Newmachar. They had a referee there; I was just a spectator.

One of the boys hit his ball to a par-5 and it plugged on the bank of a bunker in long grass. 'Thank goodness you're here,' said the referee. 'Oh my God,' I said to myself.

'He doesn't get a drop from there, does he?' asked the ref. To which I replied, 'Is that part of the bunker?' And of course it isn't. After a bit more toing and froing, I persuaded the ref to look up the book or call someone who knew what he was talking about. And eventually we got it sorted out.

Walking away, the ref said to me, 'Man, I thought you would have known what to do there. I thought a boy at your level would just have gone like that (snapping fingers).' But I didn't. I know I should. But I don't. To me, the rules change way too often for me to keep up. And if I get something wrong it can be very expensive. So, for better or worse, 'better safe than sorry' is my motto.

There was one time I did take a chance when it came along though. I was in the shop at Banchory late one afternoon in 1989 when one of the members, Malcolm Tocher, came in. He was a dentist and he had a couple of young ladies with him. They were both dental nurses at the time. One of the girls was called Marian. I was immediately impressed, although it must be said that, after a day at the Banchory show, she was kind of half-cut and a bit giggly. I got her number though. And I called and asked for a date.

Now, that was unusual for me. As far as girls were concerned, I had never really bothered. All of my spare time was spent on the range hitting balls. And that isn't exactly a great spot for meeting women.

And the first date? Well, it didn't exactly go to plan. I was playing in the Ram Classic at Royal Aberdeen and the plan was to meet up after that and go to the pictures. But there was a bit of a delay at the tournament. So I was struggling to make it on time and, as a result, driving too fast away from the course.

I know I was driving too fast because the nice policeman who pulled me over told me I was. I hadn't been driving long at that point – I was only 20,

I think – and I was s-----g myself. And just to make things worse, my name was on the side of the car. Sandy Thain, a local garage owner, was my sponsor at the time.

'In a hurry lad?' asked the copper.

'I'm really sorry,' I said. 'I've got a first date tonight and I'm late. There was a delay at the golf.'

'Oh, you've been playing have you?'

'Aye, I've been playing. Aye.'

'How did you get on?'

'Actually I'm leading.'

'Well done. Good for you.'

At which point he says, 'Just slow down. There's no need for that speed. On you go, on your way.'

He was a nice guy. I think he saw I was shaking like a leaf. And yes, I was late. And no, I can't remember the name of the movie!

Anyway, my lateness can't have been too bad that evening. And, as they do, things progressed from there. A few months later I moved into Marian's flat in Aberdeen. And when we got married in October 1991 we bought a house in Cruden Bay. My first couple of years on tour we lived up there.

The wedding reception was at the Marcliffe hotel and the ceremony was in Lumsden, where Marian is from. She's actually from Kildrummy but the nearest church big enough was in Lumsden. My best man was my older brother, Stephen. I had been his best man exactly a year before. I remember that well because that was also the day I proposed to Marian.

I think she said yes right away. I can't exactly remember how it all happened. I'm just hopeless when it comes to things like that. Thankfully, Marian isn't. There are some things I can remember, but some I can't.

For example, I can remember exactly where I was the last time Aberdeen won the Scottish Cup. I was playing in a pro-am at Clydebank & District. And I was on the fifth green with my caddie, 'Shifter'.

Overlooking the green was a big block of flats. And through an open window we could hear the radio commentary on the final against Celtic – Shifter's team. It had gone to penalties. I asked my playing partners if we could stop and listen. So we did. Then up stepped Brian Irvine to score the winning penalty for the Dons.

As you do in such situations, I turned to Shifter and said, 'Get it up ye wee man,' or words to that effect. To which he responded by throwing the pin at me. It whizzed right past my head and stuck in the green. After a quick repair job we were on our way. I remember that perfectly!

Unfortunately, my memory for other, more important, things is less reliable. At least I can remember we went to Mallorca on our honeymoon and that I didn't take the clubs.

And yes (again), I know how lucky I am. I knew that very early on in our relationship. My wife is just a brilliant person in every way. She has made my professional life so easy by being so organised. And as a mother she is different class. The boys are as good as they are and as well mannered as they are because of her. It's not because of me.

I remember the first time Marian met my parents. Right away, my mum said how much she liked her. 'She's lovely and she looks after you,' she said. 'You're not going to do better than her.'

And you know what? My mum was dead right.

On Tour

I t was time to step up. After playing what I felt was some pretty good golf in Scotland over the previous two years, the campaign to get my European Tour card for the 1992 season began with 36-holes of pre-qualifying at Bolton Old Links. Rounds of 68–74 saw me finish tied for third there, easily good enough to get me on the plane to Montpellier in France and the six-round ordeal known as the tour qualifying school.

Everything you have ever read about the horrors of 'Q-school' is probably accurate. Even if you go there confident and playing well – as I did – it is nae a great experience. Instead of trying to play well as you would normally, it is easy to fall into the trap of trying not to play badly. Such is the pressure involved in trying to finish in the top-40 of what starts out as a 180-strong field.

So it was a huge week for me, one that I'm glad to say I've never had to go through again in the more than 20 years since I was there. I had some great help too, in the shape of David Thomson. It was, as ever, my great friend Stewart Spence's idea that David should accompany me. Stewart has been so generous towards me over the years and this was no exception. He paid for our flights and the hotel room we shared all week.

David, who is now the pro at Skibo Castle near Dornoch, was coaching me at the time and he came to France as my caddie. He was brilliant all week, both on and off the course, saying all the right things at just the right times. He didn't get too involved with the clubbing on the course – we both felt it would be best if I did my own thing as I would have normally – but he chipped in with the odd helpful comment. Really, having him there to play everything down and join me for a low-key dinner every night was a massive help. Looking back, I can see how good he was at keeping my mind on the right track. Of course, he knew only too well what I was up against and going through, having been to the school himself on more than one occasion.

To be honest though, I've never been one to get too bothered by pressure or nerves. I think that goes back to the beginning of my career. When you turn professional with a handicap of five, anything good that happens thereafter is a bit of a bonus. So no matter what situation I find myself in, I see it as a plus, something I could never have expected back on 1 April

1986. Although, to be honest again, I was well aware that failure at tour school would mean another year of Tartan Tour pro-ams. That was a pretty powerful motivation to succeed.

My attitude to the game actually comes through whenever I speak to the press after a round. If I've played badly, I have no problem in saying so. Golf is like that, as we all know. If you shoot a poor score, you shoot a poor score. So I'm always honest enough to say so. Equally, if I feel like I could and should have been, say, three or four shots better for whatever reason, I don't hesitate to say that either. I tell it like it is.

Anyway, as is always the way of things when I'm asked to recall something that happened further back than yesterday, my memory of how I played at tour school and what I shot is hazy at best. What I do recall is that I never put myself in a position where I absolutely had to shoot a really low round the next day. I was comfortably within the crucial top-40 almost right from the start. After two rounds I was tied for twentieth spot. One day later I had slipped to thirty-third. But when the cut was made after 72-holes (reducing the field to 90 players) I was back up to 24th.

After shooting a fifth round of 72 (I'm looking this up), I was tied for 16th place with 18-holes to go. And a closing 71 lifted me up to twelfth by myself. It is funny to look at some of the familiar names around me on the leader board that day. In first place was England's Andrew Hare, but right behind him were Jose Coceres of Argentina, Ireland's Paul McGinley and another Englishman Gary Evans. All three went on to have successful careers on tour. Also ahead of me were the likes of Thomas Levet of France and Steen Tinning from Denmark – two more future tournament winners.

None of that was concerning me at the time, of course. I had my card and I was on the European Tour. Nothing else really mattered. I came home to even more great news too. A group of Aberdeen businessmen that included Stewart Spence, Bruce Davidson, Billy Hogg and George Lumsden got together and chipped in £11,000 of sponsorship cash to get me up and running in my rookie year on tour. I can't tell you what a difference that made to me. That first year on tour cost me nothing and everything I made was mine. They wanted nothing back. It was an incredibly generous gesture.

Over the years I have read many stories about guys who were not so lucky and couldn't afford to play the tour, even though they had their cards. Actually, I heard of one pro who had a novel way of dealing with that problem. At the start of some seasons he would go to the bank and borrow whatever amount he thought it would cost him to play the tour. Let's say, £30,000. Then every month he would simply pay off the loan. Hey, it worked for him. Thankfully, I've never been in that position. And it is because of the goodwill of others that I can say that. I feel very lucky.

The first thing I did after passing my 'exams' at tour school was get a new caddie. Her name was Marian and in a former life she used to be a dental nurse. But no more. My wife's new job was to carry a bag round European Tour courses.

For all that this was a huge adventure for both of us – I had never played the Challenge Tour remember – it didn't take long for Marian and I to discover that not every aspect of life in the 'big-time' is glamorous. It takes a while to get used to all the packing of bags and travelling. But get used to it you do. It is like any job, within a few months you are comfortable with everything that goes with it.

We weren't at first though. On the way to my debut as a full cardholder, the Johnnie Walker Classic in Bangkok, we were in the back of the plane for 15 hours. That was bad enough, but this was in the days when smoking was still allowed on flights. And yes, we were sitting amidst a cloud of cigarette fumes. It wasn't pleasant for two non-smokers.

The weather in Thailand was no more bearable either. It was roasting hot and incredibly humid. I can't say I enjoyed it much. I've never really been comfortable with those kinds of conditions. I am from Aberdeen after all. Having said that, I didn't play badly, shooting one under par for 36-holes. But that was enough to miss the cut by a shot. My career as a European Tour player was off to a disappointing start. It was encouraging too though. I hadn't played that great in conditions totally foreign to what I was used to and yet I failed to qualify by only a shot. It was beginning to dawn on me that I had what it takes to survive and make a living on tour. I certainly wasn't thinking, 'Oh my God, this is just too hard' or 'these guys are just too good for me'.

That wee boost to my confidence brought with it gradual improvement. I made the cut in my second event in Dubai, albeit I ended up well down the field. Then in only my eighth event I recorded my first top-ten finish, at the Volvo Open de Firenze in Florence. That was a great experience. I played the third round alongside Anders Forsbrand of Sweden, who ended up winning. He was a lot longer than me off the tee and one of the better players on tour back then. So I learned a lot just by watching how he conducted himself.

Funnily enough for someone who often enough feels a wee bit out of his depth in certain situations, I have never felt that on the golf course. I've never been one to worry about shooting 80 and looking like a chopper. I get disappointed when I don't perform like I know I can, but I don't lie awake at night fretting about it, not even if I'm playing with someone like Nick Faldo the next day. When that happens, I'm more likely to be well up for it, knowing that I have a chance to observe a truly great player up close and can maybe learn a thing or two from him.

Of course, life in general was pretty good at that point. How could it not be? I was newly married. I had just qualified for the European Tour. And my wife and I were travelling the world having the time of our lives. We must have been in 20 different countries – and stayed in some wonderful hotels – that first year. Can you think of many jobs better than that?

Well, as it turned out, Marian could. After about five months on the bag, she was so fed up with my on-course behaviour that she fired me. She gave me an ultimatum: either get a new caddie or get a divorce. I think she was just kidding about the second part, but I got the message.

What brought things to a head was Marian's frustration with me. It got to the stage where she didn't feel like she could ever say the right thing. So for a bit she said nothing. Of course that didn't work either. I would say, 'you're not talking to me' and things got worse from there. She felt like she couldn't win. And she was right. Eventually, she told me she just couldn't do it any more.

Which was fair enough. I was being a right pain at the time, moaning and groaning about everything. So, even though she was doing a great job, I'm sure she hated that aspect of it. She is still the only caddie who has ever given me the bullet in 20-odd years on tour.

I actually feel like I'm pretty good with my caddie. I don't give him a hard time; I give myself a hard time. I wish that was not part of my on-course character, but it is. I'm pretty poor really. I'm so critical of myself. So I do moan and groan a lot. But only at myself, never at the caddie. Only very seldom have I railed at the guy on my bag. I know it is not his fault. I'm hitting the shots. He is just giving his opinion. If I were to ask any of the caddies I've had, I would hope they would say that.

Plus, I'm not one for hitting a lot of balls when I'm at tournaments. Caddies tend to like that. The last thing they want to do is hang around for another few hours after a long round while their man beats balls. My typical routine is to hit 40-50 shots after a round, then do a bit of chipping and putting. Then I'm gone. So it's not as if I'm hard work there either.

Wednesdays are a different matter though. Or at least they used to be for me. During the early part of that first year on tour I was the classic 'range rat' on the eve of every event. But that soon changed. I quickly twigged that the day before teeing it up for real was a time to chill out a wee bit and do less as opposed to more. So I soon shifted from hitting hundreds of balls to lying in bed watching a DVD on Wednesday afternoons. I see that as much more beneficial in the long run.

Apart from our, ahem, minor blip, Marian and I were both loving every minute. And it is an experience we intend to repeat when I turn 50 and I'm eligible for (and exempt on for at least one year) the Champions Tour in the US. By that time, the boys will be out of the house, so we will be free to go our own way. The plan is to stay over there for nine months or whatever and maybe drive between as many events as possible. In other words, finally get a good look at the country.

That is for the future though. Back in 1992, one of the highlights of my season came in May, at the Spanish Open in Madrid. It was in the third round that I was drawn to play with my golfing hero, the late Seve Ballesteros. He was always the golfer I wanted to be, swashbuckling and exciting. I can even remember the moment we got the news. We were coming back from dinner and stopped to look at the draw on the wall in the hotel reception. I couldn't believe it. I was so excited. And yes, this time I did have trouble sleeping the night before.

The next day I was on the first tee a little earlier than I needed to be. I always do that actually (I'm early for everything. If you tell me six o'clock I'm there at half five). Not sure why. I just like to watch the previous group drive off and see how they react. Anyway, I was there long before Seve. When he did appear he walked towards me – it was a really long tee – swinging his putter in his hand. He looked like he didn't have a care in the world. He was just sauntering along. Meanwhile, I was almost shaking with excitement.

I was very nervous over the first three or four holes. And I struggled early. But he was great to play with. He was everything you would want your hero to be actually. I came off at the end wanting to be like him and play like him even more than I did at the start. He shot 70 and I got round in 68. So I was more than chuffed.

Speaking of Seve, later that year I was on the range in Switzerland. Gary Orr and I were mucking about in a practice bunker when the great man appeared. So we stopped to watch him. He was hitting out of plugged lies and getting balls to pop up high and land softly. It was amazing. I had never seen anyone who could do that before.

Sitting on a nearby bench, Gary and I were like a couple of school kids. We bickered over who was going to ask Seve if he could explain to us how to hit that shot. I think Gary went over eventually. And Seve couldn't have been more helpful. He showed us how to address the shot with the clubface open, not shut as I would have played it. He then rolled the clubface open even more on the backswing, then hit down abruptly. And the ball popped up every time. Fantastic. I will never forget that.

Years later, I played with Seve again in Madrid. Sadly, this was near the end of his career, when his game had deteriorated sharply. I think he was about six or seven over par for the first nine holes we played. But there were still moments to savour, one you may be familiar with from 'YouTube'.

Off the first tee – our 10th – Seve hooked his drive left, behind some trees. I had a look and there was no way he could hit the ball. Or so I thought. He got down on his knees and, using a five-wood, conjured up this low, smother hook that ran and ran nearly onto the green. I watched him hit it from the right side of the fairway. It remains the best shot I ever saw him hit live.

It's not the best shot I've ever seen though. That happened during a Skills game in Hawaii, just before the 2000 Sony Open. Sandy Lyle was there. So was Paul Azinger. And Jesper Parnevik and Sergio Garcia. We were in the right-hand rough behind a tree, the idea being that everyone had to have a go at shaping a shot round the tree from thick rough. No one could get anywhere near the green, until Sandy stepped up. We had all hit 7- or 8-irons. Sandy used a putter. I kid you not. He picked the club up steeply on the backswing and hit down really hard on the back of the ball. It cleared the tree by six feet or so, cut maybe 20 yards in the air and stopped 15 feet from the pin. Phenomenal.

Other players impressed me that first year as I got used to life on tour. I played with Howard Clark at the French Open. He had been to the US Open the week before and was in form. I think he hit every green that day and shot 71. He had 17 two-putts and one single putt for birdie. It was an awesome display of striking. He flushed it all day. Even now, whenever anyone asks me who is the best player I have ever been drawn with, I always say Howard Clark, if ball striking is all you are taking into consideration. That day is still the best I have ever seen. He was never away from the middle of every fairway and every green.

Howard's putting was another matter, of course. It was just woeful. He couldn't get the ball to the hole and kept moaning about how he couldn't adjust from the US Open a week earlier. But nobody has ever, in my experience, hit the ball better than he did that day.

Later that year, I made my debut in the Open at Muirfield. That was a great experience and a big thrill, especially as I was drawn with the defending champion, Ian Baker-Finch, in the third round. He was awesome to play with and such a nice guy. He didn't play that well, as I recall, but he did hit one shot I'll never forget. It was at the 14th, a long par-4 playing into the wind. He hit a driver off the deck right onto the green. I can still see the ball now, boring through the breeze.

About a month after the Open I felt like I had just about earned enough money to be reasonably sure of my card for 1993. So I popped off the tour for a week and played in the Scottish PGA Championship at Cardross. It was amazing how I felt there, playing with guys I had been competing against less than a year before. Even if you struggle on the European Tour – as I had in the two or three weeks before that – just playing at that high a level does wonders for your game, without you even realising it sometimes. So I won. Playing with better players had made me better.

Still, 'better' wasn't good enough. Over the first few months of 1992 I discovered that I needed shots I didn't have if I was to survive on tour. As I said earlier, I hit the ball like a typical Aberdonian back then – low and left-to-right. That was my shot. But then I'd be faced with a 2-iron from a downhill lie over water. My little low 'squeeze' shot wasn't getting the job done. So I had to change that completely.

One thing that did help me in that regard was, ironically, my total lack of experience in major amateur events, pretty much all of which are played on links. David Law, who is sponsored by my foundation, talks about how he has had to adapt from amateur golf to professional golf, which is hardly ever played by the seaside. On a links he had to keep the ball down; now he has to flight his shots more.

Having said that, the courses I encountered on tour didn't bother me at all. A lot of people complain – I'm sure quite rightly on occasion – that the general level of the courses we pros play is quite poor. Maybe they are. But where I'm playing has never been a big thing for me. Whatever the course is, the course is. And my opinion on how good or bad it is doesn't matter.

There is a tournament to be played. There is a prize fund to play for. So we might as well get on with it. I'm there to make money and go home, not be an architecture critic.

I'm sure that attitude helped me when I won the Open. As I touched on in chapter one, a big percentage of the field that week was complaining about the way in which Carnoustie had been presented. And by doing so, they talked themselves out of it. Not me though. I just got on with the job.

One difficulty I did have that first year was scheduling. When you don't really know how you're going to react to, say, six events in succession, you sort of have to wing it. And of course I wasn't really in a position to pick and choose where and when I played. Especially early on, if I was qualified for an event, I played in it. The big thing I learned was that a break for me is two weeks, not just one. One is not enough. Not for me anyway. I need to get away from the game completely in that first week, then play a few times and hit a few balls during the second. By the end of that, I'm ready to go play again. That is what I do now anyway.

By the end of the season, I felt like I had played pretty well despite a poor finish; I missed seven cuts in my last 10 events. Although I had failed to make it to the weekend 12 times in 26 starts, I had a couple of top-tens – in Florence, then at the Irish Open, where I was sixth. And the numbers were respectable. I was 83rd on the Order of Merit – well inside the all-exempt 125 – I had won just over €78k and my stroke average was 72.49. All in all, I felt ready to do it all again in 1993.

As it turned out, I wasn't. Not right away. I got off to a terrible start in 1993 and struggled for most of that season. But there was one great highlight, in the Open at Royal St Georges. To say that I finished tied for sixth alongside two truly great players in the shape of Ernie Els and Nick Price is pretty good for starters. But it was the way I hoisted myself up to that position that is so special. On the 71st hole of the championship I made an eagle two, holing out a 3-iron from over 200-yards. In fact, standing on the last tee I was only one shot off the lead. But I bogeyed the 18th and Greg Norman had a few birdies to win by four in the end. Still, that week was a big step-up for me.

At this point you are probably wondering if I'm going to run you through every detail of my two decades on tour. Don't worry; I'm not. But I wanted to give you a taste of what my life is like when I'm working. Besides, my career breaks down neatly into two distinct sections.

In the first, I went from being a five-handicap amateur to Open champion. I think that can safely be described as 'over-achieving'. Then there is the period between 1999 and 2012, during which I've won only five more times. For a major champion, that is very definitely 'under-achieving'.

To be honest (although as I write these words, the last couple of years have brought the sort of success I expected from myself after I won the Open), that I have only eight European Tour wins to my name is, on paper at least, a disappointment. Then again, if we take the Open victory out of the equation and look at what I've achieved from day one in the shop at Banchory, I'm immensely proud of where I am right now.

Sometimes, I admit, I take it all for granted. Sometimes I even get a bit grumpy about things that are inherently trivial – don't we all? But when I do, Marian is always quick to remind me of what we have. 'For goodness sake man,' she says. 'Give yourself a shake. What we've got now, we never thought we would have.'

She's dead right, of course. If you had said to me on 1 April 1986 that I would have a 20-year career on the European Tour and win at least half a dozen times, I'd have called you mad. So take it from me, I'm very aware of what I have and how lucky I have been.

I was once asked how my life had changed after the Open win. Trying to be funny, I answered, 'Well, not much, apart from the Ferrari, the mansion and the private jet.' But that doesn't go down well with most people. I know that now, but it was a joke.

The irony is, I've always been so hard on myself on the course. I'm like Darren Clarke in that respect. I think we have both been hurt by too much self-criticism. I've played with Darren a lot and I hear echoes of myself when he gives himself some stick after a bad shot. He is a much better player than I am, of course, tee-to-green especially, so it must be hard for him to deal with when he slips from the high standards he has for himself. But what we have in common is that we have both held ourselves back mentally. If there is one area of the game I wish I could be better at, even after two decades on tour, it is between the ears.

I'm one of those players who, when I'm having a bad time on the course, hits a shot that teeters on the top of a bank, then shouts at the ball to 'run down the hill, go on'. I do that a lot. And yes, it is embarrassing.

Over the years, I've had to apologise to so many caddies for my moaning and groaning. And every one of them has said the same thing in response: 'Listen, you are not hurting me, you are just hurting yourself.'

You can moan as much as you want. If you think it helps, go ahead. But you hit the shots. You pick the clubs. You're not bothering me. So you don't have to apologise.'

I hate that about myself as a golfer. And when I hear other players doing similar things and saying similar stuff, I know how stupid and childish it all appears. I always have a wee chuckle to myself because it sounds so ridiculous. My problem is that I get worse mentally the more I play. I'm always a lot worse in the third week of a three-week run than I am in the first. That is when the moaning starts. Give me two weeks off though and I'm a new man. I'll be brand new.

I'm not alone, of course. Plenty of tour pros have problems in this area. Tony Johnstone from Zimbabwe is one. He once apologised to me on the first tee because he knew he was going to be an idiot all day.

'Very sorry for my behaviour today,' he said.

'We've not started yet,' I replied.

'Believe me,' was all he said in reply.

On the other side of the coin there are guys like Barry Lane, who is over 50 but still has his European Tour card. I love playing with him. It's an education. He can hit it anywhere and everywhere, yet still he just goes on as if nothing has happened. Where I'm always trying to justify a bad shot by making comments to my caddie, I have never seen Barry do the same.

I wish I could be more like Barry. I have tried of course, but I just can't do it for any length of time. I'm a bit like an alcoholic who vows never again to have a drink. I'm ok for a while, then the temptation just gets too much for me. I can be going along fine, then a poor shot will just frustrate the hell out of me. And I lose it.

That sort of thing has hurt my performance over the years. Of course it has. Marian says it has. And so has every caddie I've ever had. So they can't all be wrong. Besides, I know they are right, even if I'm better today than I've ever been. I used to have runs of bad holes. I'd go bogey-bogey-bogey quite often, even after reading all the psychology manuals – which I have.

Many times I've sat for an hour or so and read, say, a Bob Rotella book. And afterwards I've felt so much better about the game and myself. But then I go out on the course and come to a hole where there is half of Aberdeen on the right and out-of bounds on the left. And of course I hook it OB. I can't handle that. I just don't have the mental capacity to handle that. Never have.

The strange thing is, I'm completely different away from golf. Marian is always saying I'm transformed as a person when I drive through the gates of a golf club. But apart from a brief period in 2003 – see chapter 11 – I've never taken the game home with me. I'm proud of that. Even if I've shot 84, as soon as I come out of the recording area I'm normally fine and reasonably approachable.

I like to think I'm a generous person too. I like looking after people. If we have a pro-am for the junior foundation and a lot of local pros make the effort to show up and play, I give them each a cheque. I always pay my caddies well. They take a lot of crap from me so they deserve it.

I'm far from perfect though. Who is? I'm 'mister angry' in the car, for example. I'm one of those guys who toots his horn and shouts and waves at people. The funny thing is I'm not that good a driver myself, which Marian always finds amusing. I drive too fast and I'm not that good technically. I had a few dents when I was younger.

But I hope that the person I am most of the time when I'm away from the tour is the real me, not that lunatic who can be a nightmare to be around. Or the guy who can't listen to anyone or anything because he has just hit a bad shot. I hate being that way and I hate being in that mood. But it is all part of me and part of why I am the golfer I am.

Anyway, back on tour, my career progressed steadily throughout the 1990s. The first win came in 1996 at the Catalan Open, which unfortunately was cut to 36-holes because of high winds. And, although I didn't win again in either 1997 or 1998, I knew I was improving all the time. By then I was a far better player than I was in 1992, when I arrived on tour. Indeed, for the first maybe four years of my time on the European Tour it was my short game that kept me out there – my putting was amazingly good back then. But for the next four it was my long game that took over the bulk of the work. In that respect I'm quite similar to another Open winner at Carnoustie, Padraig Harrington. He arrived on tour a relatively poor ball-striker. Now he is one of the best.

The man who made the biggest difference to my swing was, of course, Adam Hunter. I started working with him in the winter of '98 when he lost his card and decided to move onto coaching. I was his only player and he would come up to Aberdeen and stay for a couple of days at a time. So we got a lot of good work done, much of which had to be put on hold when I had an operation on my knee at the end of 1998.

So it was that, when the 1999 season dawned, my short-term expectations were pretty low. And in the first event of the season, in Dubai, I missed the cut by miles. I shot 76 the first day and just played terribly. But Adam gave me some things to work on over the weekend and, amazingly, I won the very next week in Qatar. Not that I hit the ball perfectly you understand, but when you can't seem to miss inside 15 feet, winning becomes a bit easier.

That was a huge lift obviously. And my good play continued. I had a couple of top-tens and a lot of good, solid finishes. In fact, I got to the stage where I was a bit frustrated. I felt I was playing so much better than my results indicated. But Adam preached patience and, as ever, he was right. By July I was Open champion.

The Battle of Brookline

Ask anyone who has been lucky enough to play in the Ryder Cup and they will tell you pretty much the same thing. Standing on the first tee before the first match is perhaps the most nerve-wracking place you can ever be in golf. And yes, it was like that for me when I eventually got over the ball to hit the opening drive in the 1999 matches at The Country Club. But I bet you I'm the first guy who, less than two minutes before that high-stress moment, had a fit of the giggles.

There I was surrounded by almost everybody who was anybody in what would turn out to be the most controversial Ryder Cup in history. Our opponents, Phil Mickelson and David Duval, were with me and my partner, Colin Montgomerie. The American captain, Ben Crenshaw, was there with all his vice-captains. So was European skipper Mark James, with Sam Torrance and Ken Brown, his lieutenants for the week. And the crowd was enormous and really loud. It was quite a scene.

In the middle of all that hubbub and excitement, Monty and I were almost crying with laughter. The 'problem' was the old guy who was to be the referee for the match. As we stood there he was telling us that he was not American at all; he was 'Scotch'.

'No,' said Monty. 'That's a drink. Scotch is a drink.'

Still, unperturbed by that piece of information, our new best friend – I wish I could remember his name – went on to tell us that his family was from Scotland and then proceeded to pull out pictures of his grandchildren. On the tee. Two minutes before the Ryder Cup was to start.

At that point, Monty lost it completely. He had already been rolling his eyes and making faces as only he can, but that was only the beginning. I was standing there laughing, but he was almost helpless. His head was down and his hands were on his knees. I'm not sure I've ever seen him laugh so hard and so long. Not that his amusement lasted forever mind. After four or five holes it became obvious that our fellow 'Scotchman' was not up to the job – he looked pretty old, to be fair – and after consulting with Phil and David, we had him replaced.

We are getting ahead of ourselves though. While the Ryder Cup matches are played over only three days, many months of planning and effort go into the biennial contest with the Americans, both on and off the course. My involvement that year actually started in May, four months before I was asked to hit that opening tee-shot. Along with maybe 30 other players, I was measured for the team clothing during the PGA Championship at Wentworth.

Funnily enough, Monty and I were actually fitted for all the gear at the same time that week. And again, he was hilarious. When we went in, the guy said, 'Right Colin, I'll take you first. What is your waist measurement?'

'36,' says Monty.

At which point I immediately started to snigger. I couldn't help it. The idea that Monty – no slim-Jim – could fit into trousers that size was funny.

'I am, I am,' protested Monty.

So the tailor comes back with a pair of 36-inch trousers. As he pulled them on, I could see Monty breathing in. A lot.

I'm next. 'What size are you Paul?' he said.

'38,' I said.

'You're never 38,' said Monty.

'I am,' I said. 'I don't like my trousers tight. I wear them above my belly, as opposed to under.'

At which point Monty went very quiet.

Anyway, if I had known what a great partner and mentor Monty was going to be for me over the course of the six days we spent together as Ryder Cup partners and teammates, I maybe wouldn't have been quite so cheeky. It's well known how much he went through over the course of those matches – the crowd's behaviour towards him was nothing short of disgusting at times – but one of my lasting memories of the week is how magnificently he played and how much he helped me.

Apart from the Sunday singles, every moment I spent on the course I was with Monty. And he was brilliant. I learned so much from him about what it takes to be successful in a Ryder Cup. For example, during our opening practice round, he immediately noticed I had a tendency to get 'too cute' with my chip shots if I missed a green. And he was right. If I missed a green on, say, the left when the pin was cut towards that side – 'short siding' myself in pro-speak – I would always attempt a low-percentage recovery shot. Sometimes it would come off, but most often I'd leave my ball in the long grass that surrounded every green.

I'd done that a couple of times when Monty spoke up.

'You must give me a putt this week,' he said. 'If I miss the green, I don't care if you chip it 30 feet past the hole. You must put me on the green and give me a chance to hole the putt.'

He must have said that to me a dozen times. Over and over. And he was bang on, even if, as things turned out, he should maybe have said it at least once more. In our opening foursomes match with Mickelson and Duval, Monty missed a green to the left when the cup was cut on that side of the putting surface. So I didn't have much room to play with.

Standing over the ball, I was aware of what I had to do. Goodness knows, he had told me often enough. But still I got it wrong. Although it was one of those shots where my last thought was to give it a bit more than I initially thought it needed, I misjudged the effect of the rough on the club head. The ball came off too high on the face and fell down short of the putting surface.

I was feeling bad enough about that, but worse was to come when Monty came bouncing across the green. 'I told you, I told you,' he said again and again. Although I wasn't happy at the result of the shot, I had to laugh.

I'm getting ahead of myself though. Thoughts of playing with Monty in the Ryder Cup were a long way from my mind until my Open win confirmed my place in the European side. In fact, despite the huge build-up to the matches on television and in the media, it only felt real once we were on the way to Boston.

It was an early start that Monday morning too. Marian and I were on the 6.40am shuttle from Aberdeen to Heathrow, where we met the rest of the team in the Concorde lounge. That was where we had our first pictures taken as a team – goodness knows how many we posed for by the end of the week – although both Jesper Parnevik and Sergio Garcia were missing. They met up with us in Boston.

On the plane – it was my first time on Concorde – the seats were two-and-two either side of the aisle. The arrangements were pretty interesting too, now that I think about it. Our captain, Mark James, and his wife, Jane, were in row one as you'd expect. But on the other side were Monty and his then-wife, Eimaer. The vice-captains, Sam Torrance and Ken Brown, were behind them in row two with their wives.

With the benefit of hindsight, I can see how much influence Monty had on what went on that week. Everything seemed to go through him. And he always seemed to know what was going on well ahead of everyone else. For example, in one of the practice rounds we played, I mentioned to Monty that I expected him to be playing with Andrew Coltart – the third Scot in the side – in the foursomes.

'No, I'm not,' he said. 'You and I are playing together in every match.' He knew that days in advance and certainly well before I did. Like everyone else, I had supposed that Andy had been picked to play with Monty. But Monty knew better and not for the first time when it came to the selection of the team.

Just before the matches, in fact, a journalist told me an interesting tale about Monty and his level of involvement behind the scenes. About a month earlier, in Munich, where Mark announced his two wild-card picks, Monty had been sitting with the reporter working on a story. This was very early on the Saturday morning; the picks were announced late the following day at the end of the tournament.

Anyway, as the two are chatting, the journalist asked Monty whom he thought Mark would pick.

'Oh I know who it's going to be,' said Monty.

'What do you mean you know who it's going to be?'

'I know. It's Parnevik and Coltart.'

This was a bit of a surprise. Most observers felt that the picks would go to Jesper and Bernhard Langer. Or, if not Langer, Robert Karlsson of Sweden. But, almost two full days before the announcement, Monty knew otherwise. And to this day, the journalist in question regrets not running straight to the nearest bookie.

Even now I'm still a little perplexed by it all. I would have gone with Langer – a two-time Masters champion and hugely experienced in the Ryder Cup – had it been up to me. I'm sure most people would have done the same. With the benefit of hindsight, Bernhard would have been the extra body we needed to give guys a rest during the matches. If Bernhard had played even once a day, it would have made a huge difference to others in the side.

None of that was occupying my mind as we arrived in Boston though. We went straight to the hotel, had a bite to eat, chilled out a little and were all in bed early because of the jetlag. That first night, I was up at 3am. I was thirsty so I went along to the team room for a drink of water. It had big sofas and seats and a dining area for the players. No one but us, the captain and the vice-captains were allowed in there, not even the wives. There was a big lounge for them to sit in.

The team room was great actually. There were loads of messages from European Tour players up on the wall. And best of all, we had a whole floor of the hotel to ourselves, so as I made my way down the corridor there was no danger of bumping into anyone I didn't know.

I did find someone though. In the lounge was Sam. He was pouring himself a large one when I walked in. He couldn't sleep either.

'All right Chippy,' he said.

'Just can't sleep Sam.'

'Oh it's murder isn't it?'

And away he went back to his room.

Speaking of the rooms, I'll never forget the first time Marian and I walked into ours. It was like a department store there was so much stuff in there. For me there were two pairs of trousers and two shirts for each of the next six days. There were 12 slipovers and 12 sweaters too. There were four pairs of the Nike shoes I was wearing at the time. There was a blazer. And there was evening wear too. The room was full of kit.

Marian did okay too. She had been flown to Germany just before the Open to be fitted for all the stuff she would wear during the day and in the evenings. I think it was all made by Escada. Which pleased her. She likes their stuff.

The real work started the next morning. Right from the start, the Country Club was mobbed. Even on the Tuesday practice rounds – three full days before the serious business began – there were people everywhere. We signed a lot of autographs that day, as per instructions from Mark, Sam and Ken. The idea was to get the fans and spectators on our side as much as possible. We didn't want to alienate them in any way. Even Monty was signing! I couldn't believe it. Instead of 'not today, not today' he was engaging with the audience in a positive way.

Until Friday when the matches started for real, I only saw Marian at breakfast and dinner. None of the wives saw the course until the Friday. Which was odd. Marian certainly didn't like all the sight-seeing and stuff. Not that it was all bad. Marian has always got on well with Caroline Harrington and she spent time with Dawn Brown, who is a lovely person. All in all, there was quite a family feel. Everyone, even those players I normally wouldn't get on with particularly, made an effort to bond.

That aspect of the matches is often overlooked. But I can remember talking a lot with Jarmo Sandelin and Sergio, two guys I could never have described as friends before that week. But at a Ryder Cup everyone is your buddy. It's a phenomenal atmosphere. Which is as it should be, even though it doesn't last. All week in Boston Jarmo and I had got along great. But then, at the baggage carousel in London on the way back, he totally blanked me. Obviously the team thing was over.

Adam was there all week too. He stayed in the caddie's hotel. We had paid for his trip and I know he loved being there. I wanted him to experience it as a 'thank you' for all he had done for me in the year he had been my coach. I had to laugh at his reaction to me changing the grips on my clubs on the Wednesday afternoon though. He couldn't believe I would do such a thing at such a late stage. But that kind of thing doesn't bother me. Adam was useful too. A couple of times I called him over and he was able to help me sort out a wee technical problem. But that was a bonus; it was just nice to have him there.

My boss for the week, however, was Monty. I can't really say enough about how well he played under incredible pressure. And he did it all playing with my golf balls. I was playing Strata balls at the time and he was a Titleist man. But we used mine in every match. In fact, Monty stuck with Stratas in the singles too. I remember Adam having to get me more balls because Monty had pinched mine.

Other than that, Monty was in charge. I was fine with that. Early in the week, Adam told me to let him guide me along. On the course he took control of pretty much everything. He told me where to hit on every hole. He told me which holes I would be hitting on. He even told me which side of the fairways and greens to aim for. At which I had to point out that I was not quite as accurate as him off the tee!

I learned so much from Monty over the six days I spent with him. Seeing him up close in that sort of environment was a huge education for me. He was world class. Some of the shots he hit and the putts he holed – all while people were shouting vile things at him – were so impressive. He handled the pressure so well. What a golfer he was.

It certainly helped me enormously to have Monty beside me on that first tee. I get a little nervous every week hitting my first drive, but this was something else entirely. I had known for about 24 hours that I was going to hit the opening tee-shot and I was fine about it. At least I thought I was.

It was Paddy who told me. During our last practice round he came over and told me, 'They're talking about the opening tee-shot. You're hitting it.'

By 'they' he meant Monty and Mark James.

'No way,' I said.

'Yeah, you're hitting it.'

'Because he (Monty) doesn't want to?'

'No. Because it fits better if you hit first at the odd holes and he has the even.'

So then Monty came over and told me. I immediately put on a false front of bravado. 'No problem,' I said.

'You okay with that?' asked Monty.

'Of course I am. No bother to me.'

But what I was really thinking was, 'Bloody hell.'

And right at the last minute I could see myself whiffing. Yes, missing the ball completely. Which makes sense. I know other players have chickened out at the last minute in similar circumstances.

'Just don't miss it. Just don't miss it,' went through my head as I teed up. 'Make contact and everyone will let you off.'

In the end, I hit an okay sort of shot. Slightly blocked, it finished in the semi-rough up the right side of the fairway. As I put the club back in the bag, I said to Monty, 'Sorry about that.'

'Don't worry,' he said. 'Wait till you see where this one goes.'

Mickelson was up next. And man, he missed the planet. He must have been at least 40 yards off-line, a really poor shot. I realised then that the Americans were just as nervous – maybe even more so – and that gave Monty and I an early boost.

We combined well too. That first morning against Duval and Mickelson – who strangely barely spoke to each other all the way round – we were four under par with no bogeys. That's very good round such a tough course playing foursomes (or alternate-shot as the Americans prefer to say). And we won 3&2. I was obviously ecstatic. Apart from the USPGA Championship in Chicago the previous month, this was my first competitive golf in the States.

The type of golf we had to play was pretty new to me. The Country Club was very tight and there was a lot of rough around the greens. That called for me to learn a different technique when chipping and pitching. I played a lot of 'bunker shots' from the long grass that week, as opposed to the lower running shots I would normally hit. It wasn't a huge problem though. After a couple of days, I adapted pretty well.

I wasn't short of confidence, of course. How could I be? Two months before I had won the biggest event in the game. And I had played solidly since. Plus, Phil Mickelson had paid me a huge compliment on the eve of the matches. When he was asked how the Europeans would get on with five rookies in the team, he said, 'They actually have four rookies and Paul Lawrie. Major winners don't count as rookies.' That was a pretty nice thing to say and gave me a lift.

I was feeling good though. I had qualified for the team as of right, in third or fourth position. So at no time did I feel like I didn't belong. In fact, I had a feeling that week I've only had a few times in my career: I felt like I was going to beat everyone there. I'm not the sort of bloke who says that sort of thing lightly, or even at all. But that was the vibe I had in Boston.

I certainly hit the ball well all week. Every day on the range, my swing just clicked into place. On the Friday morning I was in great spirits. Adam was on the range with me and we were having a great time chatting away to Monty. He was the same, laughing and giggling as only he can, on the range and the practice green. Which is not to say that he wasn't already in 'tournament mode'. He was. And when I started to make my way to the first tee he stopped me.

I normally get to the tee in time to watch the game ahead tee off. I have always done that. I just like to be there early. But Monty was having none of that. 'Whoa, whoa, whoa; we'll not go yet,' he said. I'm still not sure if he wanted the Americans to wait for us on the tee, or if he felt like it would be better not to spend much time there. But we didn't arrive until there were only five minutes to go before I was due to tee-off.

Even all the stuff that went with the crowd didn't bother me. Quite the opposite. It was a bit of a scrap at times but I loved getting 'down and dirty'. I remember looking around at one point and saying to myself, 'This is brilliant'. The spectators would be going, 'USA, USA'. Plus, I had been looking forward to it for months. As soon as the play-off at Carnoustie was finished, I said to Adam and Paddy (my caddie), 'We're in the Masters and we're in the Ryder Cup. How good is that?'

I liked the course too, even if it wasn't the sort of layout I normally do well on. I'm not typically the straightest driver on tour but I was that week. In fact, I drove it lovely in spells. So I wasn't struggling with anything. I didn't feel under any pressure to perform. I just felt like I deserved to be there. You don't get that sort of sensation very often. I don't anyway.

Unfortunately, not everything was so nice once the matches got going. When we got to Friday, the atmosphere changed markedly. Overnight, it went from friendly to fearsome and, too often, downright unpleasant. Which should have come as no surprise to those of us whose phones went off at 3.10 that morning, with no one on the other end, of course.

And, despite the way I was feeling and the confidence I had in my game, I couldn't help but be aware of an undercurrent of not quite contempt but certainly disapproval from certain members of the American camp. I got the sense that quite a few people were looking forward to me not playing well. Or at least fancied their chances of beating me.

Anyway, having won our first match comfortably, Monty and I were out again in the afternoon four-balls against Justin Leonard and Davis Love. I knew Justin from the Open play-off and Davis and I had a bit of history too. He had been widely quoted as saying, 'the Open got the champion it deserved' in the immediate aftermath of the championship. It wasn't a compliment either.

The match was close all the way until we got to the par-5 14th all square. Both Monty and I hit the green for two and so did Davis. I was about 50-feet away but he was no more than six feet.

I holed mine and went, unusually for me, completely ballistic. I was shouting and bawling and jumping up and down. I was, not to put too fine a point on it, quite pleased with myself.

Davis then followed me in for the half. And there was another big celebration. But I was feeling a bit guilty over what I had done and the way I had behaved. So I waited for Davis on the edge of the green. As he came up, I shook his hand and said: 'Great putt. I got a bit excited there. Sorry about that.'

'Don't you worry about that,' he said. 'Great putt. And a good half.' And off we went, the game eventually finishing all square. Which was great. It had been a brilliant day and the crowds had been relatively fine to that point.

That changed the following day. In the morning, Monty and I lost to Jeff Maggert and Hal Sutton on the last green. That was disappointing enough, but the crowds were a disgrace with Monty getting the brunt of it. I can't begin to tell you some of the vile despicable things I heard that day. Most are unprintable.

It got so bad that, when we reached the 13th and I had hit our ball into the right rough, Monty told his caddie, Alastair McLean, to do the yardage for the next shot out on the fairway. Then he could walk over, hit the shot and get back to his bag really quickly. It was that unpleasant. He didn't even feel safe leaving the fairway. And, understandably, he didn't want to be among the spectators, many of whom had already been drinking.

Monty kept saying, 'I'm obviously a threat. I'm a threat.' He was hating it all and loving it all at the same time. He does like to be the centre of attention! And to be fair there was some good banter amongst all the evil stuff. 'Visit the salad bar,' was a favourite. And I can't imagine how many times we heard 'Mrs Doubtfire.'

Even Monty had to laugh sometimes. On one hole he came over to me with a big smile on his face. Someone had called him a 'limey bastard.'

'They don't even know that's English,' he said. 'They think I'm English.'

When it came to the shots, Monty had just as much to say. But I had told him I wanted to do my own thing when it came to clubbing, just as I would do in a regular tournament. And the same with the putts. I don't even ask for my caddie's advice on lines. Only once or twice did I ask for his input. And invariably he would tell me to aim for the middle of the green. I learned that week how the centre of the putting surface is never bad. You don't have to play great in majors or the Ryder Cup; you just have to survive. Par is always good. That was Monty's philosophy so it became mine too.

I can't imagine anyone has ever been better than Monty at hitting shots the correct yardage. No one has ever been pin-high as much as him. When it came to distance control he was the best I have ever seen. He was frighteningly good. And he was the same on the greens that week. I can't recall him missing inside 10 feet. He banged them all in at an amazing pace.

Having said that, we didn't play so well against Maggert and Sutton, who at least once was guilty of putting me off. I had a wedge to the green on the 6th hole, from the middle of the fairway. As I started my backswing, Sutton decided to get the crowd going. So I stopped. But he did it again. Eventually, I had to tell him to get off the fairway.

I hit that shot to about six feet. They were about 12 feet away. And they missed. So Monty was putting for the hole. As he was standing over the ball, a guy shouted out from the crowd. Monty backed off and began again. Same thing. On his third attempt though, Monty holed it. Then he took his putter and was pointing into the crowd. I will never forget that. It was like he was holding Excalibur.

On the way to the next tee, we had to stop and wait for another group to play from a nearby tee. It was raining and I had my brolly up. Monty didn't have his. He was too busy going bananas. He was shouting and screaming at the spectators. What a state he was in. Eventually I told him to get under the brolly and calm down. Which he did.

We were one down playing the last hole. Monty hit a lovely tee-shot. They hit to maybe 50 feet from the flag in two. Which left me with a real chance to win the hole if I could get the approach somewhere close. It was a 7-iron and the yardage was perfect. But my shot was not. I pushed it about 30 feet right of the cup.

I looked at Monty as I was walking to the green and he seemed disappointed. Clearly he was thinking he could have done a lot better with that shot. It was the one time that whole week when I felt like I had let him down.

I didn't have long to worry about it though. About half an hour later we were back on the first tee with Steve Pate and Tiger Woods. It was four-balls again. Our tactics were that I would always hit first. No matter what I did, the theory was that Monty would hit the fairway anyway. Which shows you how confident he was at that time. He did hit some poor shots of course, but very few. He was almost robotic.

The big thing about that match – for me at least – was that it was against Woods. I had never played with him before. And it isn't easy to do so. It is like a circus when he is around. But the fact that this was the Ryder Cup made that easier to deal with in a way. Whether he was there or not, the atmosphere was loud and raucous. So his presence made little or no difference.

My memory of that match is that it was basically Monty against Tiger. I didn't play badly, but I just never got into the game. Pate was never in it at all though. In contrast, Tiger was awesome. But Monty holed everything. He was unbelievable. He seemed to make a 10-footer on every green.

I did get one chance to shine. And I took it. We were one up playing the short 16th. With basketball star Michael Jordan watching – he was Tiger's pal and made a lot of noise on the way round – I went first and 'stiffed' a 6-iron. It was no more than 18 inches from the cup and the nicest shot I hit all week. Suddenly we were dormie two up and couldn't lose.

When the match was over, Monty was interviewed by Andrew Castle from Sky. I remember him saying, 'We have beaten him. Look how quiet it is.'

What he meant was that we had beaten Tiger. But some – notably US skipper Ben Crenshaw – twisted it to make it sound as if Monty was saying the matches were over. Much later, Crenshaw also wrote in his book that Monty and I had deliberately played slowly to distract our American opponents. I wouldn't know how to play slowly and neither would Colin. But, all in all and given that we were four points ahead, all of the above was clever motivational stuff from Ben.

We weren't thinking it was all over, far from it. Every evening Mark was telling us the same thing: 'Focus on your own game; nothing else matters.' That was going to be especially true on the last day, which consisted of 12 singles. 'Don't look at the board,' was the message. 'What anyone else is doing doesn't matter.'

Of course, that wasn't what was getting most of the attention in the media at that moment. The spotlight was focused instead on the fact that three members of our team – Sandelin, Coltart and Jean Van de Velde – had yet to play a match.

For my own part, I have to say that wasn't concerning me much. My feeling was that, selfishly, I wanted to play five matches. And that was what I was doing. So I wasn't particularly bothered about what Mark decided to do with the other players.

Having said that, I do think it is wrong that players sit out every series of games. It is wrong that they don't get to play. Everyone should appear at least once before the singles. And clearly, most people agree with me. Since 1999, the situation we were in has never been repeated.

Still, we all knew it was going to be hard for the untried trio on the Sunday. To be honest, I couldn't see any of them winning, no matter how well they played. To go in cold against guys who had been playing all week was almost impossible. Nothing was said at the time, but I remember thinking we would be lucky to get a half point out of the three of them. And in the end we got nothing.

There was one funny moment amidst that controversy. On the Saturday afternoon Mark had to tell the three of them they wouldn't be playing until Sunday. When he said that, there was a brief silence. Then Jarmo piped up. 'That's fine,' he said. 'But if I'm not playing in the singles I'm going to be really pissed.' Everyone laughed and that broke any tension.

The other thing energising the press was the infamous 'good luck' note from Nick Faldo. He and Mark had been going back and forth in the press over the weeks and months before the matches. Faldo obviously felt that he should be picked; Mark in the end felt otherwise. So there was a bit of bad feeling there. And when Faldo's note arrived Mark supposedly threw it in the bin without anyone seeing it.

I know I certainly never saw any note with Nick's name on it. But I didn't read them all; there were so many. So it could have been on the wall as far as I was concerned. I did read Bernard Gallacher's message. And another from Peter Baker.

The other big decision on the Saturday evening was the order of play for the singles. I remember Mark giving a pretty passionate speech about how well we had done to be four points ahead, especially as we had arrived in the States as underdogs. Just before the matches, Payne Stewart had made a comment to the effect that the European players weren't even good enough to caddie for the Americans. That didn't go down too well as you can imagine and in the middle of Mark's speech, a voice piped up from the back of the room. It was Miguel Angel Jimenez. He was sitting there puffing away on his usual big cigar and said, 'Is no bad for 12 caddies, no?' I loved that. Miguel is different class in a team room. Just brilliant.

The singles line-up was then distributed. At first I thought they had forgotten me, but there I was, right at the bottom. Number 12.

'I see I'm last out tomorrow,' I said to no one in particular.

'What? You can't handle that?' was Sam Torrance's immediate response.

But I was ready for him. 'Whoever I'm playing (it was Maggert), at whatever time, I'm taking them down.'

Sam was great with me all week. He must have come over to me four or five times a day. 'You're doing great. I'm proud of you,' he would say. That was just what I needed to hear, especially from someone like him. It meant more too because, although we have always got on fine, we are not exactly bosom buddies either.

So it was Maggert for me. It's safe to say he wasn't one of the favourites in our team room, not after his comment that those in the American side were 'the best 12 players in the world'. He certainly didn't play like one of that elite dozen. I was something like four under par when the match ended in my favour on the 15th green.

As we stood there, Adam came onto the putting surface to congratulate Paddy and I. As he did so, Paddy said, 'Thanks Adam, it's great to beat him.'

'Paddy,' replied Adam,' he's right behind you.'

'I don't care, it's still good to beat him.'

The sort of silly comment made by Maggert was just one of a few little niggly things that week. I remember Tom Lehman's wife leaving a golf bag in our team room so that we could all sign it. But when she came to collect it on the Saturday evening it was blank. She wasn't impressed. But it had been stuck away in a corner and nobody noticed it. Honest.

In the end, of course, my win in the last match came after the destination of the trophy had been decided. But that didn't make me any less proud of the way I played against Maggert. On the Sunday morning I was thinking the deciding match was going to be mine. So I was pretty hyped up to play well and win.

At breakfast that morning I sat with Monty. It was just the two of us (and Marian) as we were the last two off. He whispered to me that he thought it was 'coming down to us'. So he felt the same way I did. Despite the four-point lead we had, he knew it was closer than it looked on paper. He gave me a boost too. 'You can handle it,' he said. 'There's a reason you and I are down at the bottom.' Which was a nice thing to say.

I got another lift on the first tee. Although the scoreboard was a sea of red (the US colour) by the time I arrived, the sight of Maggert gave me confidence. I have never in my life seen a more nervous looking golfer. Clearly, he too thought we were likely to be the deciding match. And clearly he didn't fancy it. He was in a terrible state.

As for the scoreboard, I wasn't surprised. At our team meeting the night before, Mark had impressed on us how likely it was that they would come back strong and early. It was their only chance to win. So the plan was not to look at the scoreboard. No matter what. Focus on your own match was the message.

Of course, the first thing I did when I got on the tee was look at the scoreboard. I remember saying to Paddy, 'Shit'.

'You're not supposed to be looking,' he said.

'How can you not look at that?' I responded. 'It's right in front of us and there's red everywhere.'

After that though, I pretty much followed instructions. By the turn I was four under par and five up. I remember making a great putt at the seventh hole, about a 20-footer, that must have broken his heart. He didn't give up though, or at least his girlfriend didn't.

I pushed my drive off the 13th tee and it was headed towards a pond. 'Get in the water,' yelled the girlfriend. At which point, Marian – who was standing almost right by the future Mrs Maggert – responded, 'Shut it bitch'. As I've said many times, don't mess with my wife!

The only other match I saw anything of was Monty's against Payne Stewart. They were right in front of us. I could tell from Monty's demeanour and his body language that some bad stuff was going on. The crowd by this time was basically out of control, to the point where Monty's Dad was forced to walk in at the turn, so upset was he by what was being said about his son. All in all, it was a sad day for golf.

At this stage, I wish I could tell you more about the infamous American stampede across the 17th green in the wake of Justin Leonard's huge putt. But I can't. I simply wasn't there, although I obviously heard a lot about it later in the locker room.

It was bedlam up there as you can imagine. We were all in there: players, caddies, wives. And there was a lot of greetin' (crying) going on. Jesse (Mark James) was in tears. So were Sam, Ken and Sergio (who was crying all week to be honest). I wasn't though and I'll tell you why.

I'm the sort of person who gets emotional when something is won. Even if I'm watching on telly, I get choked up when someone wins a big event. But getting beat? I don't see that. So I was one of the few players not in tears.

1980
Five-a-side team, Alehousewells Primary School.

1989
Scottish Assistants' Champion, Cruden Bay, 1989.

1990
Winner of the Scottish Under 25s Championship, Deer Park, 1990.

1991
Winner of the Daily Express National Pro-am (Carnoustie), 1991.

1992
Scottish PGA champion, 1992.

1992

Peter Davidson (Commercial Director, Scottish Brewers) presents me with the Scottish PGA Trophy, Cardross, 1992.

1993

Previous winners of the Scottish PGA, 1993.

1994-95
*With David
Whelan and
David
Leadbetter,
Lake Nova,
Orlando.*

1995 SPGA
*SPGA Masters,
Downfield,
1995.*

1996
*Arriving at
Aberdeen airport with the
Catalan Open Trophy, 1996.*

1999
*Michael's Christening,
Kildrummy Castle
Hotel.*

1999
Marian and the boys.

1999
Craig and Michael with the Claret Jug.

1999
Me with my parents, James and Margaret, 1999.

1999
Opening Ceremony, 1999 Ryder Cup.

1999
Ryder Cup Dinner.

Gary Player
GROUP

August 18, 1999

Paul Lawrie
c/o International Management Group
Pier House
Strand on the Green
London
W 43NN
ENGLAND

Dear Paul

THE OPEN CHAMPIONSHIP

Just a wee note to congratulate you on a great win at The Open Championship this year at Carnoustie. I appreciate how significant this win is for you and on behalf of the Player clan wish you continued success with your career. Remember " the harder you practice the luckier you get."

Yours Sincerely,

GARY PLAYER

GJP/lccorr/0818laurie

cc: Marc B. Player, Black Knight Inte

'DUNLUCE'
BALLENCLIFF ROAD
SUNNINGDALE
BERKSHIRE
SL5 9RA
19th JULY

DEAR PAUL,

I THOUGHT I'D DROP YOU A LINE TO CONGRATULATE YOU ON YOUR FANTASTIC VICTORY LAST WEEK AT CARNOUSTIE.

TO HAVE LIFTED THE 'CLARET JUG' ALOFT IN SCOTLAND MUST HAVE BEEN A VERY SPECIAL MOMENT FOR YOU.

IF YOU ARE AS 'COOL' IN THE RYDER CUP AS YOU WERE IN THE PLAY-OFF THEN THE AMERICANS HAVE NO CHANCE AT BROOKLINE!!

WELL DONE AGAIN.

BEST WISHES,

DARREN CLARKE & FAMILY

Hiberni

Football Clu

4 August 1999

Private and Confidential

Paul Lawrie Esq
Newmacher Golf Club
NEWMACHER
Aberdeenshire
AB21 7UU

Dear Paul

As an adopted Aberdonian, I was thrilled to see your fantastic Open win. I was sitting in a restaurant in Copenhagen along with my players as the drama unfolded. Believe it or not I had Van de Velde in the sweep, and despite my Aberdeen years, I desperately wanted to lose the money. I have French players at the Club as well as a couple of English lads. Boy did I stuff it down their throats when you clinched it! Everyone will want a piece of you now and I'm sure you'll take it in your stride.

I hope you keep on winning and if you're in Edinburgh and fancy a look at the 'Hibees', give me a call.

Yours in sport

Alex McLeish
Manager

JOHN JACOBS PROMOTIONS

J. R. M. JACOBS, O.B.E.
R. JACOBS

TEL: 01703 282743
FAX: 01703 283380

VAT REGISTRATION No. 233 9103 57

STABLE COTTAGE
CHAPEL LANE
LYNDHURST
HAMPSHIRE
SO43 7FG

20 July 1999

Mr Paul Lawrie
38 Coull Green
Kingswell
Aberdeen AB15 8TR

Dear Paul,

You will have countless messages of congratulations. Very, very well done!

The way you play and the self control you exhibit makes certain this will not be a one-off. May you go from strength to strength.

Very Sincerely,

John Jacobs.

MANCHESTER UNITED

The Manchester United Football Club plc, Sir Matt Busby Way, Old Trafford, Manchester M16 0RA

AF/LL

23 July, 1999

Mr Paul Lawrie
38 Coull Green
Kingswells
ABERDEEN
AB15 8TR

Dear Paul

Just a wee note to congratulate you on your magnificent victory at Carnoustie last week, what a performance.

On behalf of everyone here at Manchester United, but especially from myself, it was great to see a Scot thrilling the whole nation, we seem to be making a quite a habit of it of late! Well done.

Yours sincerely

Alex. Ferguson

Sir Alex Ferguson C.B.E.

Telephone: 0161 872 1661; 0161 930 1968. T
A subsidiary of Manchester United PLC. Registere

The Scottish Football Association

6 PARK GARDENS   GLASGOW   G3 7YF   TELEX: 778904

Please respond, if required, to Telefax: 0141 353 1047

FACSIMILE TRANSMISSION

Number of pages including this one: . . . . 1 . . . . . Date: . . . . 20th July, 1999

To: . . . . . Paul Lawrie

Organisation: . . . . . New Machar Golf Club

From: . . . . . Craig Brown

Reference: 149/CB/AA

MESSAGE:

Dear Paul,

Congratulations on the wonderful personal achievement and terrific honour you have brought to Scotland. The players, officials and staff of the Scottish International Team extend their heartiest congratulations and very best wishes.

Yours sincerely,

Craig Brown

CRAIG BROWN
INTERNATIONAL TEAM MANAGER

1999
*Opening match,
1999 Ryder
Cup.*

1999
1999 Ryder Cup.

1999
1999 Ryder Cup.

1999
Team room, 1999 Ryder Cup.

2000
Seve Trophy.

2000
The Roxburghe Challenge with Jesper Parnevik, Sergio Garcia, Hugh Grant, Alan Shearer and the Duke of York.

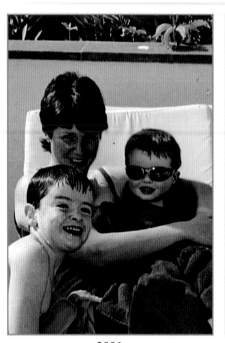

2001
Marian, Craig and Michael,
Portugal 2001.

2004
With Craig and Michael, in Dubai 2004

2004
In the garden at home.

2005
Playing football in the garden with Craig and Michael.

2009
Craig qualified for the 2009 Junior Jug Final.

2010
Open 2010, Andy Forsyth (caddie), Adam Hunter with myself and Marian.

2010
*Marian and myself on the West
Highland Way 2010.*

2011
*Opening the new practice facility
on Shetland.*

2010
Craig and Michael's first round on the Old Course (Swilken Bridge).

2011

Walking the West Highland Way, August 2011. Left to right: Alan Reid, Marian, Val Reid, myself, Audrey Morrison, Brian Morrison.

2011

Congratulating Craig on his first round win in the 2011 Scottish Boys at Dunbar.

2012

Marian and I celebrating with my caddie Davy Kenny after Europe's victory at the 2012 Ryder Cup.

2012

With the European team captain Jose Maria Olazabal.

I tried to cheer Jesse up by telling him he was 'the best captain I've ever played for in the Ryder Cup'. He had a giggle at that. I was kind of, 'come on boys, give yourselves a shake'. But they were all very emotional. Some were even saying they would never again play in America, so bad had the whole experience been.

That was understandable in the heat of the moment. But I never took it too seriously. Everyone was just so gutted to have lost from 10-6 up. And what tends to be forgotten is how well the US side played that day. They were exceptional. If you look at the scores, almost all of them – but not Maggert – were five or six under par. So any criticism of our players should take that into account.

The closing ceremony was horrific. I walked in opposite Davis Love, who had the biggest cigar I have ever seen sticking out of his gob. That we should be put together was ironic, given what he was supposed to have said about me after the Open. But we had played together earlier that week without incident so we should have been okay. Should have been.

I'm not proud of this looking back, but at that point I was assuming he had actually said what he was supposed to have said. As we were walking down there, he turned to me and said, 'It must be fantastic being the champion golfer of the year.' In other words, a nice thing to say.

I was having none of it though.

'Thanks very much,' I said. 'It's something you may never experience.'

Thankfully, in all the noise, I don't think he heard me. I think he would have reacted if he had. But I can't believe I said that now. It is an awful thing to say. But it came out amidst all the whoopin' and hollerin' and backslapping that was going on around me. I let myself down there. And I regret it hugely now, especially as he was shaking my hand as I said it.

It would be another five years before Davis and I finally put his quote to bed. We were drawn together in the 2004 Open at Royal Troon and it came up again in the press. He came over to me on the practice green and said, 'I don't know if you've read the papers this week but what I am supposed to have said back in 1999 has resurfaced again.'

I said I had seen the headlines.

'You just need to know two things, ' he continued. 'One, I did not say what they are saying I said. And two, my father was a PGA Master Professional and he didn't bring me up to say things like that about a fellow player. I just need you to know that.'

I told him I had no problem with it. And I thanked him for coming to talk to me. But it did take him five years to do so. If I had been quoted saying that about a fellow professional, I would have made sure he knew I hadn't within an hour. Not five years later. So I'm not sure why he did it when he did. Maybe because he felt like it might affect his play that week. Who knows?

Anyway, we got through the ceremony – it seemed endless – and escaped back to the clubhouse. It was there that Jesse gathered everyone together and made a wee speech. He thanked everyone for their efforts. He said he had made mistakes and could have done some things better. (Which I don't agree with. He was brilliant.) It was all over in a couple of minutes. But it was a nice thing to do.

Things were a little livelier back at the hotel, where, after a slow start, we had a few drinks and a nice time. Bernard Gallacher was there. And so were Ken Schofield and George O'Grady from the European Tour. There was only one little incident, when David Feherty was allowed into the team room.

David, who played in the 1991 Ryder Cup, had been commentating on the matches and is Sam's best mate. So ordinarily he would have been welcome. But there was one problem. It had been David who first coined the nickname 'Mrs Doubtfire' for Monty. And Monty knew this only too well. When he saw David he stormed out and went to his room for a sulk.

Eventually, it was sorted. David volunteered to leave and I was sent to get Monty from his room. It was all a bit childish and, at the time, very funny. So it didn't completely ruin the evening, although it would have been a better party had we won.

Looking back, I can see how much I enjoyed the whole week. It was brilliant apart from the end result. And it was everything I expected it would be – and more. Even though you go into a Ryder Cup knowing it is a huge event, it's even bigger than you think.

Look at what it does to players. We play every week for huge amounts of money, yet we are reduced to babbling fools by the thought of playing for nothing other than a team and a point. And you know what? I couldn't wait to do it all again. Throughout the 13 years that passed between my first Ryder Cup and my second (see chapter four), it was always a huge regret to have played only once. Of course, that 'failure' was solely down to me. For a depressingly long period, I just wasn't good enough. I have to be honest about that. But I never stopped trying to get back into Europe's colours. I knew I was young enough (even at 43!). And, more importantly, I knew I was good enough. And, as things turned out, I was right on both counts.

America & Me

First things first: Although I've flown across the Atlantic to the United States many times during my professional career, I can't claim to know the country at all well. For me, America has always been a blurry succession of airports, hotels and golf courses, many of which bear a striking similarity to each other. So if I say to you, 'I don't like America,' know that it is not that great nation or its people I'm referring to, but the week-to-week sameness I found on the PGA Tour, both on and off the course.

That's an important distinction. And not to say that some of the things I encountered during my ultimately unsatisfactory PGA Tour career didn't drive me crazy. They did. With my name, or the American mispronunciation of it near the top of that list. So it is that, whenever I've played in the US, I have suddenly been transformed into Paul 'Lowry' rather than Paul Lawrie.

Now, I know that doesn't sound like much. But it really did irritate me a great deal. For a long time, I saw it as a lack of respect. I mean, come on, it's not that hard to get it right. 'Law' has never been pronounced 'Low' has it?

Part of the problem was that, when I first went to the States as Open champion to play in the 1999 USPGA Championship at Medinah, there was a player on the PGA Tour called Steve Lowery. So right away, I used to get 'Hey Steve' yelled at me out on the course. Which was even stranger than the pronunciation thing. Steve was about four stone heavier than me and wore a goatee beard. So getting the two of us mixed up was a bit of a stretch to say the least.

Anyway, the whole thing really bothered me. I felt like I had a responsibility to go to America and play. And not only play – but also play well. So it was hugely frustrating to me that no one seemed capable of a) getting my name right and b) recognising that I wasn't Steve Lowery. I can't tell you how much it got to me. And how much I used to go on about it.

On that first trip I can remember Marian saying to me, 'For God's sake, who cares if they don't know your name?' The good thing is, I can laugh about it now. I'm past the stage of caring. Which is just as well, because nothing has changed. When I sat down for a press conference before that

'99 USPGA, the PGA of America guy sitting next to me said, 'Lowrie'. And nearly 13 years later, after my opening round of 69 at the 2012 Masters, the same thing happened again. I was introduced as 'Paul Lowrie'. The difference is that, in 1999, I got angry. In 2012 I just rolled my eyes and smiled.

So I've changed. I've had to, of course. And it isn't just in America where there is confusion. When I was playing in Abu Dhabi in 2011, I hit my second shot at the eighth hole to the right of the green, my ball finishing up near the gallery ropes. Three English guys happened to be standing there and as I walked over, one said to the others, 'Oh good, here comes Paul Lawrie, Peter Lawrie's dad.'

I had to laugh. The Irish European Tour pro Peter Lawrie is certainly younger than me, but not that much! So I went over to the three lads and asked them if I looked old enough to be Peter's dad. They were embarrassed and apologised immediately. I told them not to worry. And we had a wee laugh. But the point is, 10 years earlier, I wouldn't have handled it like that. I would have chewed the guy out and been upset by his comment. So I am a bit more laid back than I used to be.

But that wasn't the way I was feeling in 2000, the time when I decided I would take up the PGA Tour card on offer as a result of my Open win at Carnoustie. I went over there for two main reasons: I had an obligation to go as Open champion and I felt that I could do well.

That wasn't always the case, of course. When I first got my European Tour card I would have been wasting my time in American conditions, where the fairways and greens are generally so much softer than we play in Europe. Back then I hit the ball much lower than I do now. There was not much variety in my shot-making either; I certainly couldn't hit draws and fades on command. My staple shot was a low fade. My downswing was also quite steep and I took huge divots out of the turf.

But by 2000 I knew I had all the shots. I knew I could hit the ball far enough and high enough to do at least reasonably well. Not everyone seemed to know that though. I can still remember watching golf on Sky when Philip Parkin, the former British Amateur champion, said there was 'no way' I could compete, 'Paul hits the ball too low.' Which showed an unbelievable lack of knowledge on his part. Of course I could hit the ball as high as anyone else. That, as you can imagine, pissed me off more than a little.

That was me back then though. I allowed myself to get wound up by the fact that one guy thought I couldn't get the ball out there on a high trajectory. Now – while I still think Philip's comment was a bit on the thoughtless side – I wouldn't let it bother me even a little bit. Whatever I may think about someone's opinion, he is entitled to that view. But back then I was different. I didn't let anything go. Everything annoyed me, everything. Looking back, I was a psychologist's dream.

Luckily, I had my own unofficial 'shrink' in Adam Hunter. Adam wasn't just a swing coach, he had been a player too, good enough to win on tour. So he knew what it was like to be a competitor. And he knew the destructive path I was on. Eventually, he turned to me and gave me the lecture I needed to hear.

'Listen, do you realise where you're headed here?' he asked me. 'Honestly, do you realise? I'm your friend and no one else is going to tell you. I'm telling you. You're going to be in trouble if you keep going the way you're going. Just let it go. Just play golf. If you shoot 75, you shoot 75. Your kids and Marian will still love you. Just play golf.'

He was right, of course. Spot on, in fact. I was way too easily offended by even the most insignificant throwaway comment. But what was making it difficult for me was that I knew how wrong these people were. I had won the Open. And you don't win the biggest event in any sport without being at least half decent.

Looking back, I was right about that. I took the view that I could hit all the shots you needed to perform well on any golf course. I could hit the ball high and low and I could hit fades and draws. If you can do all of those things you can play at least decently anywhere. Think about it. Golf balls don't know where they are, whether you are in Scotland, the US or China. It sits there on a little square of grass in all of those places, asking the very same question of any player.

I wasn't perfect though – far from it. Although I had all the shots, I had a really bad one in there too: the snap-hook. At my worst, I'd hit that shot two or three times a day. But Adam and I worked our bollocks off to get rid of it. Nowadays I hit maybe two or three snap-hooks a year. But it was a long struggle for me to rid of it.

As I said, my staple shot was a 'hard fade'. I'd typically tee up on the right side of the tee, aim down the left side and try to cut the ball back into the middle. The real key to my success was my short game. Back then I was mustard around and on the greens. For the first few years of my pro career I was not often outside the top-20 in the putting stats.

That's the biggest difference in my game between then and now. I used to be able to hit, say, as few as nine greens and still shoot 68. These days I consistently hit 15–16 greens in the correct number, then struggle to shoot two-under par. But that's what the game is. It's about getting the ball into the hole. And I was one of the best at that for a long time. Like so many others, I didn't realise how hard golf can be until I had trouble on the greens. It's the easiest game in the world when you can roll the putts in.

But I'm digressing. Towards the end of 1999, I made the decision to take up my PGA Tour card and commit to playing at least a good chunk of my golf in the States. It was a big decision, one I'm not sure Marian was completely behind, but I felt that five years of unrestricted play on the world's biggest and most lucrative circuit was too good a chance to miss.

My first event, the Mercedes Championship, was in Hawaii and I finished T-8. Not bad. Not bad at all. The next two weeks were not so much fun though. I missed the cut at both the Sony Open and the LA Open, before making it all the way to the quarter-final of the World Match Play at La Costa, where I lost on the last green to Tiger Woods having been one up with two to play. He finished par-par to my bogey-bogey.

That was obviously disappointing. I should have won, a fact Tiger actually acknowledged. After the match, Adam and I were in the locker room. I was sitting with my head in my hands saying over and over, 'I should have beaten him; I should have beaten him.' I was staring at the floor and didn't see Adam trying to get my attention as Tiger had appeared in the middle of my little rant. When I did look up, I was mortified.

'Sorry Tiger, didn't see you there,' I said.

He just smiled. 'No problem,' he replied, 'you're right.'

What helped make the difference was that Adam joined me in LA. I had struggled with life off the course in Hawaii. The PGA Tour isn't like its European equivalent in terms of sociability. Where the players in Europe tend to stay in the same places and eat dinner together, it is very different in the States. Over there, because there are so many more hotels, everyone pretty much goes his own way.

That was why, after two weeks on an admittedly stunning group of islands in the middle of the Pacific Ocean with Adam, I realised I couldn't do this alone. So, as I said, the problem was not America per se; it was the fact that I was over there so far from home by myself. Quite simply, I was lonely and a bit lost.

It was a strange feeling for me. Normally, I'm quite happy in my own company. At events on the European Tour where mates like Stephen

Gallacher, Alastair Forsyth and Gary Orr are not around, I'm content enough to take room service and watch a DVD. No problem at all. I won't feel lonely in that situation. I won't feel as if I want to go home. But in America it was different somehow. Maybe because I was just so far from Scotland.

Anyway, I was home again after the match play. And I didn't go back to the States, until the Players Championship in late March, just before the Masters. Adam came out to Augusta along with my close friend and long-time sponsor, Stewart Spence. So that was fine. When people were with me I was okay. I still didn't particularly enjoy the environment in which I found myself, but I could get by. But the weeks on my own were murder. Seven days is a long time when you're somewhere you would rather not be.

There were exceptions, however. And the Masters was definitely one of those. It is just an awesome event. I liked it straightaway, everything about it. That first year I remember falling in love with the par-3 course. Even during the tournament I played it quite a few times, just me and Adam and my caddie.

The first thing that strikes you about Augusta National is the conditioning of the course. Everything is just so perfect. And the greens have to be seen to be believed. Plus, one thing no one tells you is how much faster the putting surfaces can get between Wednesday afternoon and Thursday morning. In 2000 I swear the first green I putted on in the first round was 10 feet quicker than it had been the day before.

Not surprisingly, I struggled that first year. I missed the cut with rounds of 79–74. I couldn't get the speed of the greens at all. I even putted off a couple of them. But I loved it, all of it. The clubhouse. The traditions. Just everything.

A big thrill that first year was when Sandy Lyle took me up into the champion's locker room. Stewart was with me. I had invited him to go because of all that he had done for me. Stewart actually stayed with us that week and wherever I went, he went too. He just loved it, every minute of it.

So Sandy took Stewart, Adam and myself upstairs. I couldn't believe how small the locker room was. It is just tiny. Then he gave us a bit of a tour of the whole place. I love all that history stuff, all the pictures and trophies and memorabilia. It is just a very special place. All of which is hard to believe when you arrive at the front gate. Until you are inside and driving up Magnolia Lane, the town of Augusta is nothing special, believe me.

Typical of me, I have no memory of whom I played with that first year. But I do remember playing with Tom Watson maybe two years later. He was really cool. A couple of times he said to me, 'Knock it in'. Stuff like that. Only two pros have ever said that to me in my whole career – Watson and John Daly.

I had five years of playing in the Masters between 2000 and 2004 and I didn't get back until 2012, which gives you some idea of how my career was going during that eight-year gap. But I'll never forget the experience of playing. We even had time to have some fun.

In 2001 I played with Padraig Harrington in the par-3 contest. We were last off and neither of us performed that well. Walking from the eighth green to the ninth tee I said to Padraig we should let our caddies hit the tee-shots. Many of the players have their children, or a friend or relative on the bags in what is a fun and low-key, albeit still competitive, event. And on this occasion Padraig had his Dad caddying and I had Marian's Dad, Bert, shouldering my clubs. The crowd round the last hole was enormous – must have been 20,000 strong – so there was going to be some pressure on them as you can imagine.

Padraig's Dad was first. He stepped up and hit a lovely shot onto the front of the green. Clipped it nicely he did. He had obviously played a bit over the years. Then it was my caddie's turn. Now, Marian's Dad plays off 18, so I was a wee bit worried about what might happen.

As it turned out my worst fears were realised. Well, not my worst fear because he stayed upright. But the shot Bert 'hit' left a little to be desired. The divot, in fact, went further than the ball. He must have hit at least six inches behind it. And the divot – huge thing it was – ended up floating in the pond in front of the tee.

I had another laugh one year at the US PGA Championship. I'm not sure what year it was but it was the time British Airways lost my clubs! They didn't arrive until Thursday night, after I'd played my first round. I was playing Callaway clubs at the time, so they put together a set for me. They gave me this wood, a steel head 4+ that had a longer than normal shaft on it. I hit that thing miles.

So I'm drawn to play with Greg Norman. I hit that club off one tee and he remarked to my caddie, 'Man, your guy hits that 3-wood a long way.' To which Paddy replied, 'It's actually a 4-wood Greg.' We had a chuckle about that.

We had an even bigger laugh later that day though. Beside one tee was a portaloo and Greg disappeared inside. When he shut the door I put two tee pegs across the lock so that he couldn't get out. He was banging on the door until someone came to rescue him.

'Did you see who did that?' he asked me as we walked up the fairway. I, of course, pleaded ignorance. So Greg, if you do happen to read this: Sorry mate.

Sadly, moments and occasions like those were few and far between for me in the States. But it would be wrong to say that I hated every minute. To be fair; on the course I was having a reasonable time right from the start in 2000. The golf side of things was great. The courses were great and they were always in fantastic condition. I always putted really nicely because the surfaces were so consistent and so true. Everyone got a courtesy car. And I was looked after unbelievably well. Yet still I wasn't a fan of it all.

A big part of my loneliness, it goes without saying, was being away from Marian and the boys. Craig and Michael were very young at that time and I hated being away for weeks on end. Leaving them at home was huge for me. Many times I would be standing in an airport waiting for my bags and wishing I was on another plane back to Aberdeen.

I wasn't alone in that either. One time I remember Monty and I arriving somewhere on the same flight. By the baggage carousel there was a list of departing flights. We stood in silence for a minute. Then he said, 'Are you thinking what I'm thinking?'

And I was. 'Yeah,' I said, 'I wish I was on that flight to Scotland.' And that was the two of us just arriving. Strangely enough, we both missed the cut and flew home early. Mentally, I had no chance of doing well over there. Which was as much my fault as it was anyone on the PGA Tour.

The harsh truth is that I was – at that time in my life – very unsociable. Not because I won the Open but simply because I'm naturally shy. I have never been one to put myself about and meet people. If I had to go to an official function and introduce myself to others I would do the bare minimum when it came to talking. And I wouldn't go out of my way to go in the first place either.

Today – yet again – I am very different from the Paul Lawrie of 2000. I've no problem attending dinners and even getting up on my hind legs to speak publicly. But 12 years ago I just didn't want to. I didn't want to make small talk with people I didn't know. Especially if my game wasn't at its best, I was hopeless in those situations. It always seemed like I was constantly being asked what was wrong with my swing or my driving or my putting. I found all that sort of thing such hard going.

Okay, back in America, I had missed the cut in my first Masters. And not long after that I suffered a painful groin injury, one that prevented me from playing in the US Open at Pebble Beach and ended up putting me on the sidelines for a bit. That was bad enough – I still haven't played Pebble Beach – but I was drawn to play alongside Jack Nicklaus in the opening two rounds. That was good enough, but it would have been made even more special by the fact that Jack was playing in his last US Open.

To say I was gutted at having to miss that event is an understatement. But I could hardly walk. And I couldn't get up stairs. I suppose I could have had an injection that would have allowed me to play, but I didn't do it. In the end, I didn't want to go there and just make up the numbers. But I should have done it. It didn't matter how I played. Not really. It would all – quite rightly – have been about Jack. But that was me back then.

Back in the real world, all that time off left me with a bit of a problem. Like everyone else on the PGA Tour I was obliged to play in at least the minimum number of 15 tournaments if I wanted to retain my membership. But because I missed so many weeks, I suddenly wasn't going to be able to do that. My plan had been to get to 15 in the US relatively quickly, then play the rest of the season in Europe. But I didn't do that. In fact, it didn't take long for the PGA Tour to get in touch. Their player liaison Sid Wilson – a really nice guy – contacted IMG to ask why I hadn't played between the Masters and the Open at St Andrews. So there was some back and forth and eventually they agreed to let me off with three of my missed events. If I played in 12 counting tournaments I would be fine for 2001.

The trouble was I had missed six of my planned PGA events when I was injured. So now I had to play three events over there not originally on my schedule. And guess what? I didn't want to do that. As far as I was concerned, 12 wasn't doable. I wasn't going back to America. I didn't like it there. I was going to stay in Europe.

Needless to say, that stance didn't go down well at PGA Tour headquarters in Ponte Vedra, Florida. Especially as I hadn't been doing too badly in a playing sense. If I had played the required number I would have retained my card pretty comfortably. I think the commissioner Tim Finchem took it as something of a personal insult. And I can see his point to an extent. They were letting me away with three events and I wasn't budging an inch. So he was like, 'bollocks to you then' and he banned me for the following season. All I would be able to play in were the three majors and the World Golf Championships, none of which are run by the PGA Tour.

At this point, of course, I was getting a lot of advice. My manager at the time, Adrian Mitchell of IMG, felt like I should find three consecutive events I could play, go over there and get it all done and dusted. But I wasn't interested. The number of events didn't matter to me. It could have been eight instead of 12 and I still wouldn't have returned. I just wasn't going back. I wasn't enjoying it. I was never going to enjoy it. I wanted to play in Europe.

I should have taken Adrian's advice, of course. I regret not doing so. Had I jumped through the PGA Tour's hoop and played the three events they wanted, I would have been in charge of my own destiny going forward. I could have continued to play in the US during 2001 or I could have resigned my membership. Either way, no harm done.

My mistake – as I'm sure all of you reading this long ago concluded – wasn't not going back to the States towards the end of the season; it was going over there in the first place. As per usual, in fact, I should have listened to Marian. My wife has a great instinct for both people and what is the right thing to do in certain situations. When we sat down to discuss this whole thing at the end of 1999, her feeling was that it wasn't a good idea. But she knew it was up to me. So she told me it was up to me, that I had to do what I wanted to do and that if I felt like I could do it, kick on.

I get asked about Marian a lot, in fact. And the answer to the most common question is that she has always been incredibly supportive of me and my career. If I want to go and play six events in a row and not come home because I feel that was the best thing to do, she never complains.

Adam, on the other hand, thought I should have gutted it out in 2000, kept my card and continued to play in the US. He went to college over there and so liked being in the States. He would have loved to be in the position I was in. He was a 'tomayto' kind of guy, as opposed to 'tomahto'.

Now, at this point, I don't blame you for thinking I needed my head examined back then. To most people, the prospect of spending a few weeks in the American sunshine, playing some golf and being spoiled rotten in the process doesn't sound like too bad a deal. And it isn't. But I wasn't thinking rationally. My mind was made up. My relationship with the PGA Tour was over.

Ah, but it wasn't. Not quite. And if you think the way I behaved in 2000 was bad enough, things are about to get worse.

Having served my ban from membership in 2001, I was free to rejoin the PGA Tour in 2002. I still had the exemption from my Open win, one that would last through the end of 2004. So I did rejoin in 2003, but with the unspoken aim of entering only those events just before each of the majors, so that I could prepare in American conditions and get over the jetlag. I certainly had no intention of entering the 15 events I was supposed to.

So that was what I did. I played in the Bell South event in Atlanta the week before the Masters – and finished T-9 – and the FBR Open (T-42) preceding the US Open. So far so good. But at that point Mister Finchem caught on to what I was doing.

At first, the tour asked me for my schedule for the rest of the year. And when I wouldn't give it to them they concluded – correctly – that I was abusing the system more than a little. They realised that my motivation was simply to prepare for the majors; using my 'membership' as a way into events I probably wouldn't have been invited to. We're talking four years on from my Open win remember; I wasn't exactly front-page news at this point.

In my – slight – defence, we did come clean with the tour after the US Open. I could have made up a fictitious schedule, one that met all their requirements, then simply withdrawn from each event as they came up. But I didn't do that. I came clean. At which point they quite rightly said I couldn't do what I was doing. Which is fair enough. The whole thing was pretty poor on my part. I was being a wee bit devious. More than a wee bit actually.

Looking back though, I have no regrets about my time on the PGA Tour. I went there, tried it – and just didn't like it. At least I know for sure. There are no doubts, although I still smile when I think back to when I was exempt over there. So many guys on the European Tour would have paid millions to have my five year exemption. But I would have given it away for nothing. If I could have signed it over to someone who wanted it, I would have. I didn't want to play the PGA Tour. It wasn't for me. I would rather be at home in Europe and get back to Aberdeen on a Sunday night.

Today, nothing has changed. I still know that the way of life on the PGA Tour is not for me. So no matter what I do in the rest of my career I'll never again be a PGA Tour cardholder, even though the arrival of more World Golf Championships makes it a lot easier to retain that membership. To play the bare minimum is less time-consuming but I still wouldn't do it. It's 'been there, done that' as far as I'm concerned.

Marian & the Boys

As I revealed to the world in chapter five, I first met the most important influence on my life when she arrived in the professional's shop at Banchory GC 'fresh' from a day out that may or may not have involved alcoholic beverages. At that time, Marian was a dental nurse and I was a down-at-heel assistant golf professional earning about £40 a week. Her boss, Malcolm Tocher, had taken her and a friend to the Banchory Show and they popped in at the golf club so that he could show me the new clubs he had just purchased in America.

That is always nice, of course. When a club member values the opinion of the club pro so much that he wants him to peruse the merchandise he has bought somewhere else, it always gives said pro a warm, fuzzy feeling inside. I mean, it is always interesting (!) to see how much profit has gone elsewhere.

Not that I could have cared any less about Malcolm's clubs that day. One look at Marian and my interest was immediately diverted elsewhere. And, even though she was more than a little giggly after consuming what I later learned was quite a few Bacardi and Cokes, I managed to get her phone number.

It took me a wee while to pluck up the courage to ask her for a date, but eventually I managed. At that time my experience with the opposite sex was strictly limited. I was much too busy playing golf and practising to have much time left over for the fun things in life. So Marian was my first serious girlfriend. I was maybe 20 when we met and she would be 22.

Anyway, as I detail elsewhere in this book, the first date nearly didn't happen when I was stopped for speeding on my way to meet Marian. But happen it did – courtesy of a very kind and understanding police officer – and that was it for me. We got on well straight away and we went out a lot. So obviously my addiction to practise wasn't that strong. I remember we spent a lot of evenings in her flat after she had made dinner. I would pick her up from work and we would go from there.

Of course, I knew right away I had found a woman with whom I could spend the rest of my life. The key being persuading her that spending her life with me, in a world that revolved around the striking of little white balls around large green fields, was an idea worth pursuing.

Happily, we were on the same wavelength as far as that particular subject was concerned and, after a while, I moved into Marian's flat in Aberdeen. I actually proposed marriage in October 1990, on the day I was best man at my older brother, Stephen's wedding. And no, I don't remember the exact details, although I can exclusively confirm that she wasn't marrying me for either my money or my dashing good looks. But exactly one year later, Marian and I were married. The honeymoon was in Mallorca. And only a few weeks after that I was the proud holder of a European Tour card.

All of which meant we had some decisions to make. I certainly didn't want to be on the road as much as I was clearly going to be without Marian. So, after a bit of a debate, she quit her job and came with me. At first, she was caddie as well as wife. But that proved to be one job too many and one had to go. Thank goodness she chose the former. And that was how we lived our lives for my first three years on tour. We went everywhere together and had what I now look back on as the most fantastic time. It doesn't get any better than being newly-wed and playing golf for a living all over the world with your wife by your side. No job could ever beat that.

Marian fell pregnant with Craig in August 1994 but continued to travel with me until he was born on 1 May the following year. Michael was born on Christmas Day 1998. Craig was a conscious decision for both of us. Marian had actually had enough of the jet-set life by then anyway. Never the best of travellers, the thought of not getting onto yet another aeroplane held a certain appeal for her. So starting a family made sense. The time was right for both of us. We had enough money. And we were old enough to handle the responsibility of parenthood.

I was at the births of both Craig and Michael. And yes, I cried at both. I find I'm getting more emotional as I get older. I assume that is normal. When I was younger I couldn't imagine crying at anything really. And I still don't see losing on the golf course as a reason to break down. Winning is a different matter mind. That I can understand. But I was in tears when I first saw each of my sons.

Since the boys came along, of course, life on tour has been very different for me. We are together as a family on the road only maybe three or four times a year these days, so I've become used to being a solitary traveller. Which is fine. But it only emphasises how brilliant our professional lives were before the kids came along.

Because I've been away as much as I have, Marian has been very much the dominant presence in the lives of Craig and Michael. We have never employed a nanny or a cleaner – we have a wee laugh to ourselves when we see players on tour with only one child employing a young girl to help with the extra workload – so she has very much been a hands-on mother. Which I'm sure they (one day) will say has been one of the biggest breaks of their lives.

Marian might just be the most sensible person I have ever met and, although I'm sure the boys think she is overly strict at times, she has been a hugely positive influence on their characters and behaviour. We are both no fans of badly behaved children, especially in public settings. And I'm proud to say that I've never been approached by anyone reporting to me anything of that nature perpetrated by either Craig or Michael. Again, that is down to Marian far more than me.

Quite early on, in fact, we sat the boys down and tried to explain to them that because I'm reasonably well known in the Aberdeen area they would be subjected to more than the ordinary level of attention from others. So they would have to be aware of that and behave themselves. Their behaviour would reflect on all of us. The last thing we wanted to hear was that the Lawrie kids were a nightmare. And, to be fair, they have both been great in that regard, possibly because they have had it drummed into them since they were nippers.

The boys always know where they stand with both of us. Which is both good and bad of course. Generally speaking, I'm the easier touch of the two, the one more likely to spoil them; possibly because when I'm away I miss them. But I'm only the 'sugar daddy' if their behaviour is up to scratch. That's the deal we have.

When it comes to child rearing I don't have any deep philosophy to offer. But I know what I like to see and, perhaps more importantly, what I don't like to see. One thing I really hate is when children eat with their mouths open. In fact, I hate it when adults do it too. Noisy kids are another no-no for me. I don't mind them speaking up when they have something to say; that's fine. But when they start misbehaving and jumping on chairs I draw the line. My kids are not angels – far from it – but they never once did that in a public place, never. They have their fun, but at the right time and in the right place.

Then there's the kid kicking the back of the seat in front on an aeroplane. The parent or parents can see what their child is doing. But when you speak and ask them to tell their delightful offspring to cease and desist they look at you as if you have just landed from another planet. That sort of thing bugs me.

One thing about Marian also fits every cliché you have ever heard about we Aberdonians. She has never been a big spender of money. In fact, it takes a lot of effort on my part to get her to buy stuff for herself. So she is very 'low maintenance', unlike many tour wives and girlfriends I could mention! I just shake my head in wonder at some of the stories I hear my colleagues telling about how much their wives/partners like to spend routinely.

Where I can be quite spontaneous and jump into things quickly and without enough thought, Marian looks at things from every angle before reaching a decision. There have been many times when I've come home from a trip full of what I think is the greatest business idea ever. And 99 times out of 100, she will listen, sigh and tell me to give myself a shake. And, by the way, here is the knife – away and peel those potatoes. I need to hear that sort of thing sometimes. I need to get a grip and realise that life on tour is not real-life at all, but as Lee Westwood recently called Augusta National and the Masters, 'Disneyland for adults'.

So when people ask me what Marian is like, the word 'straightforward' always come to mind. My wife is simple to understand and thinks in straight lines. She is not 'made up' or false in any way. She's normal and the most down-to-earth person anyone could ever meet. She doesn't like flashy stuff. She doesn't go out and spend money for no reason.

Which is not to say she is a female version of Scrooge. Far from it. She is just practical when it comes to our finances. If Marian needs something, she buys it, but wanting something is not very often enough to get her reaching for the credit card or chequebook. She even gets a wee bit upset with me sometimes, when I come home with a gift for her.

Here is what my wife is like when it comes to treating herself. We were in Dubai once on holiday and visited a jeweller. Marian had a diamond necklace she wanted to get converted into a ring. Which was fine. She also had a ring that was half encircled by diamonds. I wanted to get them all the way round for her. And eventually I talked her into getting that done. But when I asked if there was anything else she wanted, that was it. She was done. I'm very lucky. I married the right woman and she turned out to be sensible with money.

Which is not to say that there have not been moments and times where it is made quite clear to me that I have messed up on the present-giving front. The 7th January this year – Marian's birthday – was one of those times. I had a lesson booked that morning but was sitting watching Sky

Sports News on the television. Marian was in the corner doing some ironing. Then Kirsty Gallacher – daughter of Bernard, cousin of Stephen – said, 'Good morning everyone, It's Saturday 7th January.'

Of course, then it clicked. I looked across and said, 'Happy Birthday. I'm so sorry I forgot.'

'Oh, that's okay. Don't worry.'

But I could tell it wasn't. Suddenly the air was a wee bit frosty. I felt terrible.

Anyway, after a coaching session with Andrew Locke, who was then the teaching pro at Inchmarlo and who still keeps an eye on my swing these days, I stopped at a florist in town. I said to the woman I needed a really nice bouquet of flowers.

'How nice?' she said. 'And what price range are you looking at?'

I said, 'It's an I-forgot-my-wife's-birthday bouquet.'

'There's no amount of flowers in here that covers that.'

But it was the best I could do. I bought the flowers and got cards for both the boys to sign. And yes, I still feel terrible.

I'm sure our sons have learned a huge amount just by being around Marian so much. She's done such a great job bringing them up. It goes without saying that I think she is a fantastic mother, partner and friend.

She is also a good cook, but hates cooking. Which is one reason why we eat out a fair bit, most often at Deeside Golf Club, where we are members and which is just down the road from our home. So we are there a lot, a fact that has not escaped the notice of one of the chefs. One night we were sitting at a table having just eaten when he remarked to Marian that she must have a very clean cooker. I laughed at that. Brilliant.

My wife is also a bit of perfectionist and likes to take control in certain situations. Not in a bad way. It is just that she likes things done right. There is also a bit of obsessive-compulsive disorder lurking in her make-up. I laugh at her need/liking to have all the coat hangers in our wardrobes facing the same way and that all my shirts also have to face in the same direction. Or is that normal?

Marian is at her happiest, however, when she is outside in our garden wearing wellie boots and up to her knees in mud. She and her parents tackle any and every job around the house and garden. I tend to adopt, ahem, more of a supervisory role.

Both Craig and Michael played a lot of football growing up, just as I did. But both have given the game up – again as I did – to concentrate on their golf.

Michael especially had some ability with a ball at his feet. And he was good enough to be involved with the Aberdeen FC youth set-up. But he decided that it wasn't for him, just as his brother had done. I must say though, I've never pushed them into playing golf. In fact, I was a little disappointed when they gave up the football. But it has to be up to them. There is nothing worse than seeing kids playing sports only because their parents push them into it. I hate to see that. Sport is there to be enjoyed, not endured.

As far as their full swings are concerned, I consciously take a back seat when it comes to Craig and Michael. They both work with Billy Fyfe. Where I contribute is their short games and a bit of course management. I do go to their lessons with Billy though, but only so that I can comment on what they are working on when we later go out to play.

The boys play most of their golf at Deeside GC, but are also members at Royal Aberdeen. Craig is the quiet one, but Michael is a bit louder and has a bit more to say for himself. But both have at least one thing in common: as golfers, they are miles ahead of where I was at the ages they are now. As I write, Craig is off scratch and Michael plays to five.

They are both competitive too. Marian and I were both bags of nerves when Craig made his debut in the Scottish Boys Championship at Dunbar in 2011. As he teed off in his first round match I was asked how I was feeling. 'Nae great,' was the reply. The old cliché about watching being so much harder than playing is certainly true, at least in my case. Thankfully, Craig handled it all much better than his parents, making it to the third round before losing narrowly to one of the tournament favourites.

I was proud of Craig that day but even more proud of him in 2012, when the championship was played at Murcar. After Craig lost by five and four in the first round – a big disappointment to him obviously – I was told by members of the press how pleasantly and maturely he had handled their questions. There had been no hint of petulance, even though he was clearly unhappy at losing. At the end of the day, that has to be more important than how well you play.

Michael too has had some experience at the national level. In 2007 he qualified for the final of the HSBC 'Wee Wonders' event held at St Andrews. That was a great performance. One year later he won the Deeside Junior Match Play knockout event and was named 'most improved' junior. Craig's successes include winning the North East under-16s title and the Deeside Junior Order of Merit. So both show some real promise. In fact, when people ask me what my hobbies are away from golf these days I say, 'I don't have any; my hobby is going for nine holes with my sons.'

As for how good each of my sons will turn out to be: who knows? While I get a lot of pleasure out of watching them develop and improve and am always available to help them where and when I can, what level they eventually reach is basically down to them. I've seen enough really good swingers to know that what really counts is what is inside a person. You can be as technically gifted as you like, but if you have no heart or desire you will never make it in golf.

What I will say, again, is that my sons are much better golfers than I was as a young teenager. But that's not saying much; I wasn't very good at all. They both have a chance though. Take Craig. If you can play to scratch at 16, then you have at least the basic ability to play good golf. So we will see. It's up to him. He is not lazy and works hard.

Michael is bit more of a natural player than his brother. He stands up and gives it a bit of a hit without having to think about it too much. Craig takes more time and is a little slower over the ball. The good thing is they both love to win and they both love to beat their old man.

Every year we go on holiday to Dubai over Christmas and New Year. And every year we stay at the Jebel-Ali resort. It has a nine-hole course. So we play a lot of golf over the 12 days or so we are there. We always have a competition. I keep our scores for every round. This year I played off plus three and the boys used their club handicaps.

So we get to the second last hole on the last day. Michael was one ahead of Craig and I was three back. And we all knew the situation. On the 17th Michael hits long and left and chips stiff for a par-3. Craig has a 12-footer for birdie, which he makes. Cue the fist pump and off to the last in the buggy. It was serious stuff.

Needless to say, I finished third. Which was pleasing to me because I was a good bit under par for all the games we played. So they both performed well to beat me. All of which is really good for me, of course. Ever since we started going there, I have played better early in the season.

As for the academic side of life, both my sons have already far outstripped my pathetic efforts at school. I couldn't stand the place, if I'm honest. I left before taking any exams. So I have no qualifications, not one. I didn't want to do it. And I didn't want to be there, traits my sons have thankfully not inherited. They take after their mother, who although not exactly an academic has oodles of commonsense.

Anyway, Michael is doing well and Craig's plan is take a gap year then do a degree in golf management at the North Highland College in Dornoch. I think the presence of such a good golf course there is just a coincidence. He quite fancies that side of the golf business and always takes a keen interest when he meets Jamie or Marcus, my managers at 4Sports.

Still, for all that, they know who is the real boss in the Lawrie household. One day a couple of years ago I was working on my short game on and around the green we have behind our house. Beside the green is a mat where I can hit full shots with a 9-iron over the house and into the garden at the front. So, at the end of my practice session, I started hitting a few over the rooftop, all with Michael standing watching.

At the time I had just started working on a wee drill Adam had given me. And, as you'd expect in the early stages of any change, it wasn't working every time. After a few shots, I thinned one and it hit the roof, just missing a window. Immediately, Michael took off for the house.

'Where are you going?' I asked, as he disappeared.

'I'm going to tell Mum,' he yelled gleefully, not slowing down for a second. And he did. He loved it that I got in trouble, just like he would have. Life at the Lawries is never dull.

Media – Social & Otherwise

When Jock MacVicar, the long time golf writer for the *Scottish Daily Express*, was honoured with the Scottish PGA Lifetime Achievement award early in 2012, he mentioned me in his short speech. 'Paul is a perfect example of a player who is great with the press,' he said. 'Of course, that wasn't always the case.'

As ever, Jock was spot on in his assessment. I've gone from being someone who was deeply suspicious of any and all forms of the media, to what I am today – understanding of the job these guys have to do and the important role that they play in both professional golf as a whole and my life in particular.

Before I won the Open, of course, my contact with the gentlemen of the Fourth Estate was limited. Not only did I not talk to them very often, when I did it was never for very long. So, not surprisingly, they never really got to know me and I never really got to know them. It wasn't that we were unfriendly, just that we weren't that friendly either. While it was a little more than a nodding acquaintance, an acquaintance is what it was.

As you can imagine, that all changed pretty quickly in the immediate aftermath of Carnoustie. Talk about being thrown in at the deep end. Overnight, I went from being perfectly happy in my almost complete anonymity, to being inundated with requests for interviews, autographs and photo shoots. It was quite an adjustment; one you won't be surprised to hear I was ill prepared for. And, at times, didn't handle too well.

The most immediate thing I noticed was the sudden interest in my bad play or at least the days when I performed some way short of my best. Before I became a major champion the only time I ever saw or spoke with the press was after a good round. So I was in fine fettle and, generally speaking, so were they. It was good news all round.

In the wake of my newfound status, however, that changed. No matter what score I shot, there was always a group of reporters waiting for me outside the scorer's hut after I had signed my card. Soon enough, I discovered that had at least the potential to be a problem. When you have just shot, say, 77, it is hard to come over as happy and upbeat. Describing the various ways in which you have dropped shots and made bogeys, it is all but impossible not to sound at least a little whiny or upset. And I wasn't very good at either, especially right after a round, a time when I hadn't had a chance to gather my thoughts.

But that, along with so many other things, was what I had to learn. It was the same with company days, or standing up in front of an audience to make what I hoped would be a witty and entertaining speech. All of those things take practice. And when you practice you make mistakes. The key is, when you do that, you must learn from those mistakes and, at the very least, not make them more than once.

One of the things that frustrated me most – and still does, only not as much – is the extent of the misconceptions some people have about me. For example, I have more than once been accused of thinking of myself as a 'world class' player. Nothing could be further from the truth. I don't see myself as that at all. Far from it. My view of Paul Lawrie – golfer – is that he is a pretty good player who definitely got lucky at just the right time, but who has done alright apart from that.

That's another thing people don't realise. My overall career would look pretty much the same as it does right now even without counting the Open victory. If you subtract the £350,000 I won at Carnoustie from my career winnings on the European Tour, I fall only one place in the all-time rankings. So for people to say that my career has been built on one great week is clearly false. There is no way it has. But that is the impression a lot of people have.

Still, there is no doubt that I missed a few points of my own as I adjusted to being Open champion rather than just another tour player. Looking back, I should have been smart enough to realise that things would be different and that talking to the press for, say, half an hour a day was going to be part of my job from then on. And I should have stopped reading so much of what was written about me.

The longer-term effects of the Open win on my health and wellbeing are documented in greater detail in chapter 11, but in the short-term I was completely taken aback by the fuss and bother it caused. I just wasn't ready for that. I hadn't ever had any media training before 1999 and, in hindsight, I didn't get much help from my then managers, International Management Group, during and after that momentous year either. They basically left me to get on with it, although I would exempt my manager at the time, Adrian Mitchell, from any criticism. I really liked Adrian – I still do – and I think he did a good job for me. But I didn't get the overall support from IMG that I needed.

I can understand – at least to an extent – that they were perhaps taken as much by surprise as I was by the level of attention I was getting. But it should have pretty quickly been obvious to them that I was struggling and needed some help. Help that unfortunately never really came. Not from IMG anyway.

Looking back, I wish I had done many things differently, but perhaps one of the biggest mistakes I made was not seeking professional advice on how to deal with everything that suddenly was a routine part of my life. But I don't want anyone to think that I was beside myself with anger at the media. I wasn't. Not even close. Their almost constant presence was more like an itch I couldn't scratch. So I never had a big fall-out with the press in general. It wasn't that sort of problem.

What I was rebelling against most was my loss of privacy. I've always valued that. So when I found that wanting to go home and not tell anyone what I did there with Marian and the kids was a problem, I found the whole situation very difficult. Both Marian and I, in fact, took the decision that we didn't want to see any pictures of the kids in the papers. That was off-limits. But that, many times, was exactly what the papers did want.

My mind goes back to the day I won the Open, when the lady from the *Daily Record* came to my home and asked my wife if she could sit and watch the play-off with her on television. She didn't get in, of course. But that was an example of how things were going to be with the press. Marian didn't know any better at that stage. And neither did I. But that was, to my mind, well out of order. She shouldn't have been at my house that day. That very definitely was an intrusion into my family's privacy.

It was just impossible really. I was happy enough to tell the world how many greens and fairways I hit or what my score was, but when it came to what I saw as private stuff, I just didn't want to participate in the process. I have never understood the interest people take in what I think of as no one's business but your own. I'm not interested in what David Beckham has for breakfast, so why should anyone care that I like to have tea and toast in the morning.

I've never been one to chase after celebrities either. For example, although I'm a regular visitor to Pittodrie for Aberdeen's home games, I'm not friendly with any of the players. I don't know any of them socially. I haven't been for a drink with any of them. I just support the club, go to the games and go home. I couldn't care less about anything else. That's why the people I call my real friends are 'normal' for want of a better word. My best mate is a fish merchant, for example. I would never dream of getting 'pally' with anyone because he was some sort of celebrity. That would just be sad.

That outlook – one I still hold – made it difficult for me to get my head round all the fuss and bother I was subjected to after the Open. I was getting asked questions on all sorts of subjects, especially politics. Which is a right laugh. Anyone who knows me knows how little interest I take in that area of life. But suddenly, I was an 'expert', all because I won a golf tournament. I found that very hard and a bit of a joke really.

Understandably, my reaction to that sort of thing was misunderstood at the time. Which was my fault. I could have handled it better by just giving some sort of non-committal answer instead of making it abundantly clear I had no patience for the question. I must have come across as abrupt and downright rude at times. That was never my intention, but I can see now why people thought it was.

Going to dinners was another problem for me. As you can imagine I received a pile of invitations when I was Open champion. And again, I didn't react well. 'Why would I want to go to dinners?' I asked myself. Why would I want to go a dinner just so that I could sit and chat for three hours to people I didn't know and would probably never meet again? So I didn't go to any of them. And that, I'm sure, only added to my growing reputation for standoffishness. It wasn't that though; I just didn't have a clue.

The great irony now, of course, is that I really enjoy a night out at a good dinner. I've even become – or so I've been told – passably entertaining when asked to say a few words to the assembled gathering. Every year we have a dinner at the Marcliffe hotel in aid of the foundation and every year I make a speech. And happily, the feedback I've received has been 100 per cent positive. Which has helped my confidence. Now, as long as I have time to prepare what I'm going to say, I'm more than comfortable telling my wee stories from the tour. Sorry Monty, by the way!

The key for me is preparation. I'm still not good at getting up and chatting off the cuff. Okay, I'm better than I was – which isn't hard – because at one time I was a nightmare. As I said in chapter two, way back in 2001, when we first launched the junior programme that became the

Paul Lawrie Foundation, we had a press conference at Hazlehead Golf Club. The council was involved and I was called upon to speak.

It was horrendous. First off, there was no lectern for me to put my speech on. So I had to hold on to it. Which I did. With both hands. Very tightly. That was bad enough, but not once during my stilted oration did I look up. Not once. And I read it word-for-word. There was no adlibbing.

I've made plenty of other mistakes along the way, of course. None more so than in my dealings with the media. The 'I'm going to get me a Ferrari' thing at my Open-winning press conference would come under the heading of 'things never to be repeated'. But the thing I would like to change most is the amount of time I gave to such an important aspect of my working life. I would do it very differently were it all to happen again for me.

I've tried to make up for those early days. I like to think that the golfing media – especially the Scottish lads – would back me up on that. For a long time now I've made a big effort to give them what they need. I always return calls asking for a chat. And I certainly don't ever 'blank' anyone and walk straight past. None of that was the case just over a decade ago though. Back then, I was poor when it came to giving them what they needed.

I felt the backlash of that too. Human nature being what it is, a few members of the press core took to ignoring me as much as they could. Which was fair enough. I wasn't exactly encouraging discourse back then. If a guy is told to speak to Paul Lawrie then Paul Lawrie walks past him without saying a word, he still has a story to write. And it doesn't need much intelligence to guess what sort of story he will end up doing. Even if what he comes up with is not exactly accurate, I only have myself to blame. It would have been accurate if I had taken two minutes to tell him the correct story.

I was even worse in America. I remember Scott Van Pelt of ESPN coming up to Adam in Hawaii when I was playing in the 2000 Mercedes Championships. I had refused to speak to Scott for two or three straight days and he wasn't happy. 'He can ignore us as much as he wants,' he said to Adam. 'But one of these days he's going to regret his behaviour.'

He was right too. As was Adam when he pulled me aside to tell me what Scott had said. 'I know you don't like it,' he said. 'But come on. You need to do this. It's part of your job. Besides, these people are out on tour every week. You need to give them what they need. It doesn't take that much time if you do it right. It's not even 10 minutes out of your day.'

I had an especially hard time – surprise, surprise – with some of the, I felt, unwarranted criticism that came my way. Some of it was just ridiculous and came from the most unexpected sources. One was especially disappointing.

At the time I won the Open I was writing a weekly column in my local paper, the Aberdeen-based *Press & Journal*. It was a fun thing to do. Every week I would talk to the guy, Mike Tremlett, who was ghosting my words and he would write it up for me. That was fine and seemed to work well for both parties.

But the week after the Open, as you can imagine, things got a bit hectic. The doorbell was going every two minutes. The phone was ringing what felt like every 20 seconds. There was stuff to sign. So I was a bit late in calling the *P&J* about my column. Not too late, just a bit behind schedule. I'm not sure, but I think they were a wee bit miffed.

Anyway, not long after the Open an article appeared in the *P&J* under Mike's by-line. The headline said, 'One out of Three Ain't Bad for Lawrie.' It was amazing stuff. One of the things in there was that I had claimed I would never leave Aberdeen and that the city would always be my base. Another was that I was going to abandon Europe and play full-time in the States. None of it, of course, was true. But not according to Mike. My move to Bieldside was the same as me leaving Aberdeen, at least in his mind. I mean, Bieldside is part of Aberdeen! And the European Tour thing? Well, I played more than the minimum amount in 2000, so that answers that question.

As you can imagine, I wasn't too impressed. So I called the then-editor, Derek Tucker, on the phone. He's retired now. I was in the car and had to pull over by the side of the road I was so upset. I was shouting and screaming at the guy. He was claiming that his writers had license to write what they wanted. But my point was, while that may have been the case, the writer also had an obligation to write what he knew to be true.

It was all so silly. I can't understand to this day why I was so upset. If it came out now I would do nothing. I'd laugh and let it go. I wouldn't even call.

Speaking of the *P&J*, I've been on the front page of my hometown newspaper only twice in my life. The first time I had just won the Open, but the second occasion was a lot less pleasurable. After what can only be described as a bit of innocent banter that went horribly wrong, I found myself banned from the Meldrum House Golf Club, a place where I had once been attached as the touring professional.

It all started in May 2009 with a routine game of golf at Meldrum with my sons. We had played and found the greens to be particularly poor. They were bumpy and so not much fun to putt on. Which was not that big a deal until I went through to the pro's shop for something and spoke briefly to the starter: 'what's the story with the greens?' I was genuinely interested because they were normally so good.

'What do you mean?' responded the starter.

So I repeated my view that they were really bumpy and not that good. At which point, we could see one of the green keepers, Richard, was headed into the shop along with a companion. So the starter told me to ask him. And I did.

Cue another, 'what do you mean?' He went right onto the defensive.

So I explained what I had found. The balls had been bouncing all over the place.

'You winding me up?' was his next comment.

At which point I realised there was a problem brewing. So I backed off, trying to make light of the situation. It wasn't something I wanted to go any further. And when I went back into the clubhouse, I heard him say to his friend (who turned out to be the head green keeper from another course, Old Meldrum, which is just down the road), 'cheeky bastard'. I let that go and kept walking. There was no need to get more involved. There was no real argument. No voices were raised. And there was definitely no swearing. Apart from Richard's parting comment.

My motivation was sincere. I genuinely wanted to know what the problem was. To which he could have responded with any kind of standard answer, 'yeah, we're laying whatever in an attempt to do whatever'. I would have gone away quite happy, no harm done. Actually, I had left thinking that very thing. I certainly wasn't prepared for what was to follow.

My question about Meldrum House's greens was, after all, legitimate. That same week, the boys and I played at Deeside. And the greens there were in great shape. So there was no real reason why, only a few miles away, another course's putting surfaces should have been so bad. And this is perhaps my only mistake in this whole thing. After getting his number from the head pro, Neil Marr (who at that time was my coach) I texted the course manager at Meldrum House, Kenny Harper, from Deeside saying, 'Deeside greens really good, unlike your shite.'

Now, it's important I put that comment into context. Kenny and I were quite 'pally'. He had been to my house to advise me on taking care of the practice green in my garden and we regularly engaged in similar banter. Which is what my comment was meant to be. And at first he seemed to take it that way. Soon enough, his reply arrived: 'Tiger Woods is really good, unlike…' I laughed out loud. And that, as far as I was concerned, was the end of things.

Now fast-forward a week. Marian was opening our mail and found a letter from Meldrum House, signed by three directors. It said: 'In light of your recent comments and text to our green keeping staff, we feel that it would be in everyone's best interest if you were not to return to Meldrum House Golf Club.'

Their point was that I hadn't had Kenny's mobile number and so this could not be construed as mere banter. I had had to ask Neil Marr for it. So I'd never texted Kenny before and had asked for it solely to give him abuse. Which was not true. I had no reason to have his number. I would always just speak to Kenny directly at the club if I needed any more help with my chipping green. And it very definitely was banter, at least in my mind.

It really was very strange. My text was banter and they took it as being serious; his text was serious and I took it as banter. It was a total breakdown in communication, one that could have been sorted out in a two-minute phone call between the club chairman, Bob Edwards, and myself. All he would have had to say was that Kenny and Richard were a little upset at my comments and what was going on? I would have explained and that would have been it. I'd even have been happy to ring both of them to say 'no hard feelings'. But they didn't want that; they wanted this insignificant incident, for whatever reason known only to themselves, to be a problem. They clearly saw this as a chance to break off our relationship.

I was an honourary member at Meldrum House and often used the facilities for practice. But, I must emphasise, I paid for my own practice balls. I paid for any buggy I used. And I paid for any guests I brought out there. There was never any freeloading.

Anyway, the whole thing escalated from there. I phoned Kenny right away. I still thought it was a wind-up at this stage. I told him that in the message I left, saying 'you've even got the club letterhead on the page'. Kenny never phoned me back, which gave me pause. So I called Neil Marr and asked what was going on. There was a brief silence before he told me that it wasn't a wind-up, it was serious. He had actually known for a few days and felt he was in a difficult position because he worked for these people and was coaching me.

I took that point, but a stronger PGA pro could maybe have stepped up and nipped the whole thing in the bud. But he didn't. He also could have called to give me a heads-up about what was coming. But he didn't do that either. As far as he was concerned, I could and should have been just another member and he is trained to deal with situations like that.

Anyway, I called Kenny again and this time got him. Our chat didn't go well and soon degenerated into an argument. His first line was, 'What a position you put me in.' That kicked things off. I had a right go at him on the phone. As I did with Bob Edwards when I spoke to him. My point was that they had my number and all they had to do was call. But not once did they ask for my side of the story. I'd have gladly smoothed it all over. No bother.

It got still worse when the whole thing made the newspapers. Bob told reporters that the situation could still go away if I apologised. And that, if I did so, I would still be welcome back. But that was the first time that option had ever come up. Until then, he had never given me the chance to apologise, especially at the point where I would have done so, if only to put the whole silly thing to bed once and for all.

In the end, it was all a complete mess and something I would never have wanted to happen. Why would I? It isn't as if I came out the other side looking very good, even if, as I've explained, my role in it all was nothing like it was portrayed by some at Meldrum House. In fact, the only person who was happy was Martin Gilbert. There I was on the front of the *P&J* wearing an Aberdeen Asset logo on my jumper. He e-mailed me to say I should upset clubs more often. If only Meldrum House had his sense of humour.

My professional relationship with Neil Marr didn't survive long afterwards. We did start seeing each other at another club to work on my game, but when I wrote about that in my daily website blog, Meldrum House made him choose between his job there and coaching me. Quite rightly, he chose his job. But what annoyed me most was that they felt like they could tell me what I could and couldn't write on my own blog.

Actually, the choice they initially gave Neil wasn't quite as black-and-white as I just portrayed it. They told him I could come to Meldrum House for my lesson, but I had to leave straight away. Needless to say, that didn't happen. I will never set foot in the place again, even though I did get a whole host of e-mails supporting my position, many of them from Meldrum House members.

There was one last thing. Not long after all that nonsense, Neil called me to say he wanted to select Craig for a district squad he was coaching.

My response was that it would be quite difficult. I would have to drop my son at the front gate and have him walk the rest of the way from there. So that was that. Besides, Craig had no interest in going to a club where his father is not welcome. I was proud of him for saying that.

What I wasn't so proud of was the plethora of headlines this trivia generated. I was in every newspaper under some very big words declaring things like, 'Say sorry and you will be welcomed back, Paul', 'You're barred, club tells golf star Lawrie', and 'Your tee's Out'. No matter the rights and wrongs of it all, I was embarrassed, at least in the short term, even if, over the weekend when it all blew up, I shot 66-66 at the Irish Open. Obviously I wasn't that bothered!

The good thing is that my lifestyle hasn't been altered one iota by what happened. It's water under the proverbial bridge as far as I'm concerned. I learned a lesson though. One thing has changed. Whenever I'm asked what I think of the greens at any club, I always say they are 'brilliant'. Even when I know they're not. I know now that people don't want to hear the truth. So there's no point in giving it to them.

I had another bad media experience with someone called Bill Leckie of *The Sun*. On the morning of the second day of the 2000 Open at St Andrews, just before I went out to play the press officer told me that Leckie would like to speak to me. 'No problem,' I said. 'Tell him to meet me after I'm finished.'

That was fine. And even though it looked like I would miss the cut, I waited around after signing my card and doing my usual bit with the other media guys. I was standing there when the press officer appeared: 'Bill is stuck out on the course. Can you hang on?'

So I did. Eventually, Leckie appeared. He was all red in the face and sweaty and out of breath. But we did what I thought was a pretty reasonable interview. Then, of course, the next day it turns out that he has slaughtered me in print. I was a 'flash in the pan' apparently, 'a one-hit wonder'. That was just one example of how I so often felt short-changed by the press. Of course, Leckie, a man I had never seen before in my life, has never again crossed my path. Which is maybe just as well. I'm not a big fan of a hypocrite who one minute is your best pal then the next is stabbing you in the back.

That sort of stuff was bad enough, but probably the most traumatic and disappointing experience was reading some of the comments that appeared on the Aberdeen FC chat website. I couldn't believe what I was reading on a site presumably populated by a lot of people just like me: Aberdeen born-and-bred and a huge fan of the Dons. And yes, I know I shouldn't visit any Internet sites. But I did and, in fact, still do, although I was sensible enough to get myself off 'Twitter' before I said something I shouldn't. I'm not sure why I continue to log on other than to say that, like most people, I like to be popular. I like to read nice things about myself. Who doesn't?

But what was on there was poor. I would never have believed that any fellow Aberdeen fan would think such things of me. People were calling me a cretin. One guy wrote about my foundation, saying it is not all it is cracked up to be, that it is all about me, my image and my brand and not the kids. That simply isn't so. When it comes to the foundation, I'm very proud of what I've been able to do and put back into the area that has been my home since I was born.

Anyway, I registered on the AFC site, using my own name. I wanted people to see that, when I had something to say, I was brave enough to use my name and not go under some fictitious and anonymous nonsense. And I went on and answered a lot of that stuff directly. For example, I told them how difficult it could be when you have to talk to the press every day and say the right thing every time. Things do slip out.

There have, of course, been plenty of positive stories written about me over the years, especially recently. Over the last couple of years I've played a lot of good golf, won three tournaments and, played myself onto the 2012 Ryder Cup team.

Perhaps the strangest thing about my relationship with the press is that it has gone full circle. In fact, whenever I speak to a group of young pros or to the Scottish Golf Union squad, I always emphasise how important it is to give the press the time they need. If they want you to sit down for 15 minutes, sit down for 15 minutes. It is only a quarter of an hour out of your day. It is nothing in terms of time yet it can do so much good for years afterwards.

I'm actually a fan of much of what is written about golf these days. Every month I buy all the magazines: *Golf Monthly*, *Golf World*, *Today's Golfer*, *Golf International* and *Bunkered*. And I really do mean buy them. I go to the newsagent's shop and hand over money. I'm not on any complimentary lists.

I have to be honest though. My least favourite magazine is *Golf World*. For a long time they seemed to think it was fun to have a go at me every month. There was always something about me in there that wasn't too great. One time, I remember, they awarded me first prize for 'worst winner's speech at a major'.

Not long after that they even had the cheek to ask me to take part in an instruction story. So, in the interest of building bridges I agreed. I think it was a putting story. But there was one problem. The pictures they had of me were old and the clothes I was wearing were out of date in terms of the logos on my cap and jumper. So we agreed to re-shoot them. Or so I thought. Without telling me, the magazine ran the story using the old pictures, leaving me to explain to my new sponsors why I was in a national publication wearing clothes other than the ones they were paying me to wear.

I had a similar problem with the *P&J* when we ran my invitational tournament at Deeside in 2011. I had organized five sponsors for the event, all of whom put in a good chunk of cash, as did the foundation. So when the paper's photographer arrived to take the pictures of the winner, I asked that he be shot standing in front of banners advertising the event sponsors. But they wouldn't do it, something about 'free' advertising.

I don't get that, not at all. A local guy puts on a tournament. Five local companies put in £10,000 each. Yet the local paper can't even run their picture. To me, that is madness.

At least the *P&J* is consistent though. Early in 2012 we had a wee press conference to announce that the foundation would be sponsoring three young lads from the north east of Scotland – David Law, Philip McLean and Kris Nicol – as they set out on their pro careers. We took a picture of them and myself standing in front of a board advertising the foundation. The next day the picture ran, but the board was cut out. Again, I don't get that, given how much good the foundation does in the *P&J*'s heartland. People are putting money into junior golf. But we can't be telling anyone about that?

As things stand right now, I'm not talking to the *P&J*, which again is madness. They persist in running old pictures of me wearing clothes made by old sponsors. I've offered to pose for new photos but they don't seem to want to know. So we are at an impasse. I know I should be talking to them. And I'm sure they know they should be talking to me. But I can't let it go. I'm my own worst enemy. But I feel sure anyone else in my position would do that same.

The press eh? Can't live with them…etc., etc.

Down – But Not Out

It started just before the Masters in 2003. For reasons that now escape me, I looked around the range on tour and decided that no top player was using Callaway equipment. I'm sure that wasn't the case. Back then, as it is now, Callaway was one of the bigger players in the golf club market, so the chances of them having 'none' of the leading professionals on their books are slim at best.

But that flawed analysis was an indication of how my thinking wasn't quite what it should be. I convinced myself that I couldn't hit my Callaway irons out of the rough. They just won't go, I said to myself. I need to take two more clubs than anyone else just to get the same distance. So obviously it was the fault of the clubs. Which was why no major champions (male versions) were using them. And why I wasn't going to use them any more. I was going to find clubs that would give me a chance of winning again.

So what did I do? I did what all golfers do when they think their equipment is a problem. I went off and tried almost every other club maker I could think of. My goodness, I kept the postman busy back then. Stuff was arriving by the lorry-load. Sets of irons. Drivers. Sets of woods. You name it, I tried it. All because I had myself convinced I was playing the wrong equipment. It was madness really. And the end result was inevitable: total confusion about what I should and shouldn't be putting in my bag.

The irony was that I had actually started the 2003 season pretty well. I missed only one cut in my first nine events and racked up three top-tens, including a second at the Dunhill Championship in South Africa and a third in the Benson & Hedges International at the Belfry.

The funny – and I don't mean ha-ha – thing was that, after all my mucking about and experimenting, I ended up deciding that nothing was better than Callaway. So I called Peter Harrison, their European boss, and explained the situation. He had been good enough to release me from my contract only a few months earlier. And he was just as good – if not better – when he took me back into the fold, on the same deal I had been on previously. It would have been easy for him to take advantage of me, but he didn't. I'll always be grateful for that. I even bought him a watch to say 'thank you'. He had to get special permission from the Callaway board to accept it. But I gave it to him as a friend to say thanks, not as any sort of bribe or inducement.

By the Open at Royal St Georges that year I was really struggling mentally. For the first time in my life I felt really down. I had no energy and I didn't want to play or practise. Not even a little bit. I would never have believed I could get like that, but I did. I went to the doctor and he put me a course of tablets. But I felt no better. So he gave me more, warning me that something would have to be done if this lot didn't work.

As Marian says elsewhere in this chapter, I wasn't an easy person to live with around that time. I had always been good at leaving any golfing problems on the course or on the tour, but for a while there I was doing just the opposite.

The root cause of it all, of course, was my Open victory four years earlier. Actually, that is not quite accurate. It wasn't the winning that was causing me problems; it was the way I won. And the subsequent lack of respect and recognition. That was driving me crazy. It seemed like in every golf magazine I read there was a picture of that Frenchman up to his ankles in the Barry Burn. As a result, I put myself under enormous pressure to prove everyone wrong and to show that my ultimate victory was no fluke. I just really struggled to get my head round the thing.

Adam always said just that. And a few years later he said so publicly. In a story headlined 'Trophy Strife', published in *Golf World* (US version), Adam told the world how much the general reaction to my victory had affected me as a golfer and a person. Here is what he said:

'There is no doubt that Van de Velde gave it away. Or that he was unlucky. But that isn't Paul's fault. And it doesn't make Paul lucky either. He went out and took his chance. I kept telling him to look at the Claret Jug on his mantelpiece and just smile. They can't take it away from him.

'He's never said this to me, but, deep down, maybe he feels like he didn't deserve to win an Open. Maybe that's why he is torturing himself with it. Who knows? It's easy to say he should enjoy it more, but he has to allow himself to do it.

'The problem is his expectation level. Before '99 all he ever heard was that he was a five-handicapper who would never make it big. So his attitude was always, 'Right, I'll show you.' Everything was a bonus.

'After '99 all that changed. Suddenly, Paul was expected to win. So now he is trying to prove to all the doubters – and there have been many – that he deserved to win it. Which is crazy. He can't change people's opinions. Whether he deserved to win or not, he did win the Open. Who cares what anyone else thinks?

'Paul has played this respect thing to death. He's getting in his own way. I fear, not for his sanity, but his mental wellbeing. This is torture for him and it's hard to get him to open up about it all. He's very guarded. He knocks back any negative question by not really addressing it. And that's how he denies the existence of a problem.

'To me, his winning the Open has hurt his development as a golfer. The Open did open a lot of doors for him – the Ryder Cup for one – but it's been something of a poisoned chalice for him. And it will be until he wins another one.'

Now, I'm not saying I agree with everything Adam said there. For one thing, I would have qualified for the Ryder Cup team even without the money I earned from my Open win. But there is no doubt that there are a few home truths in there. And remember, he spoke those words in early 2007, four years after I did actually make myself ill with some of the stuff he talks about.

I even reached the stage where I said to more than one person, 'I wish I had never won it.' To which the common reaction was along the lines of, 'Oh, don't be stupid. Get a grip and give yourself a shake.' That sort of stuff.

What was making it worse was all that 'Lowery' stuff in the States. I would go over there and be just about demented by the fact that no one seemed capable of looking at my name and pronouncing it properly. I can't tell you how often I said to myself, over and over, 'I wish I had never won that tournament.'

Of course, that was nothing new. I had felt that way almost from the day after I did win the Open. I certainly felt the lack of respect. And when it took me 18 months to win again – at the Dunhill Links Championship – people were saying quite openly that I should have been totting up the victories long before that. I struggled with that actually. I had a few chances and didn't finish them off. There was an event in Korea. I finished third or fourth and should have won. And the European Tour season-ending Volvo Masters at Montecastillo was something similar. I ended up 10th or so but I should have been right in there at the death. So there was some truth to the criticism.

All in all, I had about two years of events actively wanting me to pitch up and play. I was an important part of a sponsor's plans then. But because I didn't win much or even kick-on as many seem to expect I would or should, that ebbed away. Which is understandable.

In retrospect, I think my desire to be accepted and recognised as a 'proper' major champion had much to do with my decision to join the PGA Tour at the end of 1999. I wanted to be a world player like Ernie Els has been a world player, someone capable of winning everywhere on the planet. I wanted to be a real Open champion and not just play in Europe. I thought that was important.

Part of that too, was I wanted people to recognise my achievement. It is hard to put into words exactly how I felt, but it would have been nice to get a different reaction to my victory. Let me say – yet again – I understand why it wasn't the way I would have liked it to be, but it would have been nice if even one or two could have made the effort to pronounce my name correctly. I saw that as nothing more than bad manners, and would have done even if I was not Open Champion.

I remember a group of guys in Hawaii. We were there in January 2000 for the Mercedes Championships. Adam was with me and Paddy Byrne was on the bag. It must have been about the 15th hole on the first day and I was leading. Or at least I was doing really well. So one of the group shouts, 'Great shot Lowery!'

I marched over and said, 'How do you spell Lawrie?' Which was daft of course. What was I thinking? These days I would just laugh and play golf. But back then, as I've said over and over, I cared and it bothered me. A lot. I wish I could have been more like I am now – I would have won more and played better for a start – but I wasn't. Which was a pity and, as it turned out, not good for my long-term mental health.

Also putting me under pressure was the self-imposed stuff. It is really difficult – even when you are a decent player – to live up to suddenly increased expectations. As a major champion I was now not able to – at least in my own mind – have an off-week or make even the smallest mistake. And that, when you are playing a game full of mistakes, big and small, is no way to get better.

I also had to get used to the weird notion that, if I did shoot 75, it was still news. In fact, my 75s became bigger news than my 67s. If I shot the former there might be 20 reporters waiting for me after I had signed my card; if I had shot eight shots lower there might be only three or four. That was tough. I found that really hard to understand. Plus, I'm not the best right after I've played poorly. I only need five minutes, but that five minutes is vital.

Add in the loneliness I was feeling being away from Marian and two very small boys and you have a recipe for what I found myself going through in

2003. It just all added up over a period of two or three years and in the end it was too much for me. I still shudder when I think of how many solitary evenings I spent in America hotels eating room service meals. And the thing is I knew right away I had made a mistake going over there. In only my second event – the Sony Open in Hawaii – I couldn't wait to get out of the place. Hawaii!

Hindsight being what it is, I can see very clearly all the mistakes I made in the 24 months or so after Carnoustie. But no one was saying to me, 'Stop!' It was more, 'Are you sure?' But I'm like that with lots of things. I start off with the best of intentions, get a wee bit down the track with something, then think to myself, 'What are you doing?'

The pleasure I get from being home in Aberdeen should have been enough by itself to make me ponder. I'm very much a home bird. I enjoy being away at tournaments, but I enjoy being home even more. I've always been a back row guy as opposed to a front row guy. I'm the sort of person who likes to mingle with people and have a chat. But I'm not comfortable being the guy everyone wants to talk to. And America is the opposite of that. So I should have known.

Anyway, the early part of 2003 is when all of the above came to a head. And by the summer, by the Open, I was just gone. Marian, of course, had noticed the change in me and was concerned. 'I've never seen you like this,' she kept saying. 'What's going on?'

The trouble was, I didn't really know what was going on. I had no previous experience of mental illness, even in the mild form I was suffering from. I do know what tipped me over the edge as far as my clubs were concerned though. It was one hole, the 13th at the Masters.

I had pulled my drive very slightly, the ball finishing in the narrow strip of semi-rough – or 'second cut' as it is known at Augusta National – just above Rae's Creek, which meanders all the way up the left side of the fairway before cutting across in front of the green. I can't recall whom I was playing with, but we were side-by-side in the rough. He went first and hit a 6-iron onto the front left side of the putting surface. A good shot.

So it was me to go. I took a 4-iron and hit it perfectly. And the ball finished in the water. I had hit two more clubs than my playing partner. Yet he was on the green and I'm in the drink. And I didn't miss it either. Walking up the fairway I was thinking, 'That's it. I'm done with these clubs. I can't be clubbing up like that and still coming up short. It's just ridiculous.'

And then my mind was racing.

'Callaway has no major winners.'

'No one any good is playing with this stuff.'

'No one in the top-ten anyway.'

'This is just not on.'

Of course, I got worse and worse the more clubs I tried. My ball striking was pathetic inside a couple of months. Before I knew where I was, I couldn't get out of bed. I didn't want to do anything. I didn't want to be with the kids even. Which isn't like me. Even if I'm tired after being away at events and they want to go to play golf right after I walk in the door, then we go. I never say no. Never. If they want to play, I play, whether I'm knackered or not. But back then I didn't want to play. I didn't even want to see them. I had no go in me at all.

Anyway, right after the Open I went through that first batch of tablets without feeling any more positive about anything. Only Marian, Adam and my best mate, Colin Fraser, knew what I was taking. I still didn't want to do anything. I still didn't want to go anywhere. I would come downstairs in the morning and just lie on the couch and watch the television. The only times I got up was to pee.

That went on for three or four weeks. If somebody came to the door it was, 'I'm not in.' Or if the phone rang it was, 'Tell them I'm out.' Stuff like that. I just didn't want to speak to anyone. The thing is, before I went through what I went through, depression was the sort of thing I would have scoffed at. I would have gone, 'Bollocks. Get off your arse you lazy so-and-so. Give yourself a shake man.'

I know better now. Depression – even in its mildest form – is very debilitating. I know. I went from someone who is neither up nor down 10 minutes after even a really a bad round, to this guy who could hardly get out of bed. It was such a weird time. It was horrible really. I wasn't very nice to be around.

Eventually, of course, I had to go back to the doctor. I wasn't getting any better and the first set of tablets he had given me was all gone. So he changed the prescription. The second batch I got was, I assume, more powerful. The doc said he had had a lot of success with a lot of people displaying similar symptoms to mine. He left me with a warning though: 'If these don't work we need to seriously consider sending you to talk to a specialist.'

Luckily, the new tablets made a difference within a couple of weeks. And by the end of the course I was feeling pretty much back to normal. I had more energy so I started chipping and putting and making some swings. And soon after that I began hitting balls again. That was much more like the old/real me. I have never been one for watching much telly; 10 minutes is a lot for me. Then I'm up doing something golf-related, either chipping, putting or practice swinging.

During my illness though, I did none of the above. I went a whole month without making one swing, which is unheard of for me. Looking back, that's amazing. It just shows you how powerful your mind is. I would never have believed I could be as bad as I was. Or that I would be someone who could ever be depressed. So it shows how it can happen to anyone.

The good thing was that the root cause of my problem was obvious. Goodness knows I had articulated it often enough over the four years since I won the Open. But it was a strange thing. Who would have thought that the fulfilment of a lifetime ambition would lead me into depression?

Indeed, it is only in the last few years that I've been able to let all the bad feelings go. I no longer get upset about articles or pictures that highlight the guy who lost the 1999 Open rather than me, the winner. I no longer try to change anyone's opinion, even if they do feel I was lucky. I know that I was. Jean should have won but he didn't. I mean, anyone with a six to win up the last should be able to get the job done.

It no longer bothers me that, in the immediate aftermath of the championship, no one seemed to mention how well I played that day, both in the last round and in the play-off. I had only won a couple of events before that day, yet there I was claiming the biggest event in golf and winning the play-off with something to spare and no one seemed to notice. I mean, give me some credit for taking my chance when it came. That was what first annoyed me, then depressed me.

It was a battle I was never destined to win, however. As someone told me a long time ago, 'Don't fight the press, you'll never win. They will always have the last word.' I wish I'd taken that on board a lot earlier than I did.

The good news is that I'm fine with it all now. I've let it all go. I can even laugh about it. Early in 2011 I was in Mallorca, waiting for the bus to the course. There was a scoreboard right where I was standing and a married couple was looking at all the names. The husband says to the wife: 'Oh, Robert Rock is playing. (Pause) And so is Paul Lawrie. You know, the guy who got lucky in the Open.'

At that, I turned round and said, 'I know'.

Of course, they were immediately apologetic. I just laughed and reassured them that all was well. But I wouldn't have been that way if that incident had taken place, say, 18 months after Carnoustie. I would have been really angry. I would have said something rude to them. And I would have been upset for the rest of the day. Not now though. I'm over it.

Happily too, I have not suffered any sort of relapse in terms of my depression. I still give myself a hard time if I play badly, but that's not quite the same thing. I've always done that!

Marian

Right from the start, the general reaction to how things went on the last day of the Open really bothered Paul. And yes, it was hard for me to see how much it affected him. It seemed like every book or magazine he picked up, there was a picture of Jean Van de Velde.

Then there was the thing at Buckingham Palace, when they announced him as 'Peter Lawrie'. That doesn't sound like much, but on top of all the other stuff I'm not surprised that he reacted as he did.

I've had to listen to my share of it over the years. I hear it all the time from spectators when I'm walking round following Paul and they don't know who I am. 'There goes Paul Lawrie,' they say. 'He was so lucky at the Open. Van de Velde threw it away and really should have won.'

But that is the way of things, or was for a long time afterwards. Jean was the story and Paul was an afterthought. It is hard to read that stuff over and over. When it is in black and white you can't change it. It's right there in front of you. And what can you say? You can only point out how well he played so many times before you get fed up with it all.

His bout of depression and all that club-changing stuff was a direct consequence of the Open win and all that came after. I think, deep down, Paul thought he would win more majors and really kick on in his career. But it didn't happen and he was searching for reasons why. I'm not sure how much the media contributed to any or all of that, but it was definitely a factor. He certainly never got the recognition he deserved. I mean, how often does Scotland come up with an Open champion? He should have been given a lot more praise than he was for what he achieved.

Our family doctor was great with Paul when he was ill. He took a big interest in his recovery. I remember calling him during the 2003 Open at Royal St George's because he was so keen to know how Paul was getting on and if the pills were helping.

That was not a good time though. Paul just wasn't the man I've known all these years. Before, he was always doing something, always on the move. Then, all of a sudden, he was just lying on the couch all day. I was very worried. There was nothing I could say or do to make him feel better. And he had no interest in anything. I'd be taking the boys to the golf club for nine holes and Paul would hardly notice. He would just lie there.

At first, I would try to get him going, tell him to 'get up and get on with it'. But I soon realised that was pointless. And, not having ever experienced anything like that myself, I couldn't understand what he was going through. I knew quite quickly that, no matter what I said or did, it wasn't going to make any difference. He needed medical help.

It was hard for the boys too. I'm not sure they really understood what was going on. But I'm sure they noticed the huge difference in their Dad. I was worried too about the financial side of things. I don't work and Paul is the sole breadwinner. I had no idea how long he was going to be in the state he was.

Because he never really stopped playing for a noticeably long period no one really knew what was going on. I don't think even my parents realised. They thought he was resting or just putting his feet up. So it was probably just the doctor and I who knew the extent of what he was suffering.

Even now, years later, it still worries me that he will suffer a recurrence. I remember before he won in Andalucia early in 2011, Paul hurt his foot. In fact, his knee and groin were bothering him too. I never said anything at the time, but I was thinking, 'I hope this isn't going to lead to another bout of depression' because he was just so cheesed off with everything. Everyone is always telling him what a great swing he has, what great rhythm and how wonderful his short game is, but when he is putting poorly and not even making the cut at events, I sometimes think, 'oh no, here we go again'.

That happens a lot less these days though. I honestly don't think it will ever happen again. Paul has things a lot clearer in his mind now, especially when the subject of the Open comes up.

The Paul Lawrie Foundation

The original idea came from me just wanting to put something back into a game and a part of the world that have both been so good to me and my family. That was my initial motivation but it goes without saying I couldn't do it alone. I've had an amazing amount of help over the years from Stewart Spence and others in the Aberdeen area. Stewart in particular has been vital to any success I've had. I'm not sure I'd be where I am today had it not been for his constant help, guidance and invariably wise counsel. So I wanted to be like him; I wanted people to feel for me what I feel for him. I still do, in fact. I can never thank him enough for the money and time he has given so generously to my life and career.

I actually wanted to get things going before we actually did in 2001. But before then I didn't feel like I had a big enough public profile to make it all work in the way I wanted it to. Quite simply, I wasn't a good enough player. I could see me turning up at events and kids looking at each other asking, 'who is this guy?' Although I bet they probably still do!

Winning the Open changed all that, of course. But even then it took a while to get up and running. Only when you embark on something like this do you realise just how much time and effort goes into making things run as they should. So it wasn't until 2001 that what was then called, 'Paul Lawrie Junior Golf' came into being.

There was so much to be done. Dealing with the Aberdeen council made things time-consuming too. That is not a criticism – I understand perfectly how publicly funded enterprises have to operate – but when you are negotiating with and explaining things to committees and such like, getting agreement all the way up the line inevitably takes longer than if you are dealing with, say, a benevolent dictator. But that was the way we had to do it. Without council backing, we couldn't get to the kids in the schools. And, to be fair, they were great in providing staff to help run the whole thing and participate in the actual coaching.

At first, as you would expect, it all started off in a small way. There was some coaching. I went along as much as I could. And we paid a few pros to give lessons at Hazlehead Golf Club and the Kings Links Golf Centre. The people at the Kings Links were brilliant as I recall, giving us free balls.

Holding a 'Junior Open' was one of the first things we did. Then we got into the 'Flag' events pretty soon after that.

I love the Flag tournaments. I first saw how they are done – each child gets, say, 36 shots to play with then when they have hit that many they put a flag in the ground to indicate how far round the course they got – when Michael played in the HSBC 'Wee Wonders' championship at St Andrews. So I, of course, came back raving about how good it was. As you will see reading this chapter, my role in these things is usually to have an idea then leave it to everyone else to make it work!

And it has. Now, just over 10 years later, the Paul Lawrie Foundation runs about a dozen Flag events every year, all of them with around 100 kids taking part. They are great fun, which is why they work of course. And they are still, in my opinion, among some of the best things that we do. We charge £3 to enter, which we give to the host club. And every child gets a goodie bag containing a golf ball, tees, a pencil, a bottle of water and a piece of fruit. It has always been our aim to give everyone a good deal, value for money and to take away costs for the parents. The golf clubs tend to do okay too, as a lot of parents eat and drink while the kids are playing.

At every event we give out a gold, silver and bronze medal to the winners in each age category. No parent is allowed to caddie or even give advice. That is always a recipe for disaster. Plus, it is better if the kids learn how to conduct themselves and play without outside influence. The kids are so switched on though. I was speaking to Philip McLean recently – he is a young pro sponsored by the foundation – and he told me that his nephew was a keen participant in our Flag events.

'Aye, uncle Philip, they're great. You get about 15 quid worth of freebies, which includes a ProV1.' Brilliant.

Although, on the other side of that coin, I did have one wee lad who followed me back to my car after I had given a clinic at one of the events. 'I'd have thought you'd have a better car than a Range Rover,' he said. I would never have said that to an adult at his age.

Then again, most kids are terrific. I appreciate their honesty. I was at a school visit once and was sitting with the Claret Jug answering questions from the floor. One lad pointed at the trophy and said, 'Are you telling me you've only got one of them?'

'Yes,' I said.

'That's not very good is it?'

So funny, especially as the teachers were mortified. But I love it when stuff like that happens. I try to do as many of those school visits and junior prize-givings as I can. But unfortunately I can only usually do a few in the winter. They are enormous fun. We normally do a Q&A and I'm often interviewed for the school magazine. Sometimes, we set up a SNAG golf event in the gym, in which I take part. I can't imagine how many of those SNAG sets we gave away to schools in the early days of the foundation.

We also started match play tournaments for both boys and girls, with one competitor from each participating club taking part. Now that number is two from each club. There is also an Order of Merit and at the end of each season, a finals day. The first of those was held at St Andrews Bay, but now we are at Deeside, who are very good at letting us have the course. It is the ideal venue.

One step up from the flag events – and to plug the gap between the smallest kids and those playing in the Junior Open – we have Stableford competitions for the under-15s. The winners of those get vouchers. Again, there is a season-long Order of Merit with the top-27 invited to play in a Pro-am on finals day. The foundation pays local pros to take part. I play with the top-three from the Order of Merit each year.

A few years ago we started a new national event called the Junior Jug. I contacted Peter Dawson, the chief executive at the R&A, and asked if we could buy two replica jugs from them, the idea being to hold both a scratch and handicap event. Thankfully, he agreed and in fact enthusiastically endorsed the plan. Adam Hunter ran the first few events and did it extremely well. Which was great as it was our first event out of the Aberdeen area. We had eight qualifying events all over the country with the top-four scratch and handicap qualifiers going through to the final at Dundonald in Ayrshire. And the entry fee is only £5, which includes lunch. So, again, we provide great value for money.

Later on, we got the Scottish Golf Union to use the Junior Jug as a counting event on their Boys Order of Merit. That was a great boost and gave us a new level of credibility. We also sponsor the Aberdeen Schools Championship, the Aberdeenshire Schools event, the North East Boys Championship, the North East Boys Team title and the Aberdeen District Pennant League. And, on a national level, we have sponsored the Scottish Schools Championship for the last three years and, in 2012, the Scottish Boys Championship at Murcar.

At first then, that was our market. It was all about the kids. Only later did we get into professional golf, elite amateur golf and even events outside the north-east of Scotland. But initially – although I was keen to go national, as it were – my own local area was enough to be going on with. For one thing, it would have taken so much money to operate all over the country, more than we had at the time certainly. And for another, we wanted to do everything well and we couldn't do that if we were spread too thin.

That almost happened much later, in fact. Things were on the verge of getting out of hand and we were close to not doing things properly. Which is when Marian made it clear we should stay in the Aberdeen area, at least for the foreseeable future. And that has been the right way to go. Only very, very rarely have we received any complaints about what we do and how we do it. One we did get was from a mother who was drunk. She apparently thought little of us giving the football coaches a case of wine as a thank you for their efforts while her son only got a 'shitty trophy'. What she forgot, of course, was that no parents pay any fees for the Boys Club or for strips, training, etc. And they get a free golf day at the end of season party.

Given that we wanted to do things our way, it didn't take too long for us to realise that we needed to break away from the council. Again, that isn't a criticism, just an acknowledgement of reality. They had been great at the start but dealing with the inevitable levels of bureaucracy was making me very frustrated. And, as it turned out, the decision was made for us. The council was massively in debt and during a meeting at their offices they told us they could no longer participate. They just couldn't afford to continue. I made all the right noises, of course. But inside I was silently cheering.

Anyway, at that time we had John Caven working for us part-time. He was director of golf at Meldrum House and is now at Loch Lomond. He was very good at what he did for them and for us. He has, as they say, the gift of the gab. Which was important. With the departure of the council, we had to find new sponsors. John was great at that, as well as working on the Paul Lawrie clothing collection we had at the time. For a while we were almost a full-time job for him.

When my clothing collection stopped, I took up an offer from Conte of Florence to wear their clothes on tour. But that took away a large part of what John was doing. So he went part-time before leaving to take up a job at Dundonald. And that was when Murray Carnie, who is a PE teacher well used to dealing with kids, came on board.

Murray brought a lot of enthusiasm to the role and did so much to 'kick-on' what the foundation did. He and his wife, Lynda, did a power of work on our behalf. He was great with the kids and she did all the administration for him. And all the while the foundation grew and grew. We just did more and more of everything, to the point where, when Murray and Lynda moved on, we hired Iain Powell as a full-time part-timer, if you see what I mean.

Iain works for a communications company and is a mad keen golfer. He does mornings for them and afternoons for us. It works well and he has been great for us. He has transformed the foundation website (www.paullawriefoundation.co.uk). Almost everything related to the foundation can now be done on-line, including entry to competitions. There is also a place where the kids can ask me questions – 'Ask the Pro' – all of which adds to their feeling of involvement. I'm not sure where Iain found the time to do all that, but I'm grateful that he did. Although, to be fair, I think his year breaks down pretty unevenly. I suspect that, in the summer, his 'real' job gets a bit less of his attention than it does in the winter.

Now, at this point, you may or may not be wondering exactly what Paul Lawrie does in the midst of all this activity. Well, as I said earlier, I have always been the 'ideas' man in the group. In other words, I think of ways in which we can make more money, then I let someone else do all the work!

To be fair, I do put in my share of time. I sell rounds of golf where I play with three amateurs. I pay the green fees and buy lunch and all the rest, with all the money going to the foundation. No expenses come out of foundation funds. Two years ago Marian and I and some friends walked the West Highland Way and were sponsored for every step we took. And this year we walked the Great Glen. We also run a weekly lottery, which raises huge amounts of money for us (over £30,000), especially as the vast majority of the lucky winners actually put their prizes back into the fund. Then there is our annual foundation dinner at the Marcliffe, which is now, since John left, run by Marian and Iain and held on the Monday after the Johnnie Walker Championship at Gleneagles. It raises about £25,000 annually.

Every penny we bring in goes straight back out the door. And if there is some left over at the end of each year, we find ways to give it away. One Christmas we went to Toys R Us and bought as many toys as we could. Then we took them all to the kids hospital in Aberdeen. Another time we gave the Flag event kids a present. The good thing is that, whatever we do or don't do, it is only Marian and myself who make all the decisions. There is no committee or board and no one has any say apart from us, although I do take advice when appropriate from Stewart Spence. Even then though, we make the final decision. That's how it has to be. My name is on the wrapper, so it is me (and Marian) who has to decide how things are done.

Anyway, as things grew and grew, I started to think it was maybe a bit unfair that kids elsewhere in Scotland weren't really getting the chance to participate. But it is difficult and that is why I'm delighted to see that my friend and fellow tour pro, Stephen Gallacher, has started a similar foundation in the Lothians area. I'm proud to say too that he has copied what we have done to a large extent. Which explains why he has been asking me so many questions at dinners all over the world for the last two years or so.

We've made mistakes of course. But far more has worked well than not. And nothing has ever been a disaster. We've not had any sort of nightmare scenario take place. The kids have been wonderful too. Not once has there been any sort of significant disciplinary problem.

With the success of the whole programme we started looking into other sports, something I had always been keen to do. Sponsorship requests were coming in from footballers and football teams. And when we decided to take part it was then that we changed the name of the organisation to the 'Paul Lawrie Foundation'. It didn't make sense to be 'Paul Lawrie Junior Golf' if we were involved with other sports.

On the football side of things we now have three age-group teams in the Boys' Club. We also do some coaching with the 'Player Development Academy,' which is run by Graeme Burnett and Phil O'Sullivan – whom in their spare time, work with kids on their football skills. They both have their FIFA coaching badges so they are extremely well qualified to coach the boys. All our teams get time with them every week. As do the fathers who go along to help out. They are all better coaches now than they were when they started.

We are also going to be involved with the Russell Anderson Football Academy. Russell plays for Aberdeen FC, of course. And his involvement will hopefully stop people wondering why a golfer is sticking his nose into other sports. Maybe I'm over-sensitive to some of the comments I hear, but that is the way I am.

In other sports, the foundation sponsors a junior curling team from Aberdeen. They were Scottish champions last year, which was brilliant. We also sponsor a young swimmer, Suleman Butt. He has broken all kinds of records, far too many to list here.

Back in golf, one of the best ideas I've ever had was to expand our sponsorship into the area of elite amateurs. I must admit I was being slightly selfish when the inspiration came to me though. I just felt that, I can best contribute to the development of young golfers when they have reached a certain level. So, while it's great for me to go along to all the events for kids, hand out a few prizes and maybe answer a few questions, my real area of expertise is in playing the game at a reasonable level. I'm not a swing coach, but I know how to play.

So the 'team' idea was born, one where we would select some of the best young amateurs from the area and give them every help and encouragement we can. For my part, that means playing with the lads as often as possible, all the while passing on tips and advice in course management and short game. I don't actually work with the swing coaches they already have. It's more of an 'alongside' relationship, I think.

I get a lot of satisfaction out of helping really good players like David Law, Philip McLean, Ross Cameron, Laura Murray and Kris Nicol. When I talk my way through certain shots I can see and feel them soaking up the information. Which brings me to something I hope will not sound too harsh. While I agree that in Scotland we have a group of phenomenal full swing coaches, I don't see anyone teaching chipping, putting and course management. Too many coaches haven't played at a high enough level to fully understand how to play certain shots and when to play certain shots.

That was yet another reason why Adam Hunter was such a brilliant coach. Adam knew the full swing inside out. But he had also been good enough to play and win on tour, so he knew all about the importance of the short shots and the mental game at the highest level. Which was why the foundation paid him to teach nothing but short game to the elite team. They all worked with him.

In passing, I could never understand why Adam didn't get more tour pros coming to him for help. Even after I won the Open, he never got that much extra business. It was weird. Of course, I knew how good he was and others didn't. But I'm still surprised that more were not curious enough to find out. He was the whole package.

Anyway, my role within the 'team' environment is to be a mentor of sorts to these highly promising youngsters who already swing the club to a high standard but who maybe don't yet have the more subtle tools that will take them onwards and upwards to the next level. I tend to take them out in a four-ball and play for a few quid. Sort of. The deal is that, if I win, they pay me £1. But if they win, I pay them £20. All the way round we talk about certain shots, what clubs to hit from certain tees and, of course, we work constantly on the chipping and putting.

They all get Glenmuir clothes, complete with the foundation logo. They get Titleist balls. And lots of other bits and pieces. But the big thing, I think, is me playing with them and showing them stuff they maybe hadn't thought about before. They all swing great and hit the ball great, but it's all about the shorter clubs.

Here's an example of what I'm talking about. A few years ago we sponsored an assistant pro event at Meldrum House. It was a 54-hole event with the first round a pro-am. My close pal, Colin Fraser, took a team and I was out watching on a buggy.

So we got to the fourth hole, a par-4 with a pond up the middle maybe 245-yards from the tee. I was just standing watching as this young pro pulled out his driver. We had to wait so I said to him, 'Have you got a yardage book?' Which really meant, of course, what the hell are you doing with a driver in your hands?

But he wasn't listening, or at least he wasn't aware. And of course he hits his ball straight into the water. No bounce, just straight in. Splash. He even had the nerve to look surprised. I said to him, 'How far do you hit driver?'

So he says, 'oh, 270'.

Then I asked, 'How far is the water?'

He goes to his yardage book and announces, '245'.

That is to reach the water, which is 40-yards long! And it was then that I thought there is a huge problem in this area, even when you start talking about really talented players. And virtually nothing is being done about it. I don't know how many short game/course management lessons coaches in Scotland are giving every week, but I'm betting it isn't many. It's all about hitting, the part of the game that actually matters least. The full swing isn't easy to learn, but it is the easiest. Yet that's what coaches routinely coach.

All the time I see and hear things that only confirm my worst fears. In 2009 I was out watching a young lad play a practice round before the Scottish Boys' Championship at Royal Aberdeen. We came to the fifth hole, which is a short, driveable par-4 with a bunker on the right just short of the green. The lad turned to his coach and asked him what he thought he should do. The coach – who at least was honest – said he didn't know and that he should ask me.

Now, this was not a complicated business. There were two choices. The lad could either lay-up short of the sand, or go for the green. But the coach apparently couldn't figure that out. That sort of thing used to really frustrate Adam, especially when he thought of all the money these supposed coaches were being paid.

Adam spent a fortune going to all kinds of seminars on all kinds of aspects of his profession. He wanted to get better so that his clients in turn could improve. I don't see anyone else doing that.

Another young player phoned me recently. He has just turned professional and had a few questions. One of them touched on how well he hits the ball on the range, yet he can't seem to score that well out on the course. His practice rounds were brilliant but during tournaments he just can't play as well.

I asked him how many balls he was hitting. 'I'm a range rat,' he said proudly.

Then I asked him how many balls he was hitting on Wednesdays at tournaments. 'Oh, at least 400,' he said, still thinking that hard work is what the game is all about.

'Well,' I said. 'On Wednesdays I never hit more than 100 balls on the range.'

'How do you feel prepared hitting only 100?'

'Because I'm resting on a Wednesday. I'm lying in my bed watching a DVD. You're out there tiring yourself out and I'm resting. Who do you think is going to be best prepared on Thursday morning? And how are you feeling on Thursday mornings?'

'Oh, I'm knackered on Thursdays,' he said.

At that point, he started to catch on. It was just that he didn't know any better. But no one had ever told him any different. And this kid has a coach. So, again, his coach apparently doesn't know what playing the tour is all about. The tour is not about hitting 1,000 balls per day. It's about chipping and putting and being ready to play well at the right times. And one of those times is Thursday morning.

I'm not sure I want to open up this can of worms. But as far as I can see, the area in which promising young players need most assistance is in mentoring. They need someone to pass on what things they need to know and not know. Look at my '400-balls every Wednesday' lad. As I told him, 'If you think hitting all those balls is making you a better player, you kick on with that. But if it isn't, you have to change.' And that is what his coach should be telling him.

Maybe I'm being a little too tough on some of these coaches. Maybe you have to really know what life is like on tour before you can help with this stuff. Maybe you need to know how hard the travel can be on your body. Maybe you need to know from experience not to get in too late on a Tuesday because you will be tired in the pro-am. If you're tired in the pro-am then you are tired again the next day. Just commonsense, but all those sorts of things add up when you are competing at the level found on the European Tour.

Stuff like this is why I just shake my head when I hear the question, 'Why does Scotland not produce more top players?' It's simple. Because our best youngsters are not being coached the way they should be coached. And it frustrates the hell out of me.

I'm sorry if any coach based in Scotland is offended by my views, but that is the way I see it: Too much long game and not enough short game/course management. If I'm wrong, I hold up my hands. But that's what I see.

Don't misunderstand me though. I'm delighted to be able to help any and all of the youngsters who have my phone number and can call me any time. I get a lot of pleasure out of making a difference to their games.

I remember when my old friend and boss Peter Smith came back to Aberdeen after a period working abroad. I told him all of the above. I told him that there is a massive hole in the market for someone to coach short game and course management as opposed to 'where your hips should be on the backswing'. There are lots of those guys out there. So Peter now sells a three-month programme where the pupil gets four short game sessions and so many rounds with Peter walking and offering advice. In other words, he is mentoring as much as coaching. It's the way ahead, I'm sure of it.

And, just to be clear, I'm not talking about telling kids to develop a safety-first approach at all times. If they want to hit driver on almost every hole, that's fine. But you have to know things before you go down that route. You have to be like Phil Mickelson – the most aggressive player I think I've ever seen – and accept that, two or three times a round, you are going to be in trouble off the tee.

There are no absolute rights and wrongs when hitting off any tee. But you have to pick the shot you think is right. Then, even if it's wrong, you have to go with it. And what I may think doesn't really matter, not if you have made peace with yourself before the round. Besides, it's possible to hit the wrong shot onto the green, just as it is possible to hit the right one into a bunker. The key is committing to whatever you decide.

At a session I had with a young player and his coach, the coach was trying to get me to dictate to his player what he should be doing. But that is missing the point. What I think is right for me may not be right for him. So all I can do is tell him what I would do, then let him make his own decision.

Golf at pro level is not about how many good shots anyone hits. Adam used to say that to me every day. Everyone hits only four or five really good ones. It's all about the misses and where they finish relative to the target. My aim was always to get my misses within five yards of perfect. Do that and you can really play, especially if you have an ability to get the ball in the hole in less than three shots from inside 75-yards or so. But even the best short game is not going to be any use when you miss by 20 yards and are hacking out of heavy rough all the time. And, yet again, I just don't see and hear that sort of information being passed on to our best youngsters.

Okay, back off my soapbox.

I think we were talking about my role within the foundation. At its most basic level, I'm a salesman. I'm here to come up with moneymaking ideas, so that we can then spend that cash as best we can. In other words, I used my name to get people to give me money so that I can then put it to good use.

Sometimes I have to use my voice too. It is amazing how easy it is for me to get calls returned from prospective sponsors. I can get people on the phone quicker than any of the various assistants we have had. That is no reflection on them; it is simply a fact of life. That is why, when we come up with a new scheme, I'm the one who makes the phone calls and sends out the e-mails.

All of which takes time, of course. And the level of my involvement has not gone unnoticed by at least two of my coaches over the years. Adam was certainly sceptical. If we were hitting balls and I suddenly announced that I had to go, he was never too impressed. He never actually said so, but I could tell. Bernard Gallacher has also publicly voiced his doubts over my commitment to my career. And Bob Torrance, during the brief time we spent together, told me outright: 'If you want to be a top player again, you need to ditch this foundation. It's not helping you.'

Needless to say, I disagree with all three. I don't think about the foundation when I'm playing. I've never been standing in the middle of a fairway wondering about some event or other we are running. My practice time has never been compromised either. And I'm really not sure that I would have won more without the foundation to run when I'm off the tour.

But even if all that were true, I would still want to be involved with all we've done. The foundation is just too important to me to ever think otherwise. So it doesn't really matter one way or the other.

Besides, while I take the point being made by others, I do think that there are plenty of other Scottish golfers, far more talented than I, who could do a lot more to put back something into the game that has given them such a great lifestyle. But they don't do it. I don't get that. I just don't understand why they don't do it.

Some have claimed to me that they are 'not good enough' to carry a foundation similar to mine. Others think they don't have a 'big enough name'. And that is a fair comment. I had the same concerns at the outset.

Besides, the success I've enjoyed over the last 18 months or so proved my own point, although I will concede that I'm doing a little less foundation-related work than I used to. I don't go to as many meetings as I have in the past and that has helped my golf. Iain Powell does all the hard work now and makes me look good!

So I'm more of a figurehead than I've ever been. But I'm still heavily involved. That will not change either, if only because I enjoy almost every aspect of what we do. It can be fun. Earlier this year, for example, we held a foundation sponsor 's day at Loch Lomond. We had five teams playing in a pro-am format, with five pros of course – me, Peter Smith, David Law, Robbie Stewart from the Paul Lawrie Golf Centre and Philip McLean.

We all went down together on the bus. It was great crack all the way there. And I could see that everyone involved was having a good time. So it is a great way for Marian and I to say 'thank you' to everyone who helps make what we do possible. We paid for the whole day; nothing comes out of the foundation funds.

Going forward, I'm not sure where the foundation will go, or where it will take Marian and I. Just recently we've been more into consolidation than expansion. Not much has changed for a while, so we haven't been getting any bigger. But, based on past experience, that may change. There is only one proviso: if we do stretch our resources even more than they are already, we will have to look at employing people full-time. That's a whole different proposition than what we have done so far. A huge step.

The thing is, I'm never going to be able to devote myself completely to the foundation. I'm hoping to have another seven years on the European Tour, then, when I turn 50, embark on a new career as a senior golfer. We're talking another 15 years at least. And I'm not sure I'll be looking for a job when I'm finished.

We can always do more of course. And things can always be better. But I'm happy with what we've achieved. Who would have thought 10 years ago that we would be the name sponsors on something as prestigious as the Scottish Boys' Championship, with its long list of outstanding winners (although there was one dud in 1978)? Or that we would be getting the publicity we have had as a result? That one thing has been great for us in terms of raising awareness of what we do and what we are about.

And what we are about is getting kids to play and enjoy golf. What, at the end of the day, could be better than that?

Home on the Range

– & on the Couch

The first golf lesson I ever had in my life was with Peter Smith, who was the head professional at Murcar Golf Club at the time. His assistant was Frank Coutts, who is now the pro at Deeside, where I spend so much of my time with the boys. I must have been about 15 years old and probably playing off a high single-figure handicap. I don't remember much about the content of the lesson, but I do recall my father complaining to Peter afterwards about the poor repair job he had done on the insert in the face of my driver.

Later on in my, ahem, distinguished amateur career, I had a few more lessons with Peter. But not many. At that stage I wasn't taking my golf nearly seriously enough to justify any sort of bigger commitment to improving my technique. I can't imagine what sort of player I was back then. Pretty much hopeless really.

Peter has been a friend ever since those far-off days and now does a few bits and pieces for the foundation. He is a good player, who was on the fringe of the European Tour for a few years. But, to me, he has never been able to settle on what works and doesn't work in his own swing. While I've worked on the same things in my swing over the last six or seven years, I don't think Peter can go six or seven minutes without trying something new. Which is a shame. He has a lot of talent and swings it nicely.

There is, however, a huge difference between going along for the occasional lesson and actually being coached by someone. Lessons tend to be good for giving you short-term tips that will hopefully lead to some equally short-term improvement. Real coaching, as you can imagine, is a longer-term thing, where various steps are taken towards a usually distant goal.

Since I turned professional, I've had quite a variety of coaches. In my earliest days, my first boss, Doug Smart, would take me down to the range at Banchory and take a look at what I was doing. I must admit he had some pretty funny ideas about the swing and even back then I knew enough to pick and choose what parts of his advice I would actually incorporate into my own action.

Bruce Davidson, who had gone to college in the States then returned to Aberdeen to build the driving range at the Kings Links, was another who would give me the once over now and then. Bruce, whose parents lived in Banchory when I was assistant pro there, had a sound knowledge of technique, as is obvious from the fact that he now coaches former Open and Masters champion Mark O'Meara from his long-time base in Houston, Texas. He helped me a lot in my early days as a pro, even before I was competing regularly. In fact, he actually gave Marian a job in the shop at the Kings Links when we were struggling a wee bit.

The first proper coach I had, however, was David Thomson who, like Bruce, was attached to the Kings Links. I first met David when he interviewed me for the job of assistant professional at Deeside, where he was then the head pro. We played nine holes as part of that process and I can remember him saying how good my short game was. Which was good to hear, because the rest of my game was rubbish. I hit the ball all over the place that day, yet got round in under par.

At that time, I was your typical Aberdeen-born and raised player. I hit the ball very low and left-to-right – my only shot – to keep it out of the wind and took really big divots with my irons, because my downswing was so steep and the ball was so far back in my stance. No one could hit 9-irons lower than I could. I was the world champion at that. All of which was fine if I intended to spend the rest of my career playing in and around my home city. But I didn't of course; I had wider and bigger ambitions.

David and I spent a huge amount of time together working on my game and we became good friends – as we still are today. He was and is a great character to spend hours and hours with. And, as I said in chapter four, he was on my bag as caddie when I qualified for the European Tour in late 1991.

Not that David was the perfect caddie. On our last night in France he came back to our room very late a little worse for drink. I think it was the red wine he liked. Anyway, he stumbled into the wardrobe, knocked over some coat hangers and whispered really loudly (if such a thing is possible), 'Sssshhh, Chippy is sleeping.' Who he thought he was actually talking to remains a mystery to this day. I was the only other person in the room and, of course, the only one trying to get to sleep.

So David turned out to be a better coach than a caddie. He was certainly the right guy for me at that time. And he said all the right things about how the changes he wanted to make wouldn't be easy and that results wouldn't come overnight. But I worked at it because, young and inexperienced as I was, I knew it had to be done if I was ever going to be any good as a golfer.

Eventually then, my ball flight changed, all as David gradually moved the ball up in my stance and flattened my swing. One leads to the other of course. And I would hit a lot of shots off tees in an effort to get a bit more 'behind' the ball through impact. He was the first to spot that those changes had to be made if I was to progress. Although it was probably pretty obvious. I had no flight on the ball at all back then. I couldn't get it up in the air.

David was also the first person to say to me that I needed a 'safe' shot, one I could rely on to get or keep the ball in play when the pressure was at its most suffocating. In other words, we worked on a drive I could use when I absolutely had to hit a narrow fairway. It is one I still employ today, in fact. I address the ball slightly in the neck of the club (towards the bottom of the shaft) and hit a low cut.

David also took a long hard look at my equipment. Soon enough he had me playing with clubs that were longer and had stiffer shafts. That made a big difference. Until then, the shafts in my clubs had been too whippy, which led to the club head being too far behind me coming into impact. David understood the game, having been a good enough player to get a tour card himself. Now the pro at Skibo Castle near Dornoch (where I am the touring professional), he and I still keep in touch.

There came a point, however, where I felt that David had taken me as far as he could. Telling him that I was moving on was tough, but, happily, he agreed that was the best thing for me at a time when I was starting to play a lot more competitive golf and, at assistants level, win my fair share.

In passing, I laugh when people commend me for the way I've gone about my career in golf. Many have said how great it is that I 'went to school' and took all my PGA exams before going out on tour. But I did that not because I wanted to or thought it was the best way to go, but because I had no other option. If I had been a good enough player at the age of 18 or 19, I would have gone to the tour school then, just as so many of my contemporaries did.

But I wasn't. So I had to work my way up, progressing through each level as I went along. But again, while that may appear laudable from a distance, it was the only way forward for me. On paper, I may look like the poster boy for the PGA way of things, but the reality is I had no choice in the matter. I had no plan. But if I had been able to bypass the PGA system and go straight to tour school I would have done so in a heartbeat.

Anyway, recommended by my fellow tour pros Adam Hunter and Stephen McAllister, I started to see Jim Farmer, who was based in St Andrews and was the pro at Scotscraig Golf Club. Jim had a bit more experience of golf at the level I aspired to and knew what was required to get me there.

We used to hit balls either at the Links Academy in the home of golf or on the range at Scotscraig. One of my first sessions with Jim was spent in his back shop, looking at pictures and videos of Sam Snead and Ben Hogan. He wanted me to see or at least have an idea of how those great swings worked. That would be around 1993, still early in my European Tour career.

As David had done, Jim felt quite strongly that I hit the ball too low. And, again like David, he was prepared to put a lot of time into helping me get more height on my shots. I must have spent countless hours hitting balls over trees by moving the ball forward in my stance, which put more loft on the club at impact. He also had me hit lots of shots off side hill lies, the ball above my feet. That had the effect of flattening my plane and, in time, lowering my ball flight.

Jim was – and is – a great coach and we were together until the middle of 1995. I was really struggling at that point though and looked like I would lose my card. My shots were either low and left or straight right, neither of which is a good combination of trajectory and direction. So I decided to make a change.

As I would do so often later in my career, I took advice from Adam. He had previously left Jim and was working with David Leadbetter, or, more accurately, his assistant, David Whelan. So I did the same. I remember having my first lesson with David in the week after the 1995 Open at the Chart Hills course in Kent, which was where Leadbetter had his UK academy.

The first thing we tackled was my takeaway (the first couple of feet in my backswing). I used to fan the clubface open very quickly in the backswing, then have to reverse that move with my hands through impact – no way to be consistent. David felt fixing that would make enough of a difference that I could safely keep my card. Then, once that was achieved, we would move on to the bigger stuff at the end of the season. And he was right; that is exactly what happened. I somehow got through to the end of the year – I was, thank goodness, ninth in the European Open, the second-last event of the season – although finishing 107th on the Order of Merit (the top-115 are exempt for the following season) was cutting things a little fine.

Anyway, before the start of the 1996 season I found myself at the Lake Nona club in Orlando along with the rest of Leadbetter's European-based players. Per-Ulrik Johansson was there. So were Anders Forsbrand, Mike Miller, Stephen McAllister, Adam and Ross Drummond. We hired a big van to get around in and all stayed in the same hotel. And each day we would line up on the range, get 30 minutes or so with an instructor, then be left alone to work away by ourselves.

David Leadbetter also organized his fitness trainer, Pat Eckelberry, to have a look at us and a sports psychologist was on hand also. It was a very productive time and I always came away feeling like I had learned a lot. Which was good, considering the whole package cost each of us $5,000.

That first week we worked on my backswing. It was still too upright at that point, which led to my impact position being what David (L) called 'unconnected'. He even had a nickname for me: 'Throwaway Duff.' My arms used to come well away from my body after I hit the ball, at which he would always kill himself laughing. He has a pretty dour public image, but David has a surprisingly good sense of humour, even if he is, by a distance, the worst timekeeper I've ever come across. The man will, I'm convinced, be late for his own funeral. If he arrives at all.

My short game got a lot of attention that week too. The facilities at Lake Nona were great and I took full advantage. I would spend no more than 20 minutes on each aspect of my game before moving on to something else. In that respect, I was different from the other players, a fact David picked up on. But he was a great help. He had a huge number of drills designed to encourage whatever feel you needed in your action and was constantly thinking up new ones. In that respect, the man is a genius.

All of which was great. The problem was, however, that we only got to see David Leadbetter maybe twice a year – once at the winter camp and once at the Open and then only for a few minutes. The rest of the time I was coached by David Whelan, who was very good at what he did and understood the game well having played – and won – on tour himself. He was especially adept in the area of the short game, so we got on well in that regard. Our relationship was always good.

Well, it was until one day at the Braid Hills driving range in Edinburgh. David lived in Newcastle and I was in Aberdeen, so that was about half way. I was hitting balls and David was watching. I hit a poor shot and turned to ask him what had happened there. But he was looking the other way. I remember thinking, 'I've driven two and a half hours to do this and he isn't even watching.' That was the clincher in me deciding to move on, good as David undoubtedly is as a coach.

I actually stayed with the Leadbetter group through the end of 1998, which was when Adam decided to give up playing and focus instead on his own coaching career. I remember we had dinner towards the end of that season and he told me of his plans. Even if he kept his card, in fact, he was going to pack in the playing side of things. Because of my slight unrest with David Whelan, I asked Adam to write me a letter detailing what exactly he would work on with me if he were my coach. What would he do to make me a top player?

So he did. And what a letter it was. I've never seen anything so detailed. I was convinced, which, to be fair, didn't take much. I wanted a coach who was committed to me and only me. I wanted one I knew I would get along with. And, let's face it, I had been following Adam's advice for years anyway. It was him who had told me to go to both Jim Farmer and David Leadbetter. In so many ways, he was a logical choice.

In view of all that was to follow, our career together got off to a pretty undistinguished start. For me anyway. My first lesson from Adam took place at Murcar on the morning of an Aberdeen-Rangers football match. I organised tickets knowing Adam was a big Rangers fan. They won 3-2, so at least he was happy.

Not that we were able to do much work that day anyway. It was the middle of winter and I was already feeling soreness in my left knee, pain that would lead to me undergoing keyhole surgery not long afterwards. There was a small piece of gristle in there that needed to be removed. So it was that I headed off to the Middle East early in what was to be an eventful 1999 having hit hardly any balls under Adam's guidance.

It didn't take long for me to notice that Adam wasn't like any of my previous coaches, however. He was certainly the first to send me 'lesson notes' after each session, explaining what we had done and what he wanted me to focus on. He was also the first to time my pre-shot routine as he felt I was becoming too technical in my approach to shots.

He was right of course. I was standing over the ball way too long at address, a sure sign that there was too much going on between my ears. One of my abiding memories of our time together is him walking round with his camera bag on his back, making notes on my routine as I played in events.

The first time he did that, in fact, was during the old Benson & Hedges event at the Oxfordshire. It was the opening round. I hit six greens that day and shot level par. After signing my card I walked to the range to hit a few. Adam was already there, chatting to some of the Scottish lads. He didn't see me coming, but I heard him say: 'You'll never f-----g believe what I've just witnessed. Paul just hit six greens and shot level par. What a performance. I'm going to make this guy a player. If he can do that hitting six greens, we can find him a golf swing. That's all he needs.'

At the start I was Adam's only client. So I got as much time with him as I wanted. Looking back, I think that did both of us a lot of good. We both benefitted from the many hours we spent working together. We were both learning, me about my swing and him about the swing, as we went along.

As I hope I've made clear by the many references to Adam in this book, I admired him enormously and looked up to him even more. Not physically, of course; he was not 'wee man' for nothing. But I was always asking his advice on anything and everything. And whatever he asked me to do, I gave it 100 per cent. I had total confidence in his ability. It also helped that he understood the importance of the short game – he was very good around the greens during his own playing career. On tour he would never let me hit more than one bucket of balls in a day. But I could pitch, chip and putt as much as I wanted to.

Adam loved his short game drills and was always giving me new ones to work on. He had two particular favourites though. The first was for chipping. He would throw down six balls just off the edge of the practice green. I would then hit each one, scoring five points if I chipped in, two points if the ball finished 'inside the leather' (one grip-length from the cup) and past the hole, but zero points if inside the leather and short of the cup. I would, of course, lose two points if the ball came up short outside the leather. He loved that drill.

The other was a putting drill involving eight balls. In groups of two he would space them out from six to 40 feet from the cup. I then had to hit each putt and, at worst, have each ball finish past the hole and within 18 inches. If any putt fell short or outside 18 inches past the cup, I had to start again.

That was bad enough, but I wasn't allowed to leave until I had completed the drill twice. Sometimes I would be there for hours. I know it doesn't sound that hard, but when you get down to, say, a couple of balls the pressure gets a little intense. I can remember giving him all kinds of abuse when I kept failing on the last ball. But it is a fantastic drill for getting a feel for the speed of greens you are unfamiliar with. I still use it a lot on the day I arrive at an event.

Between my disastrous first event of 1999 – a missed cut in Dubai – and me winning my second start in Qatar, all I really did was work on my short game. If ever I needed any convincing that Adam was on the right track in what he was teaching me, that victory did it.

The greatest thing about Adam though, was his commitment to me, both professionally and personally. In that sense he was also unlike any other coach I've had – or ever will have. He would do anything for me and regularly drove almost three hours from Glasgow to Aberdeen, sometimes cancelling other lessons to do so and sometimes at the crack of dawn, just to have a look at my swing as soon as he possibly could.

He also travelled with me a great deal. I liked that. And he would involve himself – at my urging – in areas that really had nothing to do with coaching. At various times he was, in effect, my manager, my press agent and the guy I used to hire and fire caddies. He was also my psychologist and my companion at dinner in a succession of otherwise lonely and faraway places. We even reached the stage where – especially when we were in America – he almost felt obliged to do some coaching, if only to justify the expense of the trip. I didn't really want or need him to do anything on the range, but that was just another indication of the strength of his character.

So he was much more than a coach; he was one of my closest and dearest friends. By the end of his life I'm not sure there was too much he didn't know about me or my career. I ran almost everything past him, such was my admiration for his opinion and perspective. In that respect, he was very similar to my best mate, Colin Fraser. Adam and Colin never told me what I wanted to hear; they would always tell me what they actually thought. So I could/can rely on them completely.

It was funny how that worked sometimes. Inevitably, Adam and Colin became friendly and they both knew how to get me to do things they wanted me to do. If, for example, I wasn't asking Adam about something because I knew I wasn't going to like the answer, he would call Colin and get him to bend my ear on that particular subject, knowing that I would then do what he recommended. So I couldn't win either way.

From 1998 until the day he died there was only one three-month gap in 2007 where Adam was not my coach in some capacity. As far as the full swing is concerned, I left Adam to go to Neil Marr. But I soon realised that

Neil didn't have the same knowledge of the short game, so I contacted Adam and asked him to have me back.

I wouldn't have blamed him if he had turned me down. Many coaches would have. But he couldn't have been nicer about it. 'I'd be delighted,' was all he said. Of course, even during that three-months when we were officially apart, I would still be talking to him on the phone three or four times a week. Sometimes not even about golf. We were still friends.

The break when it came was the result of me struggling for a long time with a hook off the tee. I would be hitting four or five snap-hooks every day. We just couldn't sort it, even though the stuff Adam wanted me to do was obviously right. The problem was I just couldn't do it, no matter how hard I worked.

It was a tough decision for me obviously, given my relationship with Adam and all that we had been through. It took me months to call him. And when I did, he was brilliant. But it was still the most difficult call I've ever had to make. 'Listen,' he said. 'I know how hard it was for you to make this call. But don't worry about it. If I can help you at all, don't hesitate to ask.'

He even offered to help me find a new coach and to speak to the new guy. I didn't take him up on that typically generous offer, but that was Adam; he always put me first. As it turned out, I did call him to see what he thought of what Neil and I were working on, a lot of which was basically the opposite of what Adam and I had been doing.

'Great idea,' he said right away. 'I don't like all of that stuff but some of it I do. And right now, where you are, it's what you need. You'll soon be driving the ball better. And from that you will get the confidence you need to play better too.'

And he was right. My driving did improve. But I was struggling with the rest of my game. Even my short game was getting worse. So after those three months, I went back to Adam for work on the shorter shots. And not too long after that, he was my full swing coach again too.

Even then he was generous. When I went back to him he told me we would continue to work on the stuff Neil Marr had been teaching me. This was despite my having been to see Bob Torrance a few times in the interim. 'It isn't what I believe in,' said Adam. 'But it makes you a better player.' The man had no ego. No matter what, he would do what was best for me, even if it hurt him.

Now that he has gone, I can't think about Adam without getting emotional. He would have done anything for me. Which is not to say I ever asked him to do anything I didn't want him to do. If it were humanly possible, he would do what I asked. He understood where I was coming from. Having been a tour pro himself he knew what it was like to have been let down by people. So when he became a coach, he vowed that his players would always come first. It wasn't just me he did stuff for; he was the same way with all his pupils. He was different class.

Not that long ago, Marian and I visited Adam's widow, Caroline. We were sitting having a cup of tea when Caroline told us she had been in Adam's office and found a sheet of paper on which he had documented every request I had made of him over however long a period, then detailed alongside the action he had taken. It was from a time when I had arranged with my then managers at IMG to pay Adam to act as my agent as well as my coach.

It was amazing to see. Everything was there from what he'd done, to who he'd spoken to and what they had said. But that was Adam to a tee. And he brought the same dedication to his teaching.

I learned not to tell him things. If I was at a tournament and he was at home and I said even one thing over the phone that he might be able to help with, I was on the line for at least half an hour more than I had planned. For example, if I told him that I had missed a green left and that had been the worst possible place to go, we were talking about what I should have done for ages. I've never met anyone like him.

His girls – Emma and Beth – loved to wind him up about his attention to detail. Adam used to run the Junior Jug for us and he would have a sheet of paper he would work from. It was all colour-coded. So he needed a lot of pens. And they would hide them from him. Or use the wrong colour just to annoy him. One time, Beth put his stapler back in the wrong place in his office and he didn't speak to her for a week. Unbelievable.

After almost every lesson he ever gave me, I would get a couple of sheets of A4 paper covered with notes. What we worked on would be there and the drills I should do to rectify the fault. How much time I should spend on each was there too. Every lesson.

In all the years we worked together I can think of only one occasion when I was downright nasty to him. I was playing at Gleneagles in the Johnnie Walker Championship. I think I was drawn with Sam Torrance and, on the first day, I struck the ball badly. Make that really badly. In fact, it was probably the worst I've ever hit it during a proper tournament. So, as you can imagine, I wasn't too happy.

Adam had walked all the way round and after I signed my card he accompanied me back to the car. I never said a word the whole way. Not one. When I got to the car I threw the clubs in the boot, took my shoes off and slammed it shut. Then I got in and drove off, leaving Adam standing there. I just left. There was no goodbye; no 'see you tomorrow'. Nothing.

I didn't get far though. As I drove away, I looked in the rearview mirror and there he was, just standing there with his camera bag. 'You prick,' I thought. So I stopped and called him on the phone. I wasn't even halfway up the drive to the hotel, where I was staying.

'I'm really sorry,' I said. 'I can't believe I've just done that.'

'It's all right,' he replied. 'These things happen. Turn round, come back and we'll hit some balls and work on it.'

We ended up hitting balls until it was dark.

I hope this isn't true, but I torture myself a bit with it. My theory is that the illness that took his life was at least partly down to the stress of looking after me. He was coaching me. He was travelling with me. He was managing me to a large extent. Maybe that was just too much. I'm sure that wasn't the cause of him getting leukaemia, but I'm certain it didn't help.

I can see him now in my mind's eye, lying in a hospital bed and obviously desperately ill. Yet he would never want to talk about his illness. Whenever I went to see him, all he wanted to discuss was my game and where I was playing next. Even then, he put me first, in a perfect example of pure selflessness, one I hope I've learned from.

I smile too, when I think of him. I think of the night a group of us missed the last shuttle from Heathrow to Scotland, so we all had to stay in an airport hotel. Mike Miller was there. Ross Drummond. Stevie McAllister. Me and Adam and a few others.

After checking in we went down to the bar. We had a couple of drinks, which is always enough for me. I'm not much of a drinker. There was a piano in the corner and Adam suddenly announces that he would give us all a song. I had no idea until then that he could play the piano.

And, of course, he couldn't. But he was hilarious. What a racket. He did Great Balls of Fire with one foot on top of the piano and one on the floor. His singing voice reminded me of a cat with its tail caught in something. He couldn't sing a note. Not one. But he had the confidence to get up there and entertain us. He was just great fun.

Even towards the end, he would get upset with his wife, Caroline, when she wouldn't tell him how many fairways and greens I had hit the previous day at some event in China or wherever. He was lying there dying and still thinking of everything except himself. He even wanted me to e-mail him the videos of my swing so that he could take a look at them. He was a great example to all of us of what a human being can be.

Now that Adam has gone, I use Andrew Locke, who is based at the Paul Lawrie Golf Centre, to keep an eye on my swing. No more than that. I don't use him much, only now and then. But he's a lovely lad.

When I went for the first lesson, I went in and he said, 'I've not slept.'
I said, 'What?'
He said, 'I've not slept. I can't believe I'm going to give you a lesson.'
I'm like, 'Come on, you're joking.'
'No, not slept. Not slept.'

Stuff like that just amazes me. But I really enjoy working with Andrew, especially now that he has settled down a bit! I visit him for maybe a couple of hours a month so that I can have a close look at my swing on the video, then I go off and work away on my own. After all this time, I know what I've got to do. I know what my swing has to look like, so in that respect Adam is still teaching me. I suspect he always will be.

Psychologists

Back in the early 1990s I had been struggling a little bit mentally on the tour. As is my way, I was being very hard on myself after every shot that was less than perfect. In other words, almost every shot. And that was having an adverse effect on my ability to score. While I should have been focusing on the next shot, I was still hacked off about the previous one. Which isn't uncommon for someone early in his career in such a competitive environment.

So we, Adam and I that is, felt it might be a good idea for me to talk to a professional psychologist about what was going through my head out on the course. Actually, that idea occurred to Adam well before I was persuaded. At first, I was like many people and thought psychologists couldn't possibly help me. Adam used to tear his hair out at my attitude. Where I would have no problem hitting balls or chipping and putting for hours, ask me to sit down for 20 minutes and talk about what was on my mind and I would invariably find an excuse to be somewhere else.

Eventually though, he talked me round. I had, I thought, nothing to lose. If I didn't like it, or felt like it wasn't doing me any good, all I had to do was stop.

At the time, Marian's brother Gary was at Moray House, the PE college in Edinburgh. And it was Gary who suggested I go to see Dr Richard Cox, who was one of his lecturers at the time. Dr Cox agreed so I drove down to see him.

I was driving a BMW M3 at the time. And I had just bought a gold Ebel watch. Anyway, after I had explained what was bothering me, he stopped me and asked me a question.

'Before you go on,' he said, 'what kind of car was that I saw you driving into the car park?'

'A BMW M3.'

'Mmmm…nice car.'

I didn't catch on to what he was doing straight away.

'Yeah it is; thanks.'

A couple of minutes later, he stopped me again.

'That's a nice watch you're wearing.'

'It is, thanks again.'

'Is it gold?'

'It is.'

'It must have been expensive?'

'Yeah, it was.'

'And what kind of house do you have? Is it nice?'

'It's alright.'

At which point I got it.

'You need to take a step back,' said Dr Cox. 'You need to realise how lucky you are to have what you have.'

And he was spot on, of course. I was losing sight of the important stuff. I had a great wife, a nice house and a few quid in the bank. Yet I was getting all bent out of shape about hitting a shot less than perfectly, or missing a few putts. His message was clear: get on with it.

Right away, I thought, 'I like this guy.' He lived in Wishaw and I would drive down to spend time with him. We just sat and talked. He would also give me tapes to take away and play at night before I went sleep. Most of the time, in fact, they made me sleep.

Dr Cox put a few rules in place. During tournaments, for example, I had to be asleep by 10.30pm. I used to be tired in the mornings. So of course he asked me why. What had I been doing? Had I been practising too hard? And what time did I go to bed? When the answer to the last question came back, 'midnight', I made some changes to my sleeping habits. He was also big on not drinking coffee or alcohol at the wrong times.

The great thing was, Dr Cox had no idea about golf. He wasn't a golfer and still isn't. We were at Carnoustie for the Scottish Open in 1996 and he was walking round while I played a practice round. It was the first time he had ever set foot on a course. And when we got to the 16th hole he nudged me and said, 'Wow, this is a narrow fairway isn't it.' It was the walkway of course, the 16th hole being a par-3. But he had no idea.

He was great for me though. Every time I left him I felt better. And he had a very relaxed attitude to money. When I asked him what he charged, he told me to pay him what I thought he was worth. So I did. Which was just as well because he never once asked for money or sent me a bill.

What I did was send him a cheque after a top-20 finish. And a couple of times he called me to complain. Not that I was not sending him enough, but that it was too much. 'This is ridiculous Paul,' he said. 'You can't send me this amount of money. There's no need for it.'

So, all in all, he was great for me. We worked on-and-off for maybe a decade or so, all with the understanding that we never had a regular contract. There were never any phone calls at tournaments. I would see him when I felt I needed to see him and that was it. Which was perfect. I hate being tied down to something set in stone. I rebel at things like that. So his attitude was ideal. And he was a huge help over the years. He figured out very quickly that my attention span was not the longest and that being told to come back at two o'clock next Thursday wasn't going to work for me. My response to that was always, 'I've no idea what is happening next Thursday so how can I say I'll be there?'

To be honest, if Marian didn't tell me I wouldn't have any idea what is happening tomorrow, never mind next week.

I don't remember why my sessions with Dr Cox petered out. But they did eventually. Maybe because he was not on tour, I don't know.

One psychologist who was on tour was John Allsop. We had one very short session, which should tell you everything about how well it went. I remember him asking me, 'what colour was your bike when you were eight years old?'

That was enough for me. I didn't know. But he felt it was important. I didn't. So we parted after 45 minutes. I'm sure he is very good at what he does, but he wasn't for me.

The next guy I worked with was Alan Fine. I had played with Philip Price at an event and been impressed by the way he conducted himself on the course. So he recommended Fine, who he had worked with for a long time.

I was with Alan for two years. He was different from Dr Cox in that it was all about the money for him. It wasn't that he wasn't keen for me to do well, or that he didn't give me his time or best effort, but nailing the deal down was important to him. I understand that. But I would rather it was left to me. I'm more likely to overpay him, so it probably cost him money in the long run.

The deal I had with Alan was that I paid him 10 per cent of my five highest cheques of the year, or 10 per cent of my second to sixth biggest cheques. To be honest, I can't recall which. Whatever, that was a smart move on his part. Even if a player performs poorly, he is still likely to have a few good weeks.

He did well out of me in our first year together. I won in Wales and generally played well. But the second year I played poorly and went down in the world rankings and on the Order of Merit. Yet he made more money that year. I paid him more when I played poorly than when I played well. Which was very clever on his part.

None of that was why I stopped working with Alan though. Along with the other players on his books, I would pay my share of his expenses at tournaments. Fair enough. But one of the invoices he sent me had a hamburger and a coke on it. That is taking the piss. So I moved on.

At moments like that, I always had a rule of thumb to go by. I would ask myself, 'Would Adam do that?' And if the answer was 'no', I'd know what to do. In that instance, Adam would have bought me the burger.

Jos Vanstiphout was next. A diminutive former pop star from Belgium, he worked with all kinds of players, most notably Ernie Els when he won the Open in 2002. I actually had two spells with Jos, both provoked by the feeling that my head was up my backside and I needed someone to clear things up for me. All to get better.

I enjoyed being with Jos and like Alan Fine he helped me a great deal. But our deal didn't end well. We were at the Masters and I had shot 77 in the first round. I was on the range afterwards with Paddy Bryne, who was on the bag and my pal Colin Fraser, when Jos appeared.

An argument then ensued about my less than perfect performance that day. And it ended with Jos calling me a 'Scottish fuckwit'. At which Colin responded, 'Either you hit him or I will.' And that was the end of Jos. Colin was beside himself. 'If you think that is making you a better player, keep him on,' he said. 'But if you want abuse like that, I'll do it for you for free.'

Marian's dad actually got quite friendly with Jos. They would have a few drinks together. Then they would have a few more. And to this day, Jos still asks after Bert. So he is not a bad guy. And to be fair, I think he employs the abusive approach with all of his guys. It was always funny watching Ernie towering over him as they argued.

My next stop through the catalogue of golf psychologists took me to perhaps the most famous of them all, Dr Bob Rotella. I had read all his books and liked them. I travelled with one for a while actually. It always made me feel better and see things more clearly.

When I contacted 'the Doc' as he is known, he told me that he likes all his new guys to come to his house for a couple of days. So I flew out to Charlottesville in Virginia, where he lives. He told me to bring my clubs because he likes to play a round as part of what I suppose is his sort of induction process.

Just before I left I took it into my head not to take my clubs. 'It'll be fine,' I said to myself. 'I can't imagine there will be any real need to play.'

So I get over there and arrive at immigration. At the desk the guy told me I hadn't filled in the address where I would be staying on the card. And of course I didn't know Bob's address. Which was a problem. I wasn't going to get in without it.

I asked the guy if he was a golfer. He was. So I asked him if he knew Bob Rotella, the psychologist. 'He lives just down the road,' I said. Never heard of him. And the guy was starting to get a bit antsy.

So I asked him if he remembered the Open at Carnoustie, the one where the Frenchman hit the ball into the burn. He did. 'I'm Lawrie,' I exclaimed. 'I'm the guy who won.'

'Hell man, so you are,' he yelled. 'Well done.' And he waved me through.

When I arrived at the Rotella home he was a bit miffed at me not bringing clubs or even shoes. But I borrowed some of his and we went out to play after I bought a shirt at the pro's shop.

'What I like to do is play nine holes,' he explained. 'Then we'll stop and have a chat about what I see. Then we'll play the back nine working on what we talk about over lunch.'

So off we went. And at lunch he told me that I was not focused enough over the ball. I was seeing and hearing far too much of what was going on around me. At the third hole, for example, I backed off my shot when someone yelled out on the next fairway. 'It doesn't matter what happens when you are over the ball,' he said. 'You should still be able to keep going and hit a decent shot.'

Fair enough. He was spot on.

On the 10th tee, he had the honour because he had birdied the ninth (he's a good player, maybe a plus-one handicap). Just as he started his downswing, I shouted out 'Boo' really loudly. He knobbled his shot about 40 yards into a bush. At which point I said, 'Bob, focusing over the ball is your problem.'

But he didn't laugh. In fact, he sulked for four holes. Not a word passed between us until, on the 14th tee, I gripped his knee and said, 'Come on Bob, it was a joke. Even if you didn't like it, you must admit that was funny.'

So we were fine the rest of the way. I actually shot six under par with clubs that were too upright and too whippy, wearing shoes that were two sizes too big and on a course I had never seen before.

Despite that shaky start, Bob and I got on great. He came to our foundation dinner one year at the Marcliffe and gave a brilliant speech. He went down very well. We paid his accommodation at the Open and he spoke for us, which was a great deal all round. People couldn't believe that we had Bob Rotella in Aberdeen.

He was, by a distance, the best of all the psychologists I worked with. If I lived in America or he worked in Europe, he would be the only person I would ever work with. And I would pay him whatever he wanted to be paid. But getting in touch with him was a problem. Especially as I wasn't in the States too often. Even going through his wife, Darlene, was difficult. When I had his attention he was first class, but it got to the stage where I wondered if all the hassle to get him was worth it.

He did clear up one thing for me. Or at least he tried to. Somehow, he was aware of what Davis Love had reportedly said about me in the wake of the '99 Open ('the Open got the champion it deserved'). And he told me that he had known Davis since he was a teenager and there was no way he would have said such a thing about a fellow professional. I still don't know with any real certainty if Davis did say it or not, but the Doc was convinced.

Funnily enough, Bob was in the mould of Dr Cox when it came to payments. There was nothing written down. His attitude was that he was really good at what he did and, knowing that, his clients would look after him appropriately. I know I did.

I started working with Jamil Qureshi in 2010 as he was out on the European Tour almost every week. I would see him at least twice during events. I especially enjoyed the hypnosis sessions we would do in my room; they were very relaxing. He was very good at everything he did, but soon enough I found that all too much, to the point where I was making up excuses not to sit down with him. I'm like that with certain things. Even if I know it is helping me, I take a notion and that is the end of it. On the other hand, everything can be going well and my form can be good and I'll decide out of nowhere that I need to speak to someone. It's weird I know. But I'm a weird person, what can I say?

Me & My Shadows, The Caddies

No professional golfer can be successful all by himself. We all need help along the way, especially these days, when the unprecedented depth of talent in the game has made things so much more competitive. It's a bit of a cliché, but those standing still are actually going backwards. Constant improvement is a must for anyone with serious ambition to succeed on tour.

To that end, one of the most important members of my 'team' on tour at any one time is my caddie. I've had a few over the years, some good, some great and some, well, neither of those two things. Still, as I said in chapter four, I like to think I've been good to everyone I've ever employed to carry my bag and fulfil all the 101 other things a good caddie is asked to do every day.

I've always thought of myself as one of the more generous bosses on tour. I don't know how much many other players pay, but I'm sure I'm one of the highest. I pay a good weekly wage and then a bonus depending on how I've played. If we make the 36-hole cut, my caddie gets five per cent of my prize money. If we finish in the top-ten, that percentage rises to seven and a half. And if I win, my man gets 10 per cent of my winnings.

I also – unlike many other players – pay my caddie a slightly reduced wage for the weeks we are not on tour. When I'm resting I want him to do the same. I think that's important. Back when I was first on tour, I took a couple of weeks off. But the guy on my bag at the time stayed out on tour. He said he couldn't afford to take a fortnight off and not be earning. Which was fair enough, of course.

But my feeling was that I wanted the man on my bag to be both mentally and physically fresh to work for me when I came back out. And he wasn't. He was tired after working for someone else over the previous two weeks. So that is why I devised the plan I still use today. When I'm home, my caddie is too. And he gets paid to rest up. Funnily enough, most of them have quite enjoyed that idea!

The other reason I like to pay my caddies well is that, as I touched on in chapter 4, I'm not always the easiest guy to work for. I know what I'm like, especially if things are not going my way. I can be a bit of a nightmare. I have apologised to many of my caddies. 'Sorry about yesterday; I was shocking,' kind of stuff.

I've even bought presents for caddies after I've been particularly unbearable. Andy Forsyth, who caddied for me for six years on tour, gave me the idea. He had been with Monty for eight months before he came to me. And every now and then, after he had given Andy an especially hard time, Monty would show up with a wee gift. I thought that was a good idea. Which is why Andy now owns a pair of expensive headphones purchased by me.

He deserved them though. It is not often I say something I really regret, but I did one day with Andy, who is one of the nicest guys you could ever wish to meet. We were at Valderrama for a tournament and there was a rain delay. On the way in, I told him to make sure and get me a spot on the range when the weather improved. With everyone back in the clubhouse, I knew it would be busy and I didn't want to be hanging around waiting for someone else to finish hitting balls.

When the sun came out a couple of hours later, I emerged from the locker room to find that Andy was still in the caddies' lounge blethering to his mates. Already, the range was almost full. Neither of those things made me happy, given my previous instructions. So I marched in and, in front of everyone, said something really nasty to Andy. I can't recall exactly what it was, but it wasn't nice. And it wasn't something I would ever want someone else to say to me, especially in front of others.

Andy got up and chased after me. 'Don't you ever speak to me like that,' he said. 'I don't care who you are and what you pay. Don't you ever say something like that to me again.'

And you know what? He was absolutely spot on. I felt terrible as he stormed off. It was ages before he came back, which at least gave me time to think of something to say. We were on the putting green.

'Look, I'm really sorry,' I said.

'Don't worry about it,' was his typically nice response.

'No, I can tell you're upset.'

'I am,' he admitted. 'It's just not like you to say things like that.'

I was so ashamed. But now and again we all cross the line don't we? I'm not proud of what I did, but I only did it once. That was enough.

On the other side of the behaviour coin, I do have some rules I expect my caddie to stick to. He is not allowed to drink much during the week. Well, okay, one is alright. But no more than that. The last thing I want is for the guy carrying my bag to be operating at less than 100 per cent.

Lateness is another no-no. Although one mistake in that regard wouldn't be a job-losing offence, twice would be. I just don't think showing up when I want him to is too much to ask.

My only other pre-round rule concerns appearance. I want my caddie to look smart and presentable. I see some of them and think they've been pulled through a hedge both backwards and forwards.

On the course, like every other I suspect, I have my little foibles. For example, as soon as the caddie has the yardage done I like to hear the numbers. I want to hear what the caddie is thinking regarding what club I should hit. I want to hear how far it is to the front of the green, how far the pin is from there and where the wind is blowing from. If I get time to think I might be miles away from what he is about to say. That's no good. So it is better to hear everything as soon as possible.

Other than that, I'm sure I'm one of the less demanding players on the European Tour. Even if I've had a bad day I rarely ask my caddies to hang around while I hit balls for an hour or so. I actually quite like to do that on my own if I've been struggling. I don't like the caddie standing there. I don't want him to chip in with any thoughts he might have on my swing or technique. Not his department.

That's why I never blame my caddie for a bad shot on the course. I almost never have and I hope I never will again. I make the decisions out there, not him. It's my decision and the consequences of that action are down to me. If it's not right, it's not right. Only very seldom have I pointed a finger at the guy carrying the bag.

On good days, of course, I'm even easier to handle. While I typically don't really hit that many balls 'on site' anyway, if I'm happy with my game I'll hit maybe half a bucket of balls, chip a few and spend only a few minutes on the practice green. Sometimes I don't even do that. It was Adam who installed that attitude in me. His feeling was that I should go to tournaments to rest and play golf, not work my butt off. So most days, whatever has happened on the course, not long after I've holed out on the 18th green, I'll be telling my caddie, 'see you tomorrow'.

That's just me though. I'm sure every pro on tour has his own way of going about his business, one that keeps him happy and ready to play. And a good caddie will very quickly adapt to whatever routine his player is used to and happiest with.

Oh, one more thing I hate from a caddie is criticism. If I've hit a bad shot I don't want to hear any tut-tutting or see any pulling of faces. It's tough enough out there without any hearing or seeing any negativity from the man who is supposed to be on my side. Besides, I've never thought of myself as a world-class player or even a superior ball striker. So I'm sometimes going to hit shots that anyone would consider poor.

One last point: I also hate to hear something along the lines of 'okay, let's go. We can birdie three of the last five on this course.' I had a caddie like that once. But just the once. I don't want that sort of phoney encouragement. Especially when I'm on the 14th and he is talking about making birdies three and four holes later. I'm not very good at thinking about two things at once. So I like to stay in the present.

I was the same when Adam and I would be on the range working on my swing. We could never work on my backswing and downswing at the same time. It always had to be one or the other. I can't do both together. I just can't. Can't coordinate the two for some reason. And I'm the same with putting. Can't work on pace and technique at the same time. Again, it's one or the other. I hear about guys like Faldo having six or seven swing thoughts in their heads at any one time and I shake my own head in wonder. I've got to work on one bit, get that right, before I can even think about moving to the next.

I suppose it will come as no surprise to hear that my attention span is not the longest. When I was in a meeting with a psychologist or whatever, Adam would always tell them beforehand, 'you've got 20 minutes. After that, he's gone'. And he was right. After 20 minutes or so, nothing is going in. He knew me so well.

It is not just psychologists either. After a hugely important meeting with my management group, I can recount almost everything that happened or was said in the first 20 minutes. After that, I'm making it up. So my caddie has to get used to that part of my character too.

The first full-time caddie I ever had was called Paul Connelly, or 'Shifter', which was the name he actually answered to. He worked for me during my two-year stint on the Tartan Tour in the early 1990s. And very good he was too. Most of the time anyway. In truth, Shifter and I had quite a stormy relationship.

I still laugh at the memory of the 1990 Ram Classic at Erskine near Glasgow. I finished eighth at that event, but Shifter didn't finish at all. Well, he did. If you count walking in from the 13th green during the second round as 'finishing'. I don't. Before disappearing, in fact, Shifter actually threw my ball at me, hitting me on the shoulder. He then dumped the bag and marched off. Marian caddied for the last five holes.

When I got in, Shifter was still there. At first I thought he was trying to apologise. Which he did, in a roundabout sort of way. But then he claimed the reason behind his sudden departure was I had said something nasty to him. Which was probably true. But my point was that, even if I had, it was hardly the first time we had exchanged conflicting points of view on the course. What made this time so different?

Anyway, we patched things up and Shifter stayed with me a few more months. What finished us, at least for a while, was my trip to Valencia for the second stage of the European Tour Qualifying School towards the end of that season. I say 'my trip' advisedly. Because Shifter didn't make it.

At 2.30 in the morning, a few hours before we were supposed to fly to Spain, my phone rang. It was Shifter. 'I'm not going,' he said. He was in Aberdeen but he wasn't coming. I was immediately suspicious and suggested that he was actually in Glasgow having spent the previous evening touring a few of the local hostelries. I turned out to be wrong about that actually; he gave me the number where he was and, sure enough, he was in Aberdeen.

But that's where he was staying. No matter what I said, he just wasn't going. 'I've had enough of you,' he said.

Which was why Marian, after a frantic phone call to her boss, got an unexpected 'holiday' pulling my bag around for a week in sunny Spain. Shifter, you won't be surprised to hear, hardly ever worked for me again after that. I just couldn't trust him. It was a great pity. Shifter was trouble at times but when he was in the mood he was one of the best caddies I ever had. Unfortunately for him, he wasn't able to knuckle down and do his job.

My first year on tour, Dave Morgan was on my bag after Marian sacked me. He had previously worked for Vijay Singh. When Vijay played in Europe they had won a few events together. Dave was very good, even if his addition was a bit dodgy at times. When he was doing a yardage he would come back, write it all down then add it up. Then I would check it. And his eyesight was not the best. But he was very experienced and I learned a lot from him. I just had to keep an eye on him.

Gary Curry was next. He was on the bag when I won my first event, the '96 Catalan Open. From Belfast, Gary was a lovely guy. I still think of him fondly, even if our relationship ended in an unfortunate way. Gary was banned for life from the tour after he stabbed another caddie, Brian Dempster, during the European Masters in Switzerland.

I, of course, knew nothing about what had happened when I arrived at the course the next morning. But (Lorne) Duncan, who is a great character and has been caddying on tour for years, told me. He came over and said to me, 'Paul, if it helps you I'll come out with you today.'

'What are you on about?' I replied.

'Gary is in jail.'

'What? He's in jail?'

And so I heard the whole sorry tale. And that was the end of Gary on my bag or anyone else's bag for that matter. I couldn't believe it. For him to be involved in something like that was so out of character. He didn't drink much. He kept himself to himself. And he wasn't loud or obnoxious. To this day, I don't know exactly what went on that night, but the bottom line is that I lost a good caddie.

Paddy Byrne was next to be on the bag for any decent length of time. I had actually arranged for Matthew Byrne (no relation) to caddie for me at the start of the 1999 season, but when I got to Dubai there was no sign of him. Another caddie said he knew of a young lad looking for a job so I hired Paddy for the week. And when we got on well I asked him to come to Qatar, where we won. After that, I hired him full-time, even though he was very inexperienced. His only previous job had been one week with Ross McFarlane in Dubai – where he lived – the year before.

Paddy was from Dublin but had moved to Dubai when his father set up business there. He was a good lad with a bubbly personality and was easy to spend time with. That is important. Players and caddies spend as much time in each other's company as husband and wife.

Adam and Paddy got on well too. That was vital actually. Adam was travelling with me almost every week at that time. So all was fine. And all continued to be fine until we were in Australia at the end of 1999. As I said earlier, punctuality is a big thing with me, so when Paddy turned up 10 minutes before my final round in Perth, I wasn't too happy. I never am when I have to carry my clubs to the range and put them on a trolley.

What made it worse was that I was in contention. When Paddy did appear his story was that he had been up all night because his father's business in Dubai was in big trouble. Not that I was too impressed with that explanation. I was really angry and barked at him not to speak to me for the rest of the day.

Not surprisingly, I got off to a horrendous start and was well over par when he plucked up the courage to tell me the truth. He had actually been up all night in the casino and had lost track of time. I flew home for Christmas after telling him I would call to say what I would be doing.

I wanted to fire him, to be honest. But Adam talked me into giving him a second chance. That was, after all, the first time he had done anything seriously wrong. But when we got to the World Match Play in La Costa early in 2000, I wanted to make a change. It just wasn't working any more. So I resolved to tell Paddy of my decision at the end of the week. The trouble was, Adam – who was sharing a room with Paddy – felt we should let him know right away. His feeling was that other caddies might find out what I was planning and tell him before I did.

Adam felt that Paddy would handle the situation okay. I disagreed, but understood Adam's thoughts. So I told Paddy after I had won my first round match. He took it pretty badly and even went so far as to thump the bag while we were on the range. And while I couldn't quite hear what he was muttering under his breath, I'm sure he wasn't wishing me all the best for the rest of the season.

Paddy was in the same mood the next day. Eventually, I had to take him to the back of the range and ask him if he could be professional and do the job. But after hearing his response and judging his attitude, I decided he couldn't. So I fired him with 10 minutes to go before my round. Adam got his trainers on and carried the bag – which he always did very well – and we won again.

When the press asked me about Paddy they wanted to know if he had done something bad. My reply must have given them something because the next day it was all over the papers making out he was involved with some dodgy stuff. I wish I could remember exactly what I said, but I can't. But the press made it sound like he had done something really awful. Which wasn't true of course. His father was furious and asked for a meeting in Dubai the following week. I agreed and he arrived with a pile of paper clippings. In one story, Mark Garrod of the Press Association had quoted Adam as saying, 'Paddy had to go.' That was disappointing as Adam had said no such thing.

I could only apologise for the way it was handled and told him the truth of what had been going on. We left on reasonable terms – and we still say hello when I see him at the Middle East events every year – but I'm sure he wasn't too happy. Paddy is his son, so I can understand that. In fact, I wasn't too happy either. Paddy and I had obviously shared a lot during 1999, so I felt a kinship with him. We actually gave things another go later on. But it was no good. We both needed to move on.

Looking back, the biggest problem – one that never really went away – was that Paddy wasn't really a caddie. He was a bag carrier. But he was a lovely lad and that made up for any professional deficiencies he might have had. At the Open he was different class even though I was still doing all the yardages and clubbing by myself. In fact, any problems we had stemmed from the time I gave him the yardage book and started letting him do clubs and stuff like that. Had I just kept it the way it was, things might have lasted a lot longer, a bit like Bernhard Langer and Pete Coleman. They were together for years and Pete never did a yardage once.

That is the interesting thing about player-caddie relationships. They are all different – similar but different. Paddy was great at keeping my spirits up. Plus, nine times out of 10, caddies and player part on less than perfect terms, so we were no different in that I guess.

The next man on my bag was Englishman Mick Doran. Mick was an experienced caddie even before we got together. He had been on Constantino Rocca's bag at the 1995 Open, when the good-natured Italian famously holed out from the Valley of Sin at St Andrews to make it into the play-off he would eventually lose to John Daly. Mick came to me from Lee Westwood though, with whom he had a hugely successful time. They won something like 15 tournaments together.

With a resume like that, it will come as no surprise to hear that Mick was – and is – one of the best caddies on tour. He was very professional and we got on really well. There was just one problem and it was nothing to do with anything Mick was doing. The thing was, I struggled hugely with the amount of wins he had notched up with his previous employers. It may seem funny or odd to hear this, but I was actually intimidated by the success he had known before picking up my bag. It put me under pressure. I felt that he would expect the same sort of play from me. And, as much as I wanted to win, I never saw myself in that league.

Adam was one who could never get his head round my feelings on that subject, no matter how often I tried to explain what was going through my head. It wasn't that Mick was too good a caddie. But he'd won a lot. And every time I hit a poor shot my mind was racing with silly thoughts of what Mick must be thinking. Was he inwardly shaking his head and wondering what the hell he was doing working for this chopper? That was how my mind was working. And it led to me feeling uncomfortable around him on the course. None of which, it goes without saying, was his fault.

There was also some friction with Mick's girlfriend at the time. She annoyed me most in Switzerland though. I hit the worst shot I've ever hit off a first tee in my life. A low snap-hook, it struck a tree that was only 40-

yards past the practice putting green and rebounded back into the middle of the fairway. That was the only good thing I can say about it though – the ball was only 150 yards or so from where I was still standing.

All of that was embarrassing enough. But I happened to look over and there was Mick's girlfriend. She was over by the gallery ropes, her arms folded across her chest and a look on her face like you can't believe. I was not amused and told Mick, 'this game is hard enough without your girlfriend standing there looking like that'.

And there is more. Mick is one of those caddies who, if his player is, for example, two over par with four holes to play, says, 'let's birdie the last four'. As I said earlier I can't abide that. It bugs the hell out of me. How can I think about making a birdie at the 18th when I'm on the 15th? That sort of thing makes no sense to me.

Combined, all of those problems meant that Mick and I were never going to be working together that long. Which is no reflection on him or his ability as a caddie. He was never late. He never showed up smelling of drink. He's a proper caddie, one of the best. But sometimes, for whatever reason, these things just don't work out. And my time with him was one of those occasions.

When Mick and I parted – he went to Justin Rose after me – I hired Colin Byrne. I had actually tried to get him before but the timing wasn't right. This time I was luckier though, or at least Adam was. He was my man on the caddie beat. It was Adam who called around to see who was available if I was thinking of making a switch, just one more example of what a good friend he was to me over the years. Every time I think of him it hits me hard how much I miss his many kindnesses.

Colin had worked for the New Zealander, Greg Turner, for a long time and I had always been a fan of the way he went about his business. In fact, the only mistake I've ever made with a caddie was letting Colin go after we had maybe three and a half years together. He is certainly the best caddie I've ever had.

Right from the start, Colin, a Dubliner, and I got on well. He is so professional, but not your typical caddie. He's not a big drinker, he's a regular in the gym and he writes a weekly column in the *Irish Times* newspaper. He saw his job as more of a lifestyle than just a way of getting by. In other words, he is very bright, thoughtful and well read. We won twice together, at the Dunhill Links and at the Wales Open. His was such a cool head to have alongside me when the pressure was on. I remember he was especially good when I won that Dunhill at St Andrews, holing from the Valley of Sin at the last to beat Ernie Els by a shot.

It was actually at the Dunhill Links that we decided to part. As sometimes happens in a caddie-player relationship, things had started to get a little intense. Colin and I had started saying little 'narky' things to each other. So there was a bit of an atmosphere between us. Martin Gilbert of Aberdeen Asset Management – my amateur partner at every Dunhill – came over to me on one hole and said, 'You two need to go your separate ways. You think too much of each other to let your friendship end in this way.'

He was spot on. One week later, I was playing for Great Britain & Ireland against the Continent of Europe in the Seve Trophy in Valencia. Before we left St Andrews I spoke to Colin and told him what Martin had said and that I agreed it was maybe time for us to part.

Colin agreed too.

'You are right,' he said. 'We have had a great time together. I think a lot of you as a golfer and a person and it's not right that we are going down the road we are on at the moment.'

We didn't part just like that though. The money at the Seve Trophy was guaranteed so I asked Colin to work for me that week as a sort of farewell. I didn't want him to lose out financially. If he had said no, it would have been no problem, but he agreed immediately. We ended up having a nice time and we parted on good terms. Which is as it should be.

Looking back though, that was a mistake for me. Colin is a brilliant caddie. He has the perfect knack of saying what he has to say at just the right moment. Billy Foster – who works for Lee Westwood – is the same. I used to love how, if I had holed a putt, Colin would give me a wee tap on the back with the putter grip once I had passed it to him. I know that sounds a little odd, but it made me feel good about what I had just done.

So what we should have done is either sit down and thrashed out the problems that were making us snap at each other, or take a short break from each other and come back fresh. But we didn't. And I will always regret that. I did him a favour though. He went off to work for Retief Goosen and won two US Opens. Not too shabby!

Colin is easily the most intelligent caddie I've ever had. I've read some of his columns and they were always well written and interesting. I never had any doubts about taking him into any environment. He could chat and make conversation with anyone. He's just a lovely guy and very good at his job.

A few years later, in fact, I tried to hire Colin back. We spoke about the possibility and, as ever, he was very honest and straight with me. 'I've got a couple of possibilities at the moment,' he said. 'If one of those comes back to me, then I'm sorry, it's going to have to be a "no".'

Not long after that, Colin called me to say he was joining up with Edoardo Molinari. Which was fine. I understood. But it was still disappointing. The only time Colin ever had occasion to raise his voice with me was during the 2001 US Open at Southern Hills in Tulsa. Playing with Tom Lehman and Greg Norman I got off to a great start in the first round and was on the leader board.

A day later things didn't go so well and by the time I reached the last hole I was two shots outside what looked as if it would be the cut-line. Walking down the fairway, I turned to Colin and asked for my mobile phone. I wanted to make sure I had a seat on the flight out of there that night.

Well, he just went mad. In fact, he went ballistic. He was shouting and swearing and everything. 'I'm not giving you that f-----g phone,' he yelled. 'I'm trying my bollocks off here and you've given up. How unprofessional is that? You can still make a birdie here.'

Oh man, he was raging. And of course he was right. When we got into the clubhouse I apologised to him. But he wasn't finished with me.

'I understand the way you feel about playing over here,' he said. 'But you're here and I can't believe you are going down the last hole thinking like that. You could have holed out your second shot and made the cut. You've got to try to the bitter end, no matter what.'

Right again. He was spot on. And I needed to be told just that. You need people like Colin Byrne in your life at times – and that was definitely one of those times. Like most golfers on the European Tour, I spend a lot of my professional life getting what I want and having people tell me what I want to hear. So now and again a dose of the real truth never does me any harm.

Anyway, when Colin left I hired Andy Forsyth. Again, like Colin, I had tried to do that before, but it hadn't worked out. At the time of my approach, Andy was working for Paul Broadhurst, who had paid for him to go through his physiotherapy exams. So, quite rightly, Andy didn't feel like he could move on. Which says a lot about him.

Second time around, things worked out better. Andy had just sacked Monty after eight months on his bag and was looking for work. We were together six and half years from the middle of 2004 on.

Andy is one of the nicest people you could ever wish to meet. He is an excellent caddie too, even if he is prone to asking an incredibly silly question now and then. I remember him saying to Phil Mickelson: 'Phil, have you ever imagined how good you could have been if you were right-handed?'

He was great with me one-on-one. He knew how to handle me, even when I was off on one of my occasional rants. One time he listened to me for a bit and said, 'You can say what you like, today I'm bulletproof. Bring it on.' I had to laugh. That's me though. I get on myself so much that it sometimes spills over to the caddie and they have to listen. I can't tell you how often I've apologised to them.

Andy was very loyal too. I know he had offers to go to other players before we eventually finished at the end of 2010. I felt like a change was needed. That happens from time to time. I still can't believe he put up with me for as long as he did. I must pay well – he was the first guy I gave 'week-off' money to – although I still regret that we never won an event together. That would have been nice. But it goes like that sometimes. Six weeks after finishing with Andy and hiring Davy Kenny I won a tournament. Weird.

I've always needed to be comfortable with the guy on my bag. I don't like it if my caddie falls ill or is injured and I have to use someone else. I struggle with that. I'd rather go home. I'm not happy with someone I don't know well. That's why I like to scout out caddies a little bit before I work with them.

It was that way with Davy actually, albeit accidentally. I was playing at an event with Gonzalo Fernandez-Costano – 'Gonzo' to his friends – and Davy was on his bag because Gonzo's man had broken his arm. I was impressed. I liked the way he behaved. He was professional and quite quiet. And I was looking to make a change with Andy. The timing was perfect.

Davy was actually on the point of packing it in and going home to get a 'real' job. He didn't have a regular bag and had decided he would stay only if he could work for a decent player. Apparently I qualify! Our first event was in the Middle East early in 2011. And, as I said, we won almost right away, some of the credit for which must go to Davy.

We get on well. He's a good pro. And he treats me with just the right lack of respect when he writes his blog for my website. I like that he is a former teaching pro too. I've been able to run a few swing thoughts by him. Hopefully, he'll be with me for a while yet.

That is one of the common factors in all of my caddies. None of them have been big drinkers. None of them are loud and outgoing. And none of them smoke near me. I don't like when they smoke. It wouldn't stop me hiring someone – Davy is a smoker – but they have to do it well away from me. I just don't like it.

I'm not one who ever eats or socializes with my caddie. Andy was the only exception to that rule. I would take him and his mate Julian aka 'the Ferret' out for a nice dinner maybe once every couple of months. We'd have a nice steak and a good bottle of wine and just enjoy ourselves. I liked doing that for Andy though. He is such a good person.

But I've never done that with any other caddie. It's not that I haven't liked any of them or didn't want to spend time with them. I just think it is best to have some space in such a close working relationship. I see too many players and caddies becoming best mates. They end up spending way too much time together and it invariably ends in tears.

One last thing. While I obviously like my caddies to be professional and know what they are about, I never want the best caddie in the world working for me. I would hate that. I'd be intimidated just as I was when Mick Doran was on my bag years ago. I would feel like I had to match my caddie's level of expertise. So I'd rather have someone who is just really good without being great.

For example, if I had Billy Foster working for me – he is widely regarded as the best caddie out there – I wouldn't feel in charge of him. I would feel that he was above that sort of thing and that it was me who was on trial the whole time. And I would be worried that he wouldn't be impressed enough by my play. Weird stuff I know, but that is how I feel.

Some Famous Names
Along The Way

As I said in chapter one, I'm not really one who pays attention to what the world has come to think of as 'celebrity culture'. I certainly don't think of myself as a celebrity, even if others might argue otherwise. And I certainly don't live the lifestyle of a celebrity. So although my job might take me all over the world to what may seem like exotic locales, the reality is invariably very different.

While I might have a nice view from my hotel room balcony, the four things/places I'm likely to see in any particular week are a) the rest of that hotel, b) the airport, c) the routes between airport and hotel, and hotel and golf course and d) the golf course. Sightseeing is for tourists. So when I announce that I'm off to, say, Paris for a few days, I don't mean I'll be taking in the delights of the Champs Elysees or the Arc De Triomphe or the Louvre. Instead, I'll spend a lot of my time at the end of yet another big green field hitting small white balls into the middle distance. In that sense, I could be anywhere.

Besides, even if I was sitting in an airport lounge waiting for a flight and someone famous walked in, I would never – and I mean never – walk over just to say hello. I just can't. And I've never really understood why people feel the need to do that. I get it a lot myself. Guys come over and say they want to shake the hand of an Open champion. And just recently I had a lady come up to me on a plane with her kids and ask me to sign some autographs. When she left, the guy opposite me asked if I was famous. 'Not really,' I said. But the lad next to him says, 'He's the golfer.' So I had two more boarding passes to sign! Don't get me wrong: I think all of that is really nice. But I also think it's a little odd.

Still, mine is not an occupation without opportunity. So while it remains accurate to say that I couldn't care less about shaking hands with some famous face or other, I've done a bit of that in my time. Hey, sometimes it is unavoidable. Which is not to say that I've always or even sometimes enjoyed the experience of meeting the great and the good from walks of life outside golf.

There was the time, a few years ago now, when Marian and I were invited to Balmoral Castle and some function where the Queen and Prince Charles were going to be in attendance. We went along more out of curiosity than anything – honest! – thinking there might not be that many people there and that it might be fun to say we had actually done it.

Well, it ended up that there were maybe 250 people in the room, all milling about to no great purpose. But when QE2 and PC arrived that all changed in a hurry. The clamour to meet and greet them was amazing. And a bit pathetic if I'm honest. Marian and I just stood back and watched with something not far removed from fascinated horror. It was a wee bit sad to see the lengths seemingly sensible – and obviously affluent – people would go to just to say hello to someone else and shake his/her hand. It just was not my scene at all.

A lot more to my taste is meeting someone like Sir Alex Ferguson, one of the most successful football managers the UK has ever produced. In fact, he might be the most successful ever, full stop.

As I said earlier, I first met Alex at the 1999 BBC Sports Personality of the Year awards ceremony, courtesy of Monty's kind introduction. That was a dream come true for me, having been a Fergie fan since childhood. I grew up watching the great Aberdeen team of the late 70s and early 1980s, the one he led to three Scottish championships, four Scottish Cup wins, a League Cup victory and, of course, the European Cup Winners' Cup and European Super Cup in 1983. Just to prove that point, I can still from memory recite the team that won the Cup Winners Cup that rainy night in Gothenburg: Leighton, Rougvie, McLeish, Miller, McMaster, Cooper, Strachan, Simpson, McGhee, Black, Weir. And the substitutes: Gunn, Watson, Kennedy, Hewitt and Angus.

And yes I was there, aged 14, in Sweden with my father and my brother to see it happen. It remains, despite the fact that we were well soaked by the end of it, an unforgettable memory. It isn't often anyone gets to see his team beat Real Madrid, never mind in a European final.

Almost every week I used to sit in the old G stand at the Beach End at Pittodrie. We had season tickets there for years. I'm not sure we fully realised how lucky we were back then. Some of the football we got to watch was sublime. Every week – it seems now anyway – the Dons would win by three, four or five goals. If they didn't, something was wrong.

Over the last few years I have met many of the guys I grew up watching and I even got the chance to contribute to captain Willie Miller's book. I was asked to write down my Aberdeen 'Dream Team'. Which I did. I think it was the team that won the Cup Winners' Cup.

The great thing about that side was they played real football. There was never any aimless 'hoofing' of the ball up the park. Which has sadly not been the case too often since Fergie left. I remember one game, back when Alex McLeish was Hibs manager. It was awful stuff and the guy sitting next to me eventually got fed up with it all. So he started his own commentary. 'Hoof, header. Hoof, header' was all he said. But he was right. It was just terrible.

Eventually, someone near me shouted out to McLeish. 'Hey, Alex, this is shite!' Which McLeish overheard. He turned round and glared at the guy. Then he smiled. 'I know,' he said. I enjoyed that. Both Willie Miller and Alex McLeish are members of our Foundation Lottery, which is really good. And so are Craig Brown and Archie Knox, which is brilliant.

Anyway, back at the BBC awards, I got the chance to meet the great man face-to-face. He was terrific to be around. Which didn't come as any real surprise as he had written me a lovely letter after the Open. And now, of course, my family and I have been down to Old Trafford a few times as his guests to see Manchester United play. He always invites us into his office afterwards for a wee drink and the boys get photographs. It is hard to put into words how nice he has been to us.

There was one time we were at the Carrington training ground. Just watching. But Fergie comes over and tells the boys to go behind the goals and collect the balls as the players practise their shooting. You can imagine how much they enjoyed that. I will never forget his generosity.

Another time there, I told the boys to hang back as I didn't want us to get in the way. Well, we were soon right in the middle of it all. Fergie and his assistant came over and stood beside us. Then he started shouting instructions. One by one the players came trotting over. And soon enough we were right there as Fergie gave his team talk for the match the following day.

When that was done, the players wandered off and Alex invited us back to his office for a cup of tea. I told him we didn't want to be a bother but he was having none of it. At which point I asked if it would be okay if the boys got some pictures with the players.

'Who do they want?' asked Alex.

So for the next few minutes he rounded up the players my sons wanted to be photographed with. Ronaldo, Scholes, Rooney. Anybody they wanted. Nothing was too much trouble.

For all that, I have always been careful not to take advantage of Alex's good nature. I know I could go to Old Trafford and the training ground and his office more often, but I don't want to do that. We go once a season and no more. In fact, it must be three years since we were there last. I think that was the time I was asked to go onto the pitch to make the half-time draw. As I was walking out there was a huge roar and when I got to the guy with the microphone he said, 'Boy, you are really popular'.

I just laughed.

'Look behind you,' I replied. On the big screen it said, 'Burnley 3 Manchester City 0.'

When we go I always take Alex a wee present. I have given him a signed Carnoustie flag and, one time, a new driver. I remember him sitting waggling it in his chair when he turned to my older son, Craig.

'Are you proud of your dad?' he asked.

'Yeah, we are,' mumbled Craig.

'Well you should be,' continued Alex. 'When you grow up you will realise how big of an achievement it was to win the Open like that.'

Unbelievable. My hero telling my son he should be proud of me. I will never forget that.

I've only once played golf with Fergie – sort of – in something he was involved with, the 'Great Scots Cup' which was played over the Carrick course at Loch Lomond. It was teams of four and a lot of Scottish sportsmen were playing. Ally McCoist was there. So was Gavin Hastings, the former rugby star. My job was to do a wee clinic before everyone teed off, then hit one shot at the par-3 14th hole with every group. I was happy to do it and proud that he asked me.

In terms of golf, not many have impressed me as much as Fergie, but Jack Nicklaus is one who would qualify. How could he not? Not only has Jack been the greatest winner in the history of the game – 18 major championship victories speak for themselves – but he has also been the greatest loser. By that I mean the class and sportsmanship he has always displayed on the occasions when he has come off second-best. And there have been a few of them. What many people forget is that, as well as those 18 wins, Jack has been the runner-up in 19 majors. Think about that. He has finished in the top-two in 37 Grand Slam events. Unbelievable.

I first met Jack – or 'Mister Nicklaus' as I called him – at the 1999 US PGA Championship at Medinah in Chicago. He stopped as he was walking through the locker room, just to speak to me as I sat lacing up my shoes. 'Well done,' he said. 'That 4-iron you hit to the last green at Carnoustie was one of the best shots I've ever seen anyone hit under pressure.'

I was speechless. Literally. The greatest golfer of all-time was impressed by one of my shots. It took me a while to take that in. But Jack is like that. He just does and says the right things without thinking about it. Over the years we have sent him stuff to sign so that we could auction it all off for the foundation. And nothing has ever been a problem. I wish I could say the same for certain other major champions who shall remain nameless. But Jack has always come through for us. He is a legend on and off the course.

Jack was also present when I attended my first Open Champions dinner at St Andrews in 2000. What an occasion that was. I walked into the room as defending champion to be confronted by an array of golfing greats. There were 27 of us in all and I had to pinch myself every time I looked up from my plate. I was one of them that night – unbelievable. I sat next to Lee Trevino and never said a word. I just listened. Couldn't get a word in. He was just non-stop.

Every year the captain of the R&A gets up and thanks everyone for coming. Then he invites anyone in the room to get up and tell a story about a pre-determined topic. And in 2000, the topic was 'your first-ever visit to the Open'.

Jack got up first. He was sitting next to Sam Snead, who had won the title in 1946 and is sadly no longer with us.

'My first visit to the Open was in 1962 at Troon,' said Jack. 'I remember it for two reasons. The first was the cold and wet weather. And the second was the number of girls who walked round watching Sam.'

Sam, who by that time was in his 80s, was sitting half asleep. But he perked up when he heard his name mentioned. 'Yep,' he said. 'And I had most of them that year too.' Everyone was roaring with laughter.

Tom Weiskopf was next up. He was sitting on my right, with Trevino on the left. Tom's first trip was also at Troon in 1973, I think. He told of being out there playing a practice round with his great friend, Bert Yancey. It was a bit foggy and a bit rainy when they got to the famous eighth hole, the 'Postage Stamp'. So both hit but when they got to the green only Yancey's ball was visible.

So they looked around for a bit until Weiskopf, as you do, glanced into the hole. There was the ball. 'Goddamn,' he said. 'I've made an ace.'

Sitting at the back of the green were two old guys on shooting sticks. 'Hey guys,' said Tom, 'didn't you see that was a hole-in-one?'

'Aye laddie,' came the reply. 'But it's only Tuesday.'

Needless to say, I didn't have the courage to stand up and tell any of my stories. But, for the record, the first Open I ever attended was at Birkdale in 1983. I went down in the car for three days with my Dad and my brother. And the first Open I played in was at Muirfield nine years later.

Nine years on from that, I was drawn to play with Gary Player at Royal Lytham & St Annes. That was pretty good in itself but was made extra-special by the fact that it was Gary's last Open. Walking down the last hole on Friday – he was missing the cut – was a pretty emotional experience for me, never mind him.

The applause started well back from the green, so I let him walk ahead and soak up the acclaim he deserved. He did all his waves to the crowd then motioned for me to join him. So we actually walked onto the green together. He got a great reception and I felt honoured just to be part of what was his day. I've got a lovely picture in my gym at home of Gary and I shaking hands as we walked up that final fairway. It's special and a moment I'll never forget.

Back in the world of royalty, one member of 'the family' who did impress me was Princess Anne. Marian and I met her at a First Group dinner and dance held at the Ardoe House hotel in Aberdeen. She was terrific company and very well informed. She asked me about Blairs College and how the golf design business was going. And she asked about my game in a way that made it clear she had at least a rudimentary understanding of golf and the psychology of the sport and how it is played at the top level. Which should not be that surprising, given that she owns an Olympic gold medal in three-day eventing. Pressure does, I'm sure, provoke the same symptoms and feelings in any competitive environment.

Just as impressive that night was how easily PA mingled with all the guests. I'm sure she had someone feeding her all the 'gen' but she still had to remember at least most of it. And she gave a fantastic speech without notes. I know how hard that is.

Seve Ballesteros is the only other golfer who, for me, comes close to Jack Nicklaus in terms of his presence and his influence on the game. While Nick Faldo won six majors as opposed to Seve's five, there is no doubt in my mind as to which of the two was the most historically significant. Seve was Europe's Arnold Palmer, the man who took the game to the masses and played the game in the way we all would like to play it. Again, while I don't mean to diminish Nick's accomplishments – he was a truly great golfer in every sense of that overused word – the efficient and almost robotic way he played was, while admirable, not what kids grew up wanting to emulate.

Seve had so much talent – and so many shots – it was frightening. And such a presence, one that kept me awake almost all night before I played with him for the first time. I'm not sure anyone else would have had quite the same effect on me. And the shots he could play. I still feel privileged to have witnessed first hand the five-wood he hit off his knees and from under a tree that first day at the 1992 Spanish Open. The man was a genius.

As such, Seve's contribution to European golf and the tour in particular should be recognised in some lasting and high profile way. Immediately after his death on 7 May 2011 there was talk of his corporate logo – a silhouette of him immediately after he holed that famous putt to win the 1984 Open at St Andrews – becoming the European Tour's logo. That would be appropriate. It's been said many times, but we are all playing for more money on tour today because of Seve. He was a sponsor's dream when he was at the top of his game – and even when he wasn't.

No matter how Seve was scoring, something unbelievable was always likely to happen, just as it did that day I played with him in Madrid. There were so many great moments. Who can forget the three-wood he hit from a fairway bunker on the 18th hole at PGA National during the 1983 Ryder Cup? Jack Nicklaus called that one, 'the greatest shot I ever saw in my life'. Which is good enough for me. Seve, no matter his faults and his foibles, was the greatest golfer Europe has ever produced – by miles.

Speaking of the Ryder Cup, back in 1999 Celine Dion was the 'turn' at the gala dinner in Boston. She sang two songs as I recall. And afterwards we all lined up to meet her. As Marian and I approached, Celine's husband – we were, ahem, on first name terms right away (!) – nudged her and whispered a few words. So when I got to her she said, 'That was a fantastic 4-iron you hit.' I thanked her and on we went. Whether she actually saw me win the Open or not remains a mystery, of course. Maybe she and Jack are pals and he told her about it.

As far as my contact with the world of show business goes, it has been strictly limited. I'm just not that interested. I did once play with film star

Hugh Grant at the Roxburghe Challenge near Kelso in the Scottish Borders one year. Prince Andrew and former footballer Alan Shearer made up the four. But Hugh – I didn't have the courage to call him 'Shug' – was my partner. He got up on the first tee, topped his drive maybe 40 yards and yelled, 'Bugger' at the top of his voice! Which just goes to show how he really does play himself in all his movies. And that my view of celebrities is the correct one – at the end of the day they are just like you and me.

Looking Ahead

The last couple of years have seen a marked upturn in my professional fortunes. Since the start of 2011, I have won three times on the European Tour, at the Open de Andalucia, the Qatar Masters and the Johnnie Walker Championship, finished second at the Dubai World Championship, totted up a few other top-ten finishes and, of course made it into a second Ryder Cup side. All of which, in my early 40s, has obviously been very gratifying.

A lot of the credit for my improved performances is down to myself, of course. I had reached a point not so very long ago where I was a wee bit lazy. I wasn't practising as much as I used to or should have been. I wasn't going to the gym. I was heavier than I ought to have been and, as a result, a bit out of shape. Then, one day, out of the blue, our eldest son, Craig, beat me over nine holes.

Losing to Craig was a shock. I had assumed it would take him a bit longer to do it. He was only 14 at the time and playing off about three or four. It was on the wee nine-hole course at Deeside. We got to the last and I realised I was two shots behind. I hadn't really paid attention to that point.

I tried a bit of gamesmanship if I'm honest. I said to him on the tee, 'you realise you're two ahead here'. He just nodded. Then on the green he had about a five-foot putt to win. I was still at it. 'You do know this is to win,' I said. All he said was, 'yeah,' before he knocked it right in the middle. That was followed by a bit of a fist-pump.

I said all the right things of course. 'Well done.' 'I'm proud of you.' And I shook his hand. But inside I was thinking, 'bloody hell, I can't be doing with this'. That is the way I am. I was determined I wasn't going to let that happen again. So that was a big wake-up call too. I felt like I was letting myself go as a golfer. And that's not me.

I was still working hard enough. But there was no real focus to any of it. It was like Apollo Creed in the 'Rocky' movie. He trained harder than he had ever done but got beat. And at the end he said to Rocky, 'I didn't have the eye of the tiger'. That was me. I was hitting more balls than ever but not getting any better.

Round about that same time, I went to the 2010 Ryder Cup at Celtic Manor as a commentator for Sky Television. That was the final kick up the backside I needed. That made my mind up. I looked around that week and decided I wasn't ready to make a living from sitting in a commentary box. So, that being the case, I had to knuckle down and play better.

I was in the gym the next week working out. I lost a bit of weight and regained some of the fitness I had lost. As for my game, I just worked a bit harder on everything. In effect, my pride had been hurt, so I took a good hard look at myself and decided something had to be done. I got myself fit. I started watching what I was eating. I spent a bit more time on the range – and, probably more importantly, on and around the practice green we have in our back garden at home. And I started paying more attention to how well my sons can play.

There was, of course, one more source of motivation: Adam. He had been ill for some time. And we all knew just how serious his condition was. Leukaemia is never something you can take lightly. But it was still a huge shock when he passed away in October 2011.

While it would be ridiculous of me to blame the decline in my play on Adam's illness, I did find things difficult without him. We went from speaking on the phone every day, to seeing each other in a hospital. Adam was the guy I went to for everything. And all of a sudden he wasn't there. Clearly that is almost insignificant compared with what he and his family went through, but it definitely had an impact on my game.

Even now, I think about him every day. More than once, in fact. When he was alive I never thought about what he would want me to do in the middle of a round. Now that he's gone though, I do that all the time. At least twice during the last round in Qatar I followed what I knew would have been his advice. I never used to do that. And it is a good thing. But it goes without saying I would rather have him with me.

Another big motivation for me is that I know his wife, Caroline, and his two girls look at my scores and follow my progress. Caroline texts me a lot to tell me how proud he would be at what I have achieved. I want to play as well as I can for as long as I can for them because I know it gives them a boost at a time when they need one.

Adam will always be with me though. On the 14th hole of that final round in Qatar he was in my head. I had missed makeable putts on each of the previous two greens. And I had another downhill putt for birdie. In that situation I would probably have been too aggressive, thinking I 'had to make one'. But I didn't do that. I knew Adam would have wanted me to stick to my routine, roll it down the hill and if it goes in, great. As it happened it went right in the middle. And that was thanks to Adam.

He was with me on the next hole too. I didn't hit a great drive and was 220-yards from the green. I hit a 5-iron from there, accepting that I was going to be short and right of the pin. I didn't have a go at something that could have led to a bogey or worse. Adam was great with the strategic stuff. And his voice will always be in my head. He never got the credit for being the coach that he was. Very few can do the whole package. He could though, because he knew all the technical stuff and thought like a player. He is the only coach I have ever had who could do both.

One last word on the motivation front. People have asked me if I feel any need to show the Americans I'm a better player than they thought I was when I won the Open. I can't say that had even crossed my mind until I was asked about it. But I did read a story recently and one of the comments on the website said that I was 'one of the top-three worst major winners of all-time'. I thought that was harsh, obviously. But equally, if that is what some people think, I need to change that perception of me. I need to show I'm better than that. Of course, even if I'm in the top/bottom three, I'm still a major winner.

And yes, let me repeat: I know I shouldn't read that stuff. But I do. And it's always disheartening to think people think that of me. But it is motivating too. I'll be trying very hard to become, in some minds at least, the worst-ever two-major winner in history.

As a result of all that extra effort and motivation – imaginary or otherwise – I played so much better in 2011. In the 81 stroke-play rounds I played on the European Tour over that 12-month span I only twice shot over 75. Just as important was the fact that I also broke 70 as many as 28 times. By the end of the season, I was back in the top-20 of the Order of Merit for the first time since 2002.

The formula for all of that was quite simple too: I just started doing everything better. Everyone was asking me what the difference was and the answer was: everything. I drove the ball better. I was longer off the tee. I was stronger. My short game has never been a problem. And my putting was a bit better.

I still don't putt as well as I used to. But that is only because I used to miss a lot of greens, chip up stiff and tap-in. I'd have, say, 28 putts and think 'what a good putter I am'. Now I'm a better ball-striker and I'm having only 30 putts. That is a pretty good number if you are hitting 14-15 greens. It is hard not to shoot at least four under par. Which is a pretty good formula for success.

Still, for all that, I must give a lot of the credit to the boys, not only for highlighting how badly I was playing but for continuing to challenge me as I worked on my game. Them being so keen has definitely helped me. I've always said that, whatever they want to do I'll do. Even if I've been away all week and get home late on a Sunday, I'll go and play nine holes with them if that is what they want to do. It is not fair on them to say, 'nah, I'm tired' when they want to play. I'm never tired when it comes to them.

The fact that they can both perform as well as they do undoubtedly helps me too. I have to work hard to beat them. I can't just freewheel out there, especially if I give them shots. I have to be on my game to win. And I have to concentrate. All those matches, I would say, have made the biggest difference to my game. Playing with them is great practice.

I don't let them win though. Never. Not at anything. It doesn't matter if I'm playing my mother, I play to win. I hate anyone beating me. They do sometimes, of course. But mentally, I can't let them win. Which drives Marian crazy at times. But if they beat me, they deserve to beat me.

Actually, neither of them has beaten me in a while now, so I must be doing something right. And I'm going to continue doing that too. I still enjoy playing the tour and I can't see anything other than a complete loss of form stopping me from competing until I'm 50 and eligible for the seniors circuit.

I would be lying also if I didn't admit that money is a factor in all of that. I'm a professional golfer, so the clue is in the title: I play golf for money and to earn a living. And right now I'm still good enough to earn a very good living. Even though I'm a long way from superstardom – I think of myself as a decent journeyman – there is every reason for me to continue as long as possible. I will be a long time retired with a bit of luck. So why stop?

Speaking of superstars, I see the professional game as consisting of maybe four levels of player. There are your legends at the top – Palmer, Watson, Nicklaus, Seve, Faldo, Tiger. One step down from that are the likes of Jose Maria Olazabal, Ernie Els, Phil Mickelson and Bernhard Langer. Great players but not quite God-like. Next are the good journeymen types, of which I'm one. Then there are the group of guys who struggle to keep their cards every year.

If I'm being completely honest, I'm not sure if even a loss of form would stop me playing. I'm certainly not one of those guys who announce, 'as soon as I'm not competitive at the top level, I'm out of here'. I enjoy playing too much to ever say that. So I wouldn't pack it all in just because I was struggling a bit.

What I wouldn't like to do, however, is drop too far down the ladder. I play in a few pro-ams every year in Scotland. And once in a while I'll play in a Tartan Tour event. But if that was my thing full-time, I'm not sure I would continue for too long. I'd be off running my foundation, I think.

Of course, as I mentioned earlier, even turning 50 is going to be quite exciting for me and Marian. Because I'm a major champion I'm guaranteed a year's exemption on the US Champions Tour. So, although I've never been a fan of long stays in America – not when that meant living on the PGA Tour anyway – we are going to devote at least a year of our lives to travelling that circuit and seeing what the great US of A is really all about. I quite fancy going to places like Las Vegas, San Francisco, New York, Washington and the Grand Canyon and doing all the touristy stuff we have never done. The boys will be old enough and out of the house so there is nothing to stop us.

One other thing is a bit of a pipedream of mine, but you never know. Both Craig and Michael are showing great promise on the course, so there is a chance one or both of them might just prove to be good enough to play the game for a living. Goodness knows, they both have a long way to go before that is more than even a possibility. But I live in hope that one day I might play in an event alongside one or both of them. Or, later on, go to watch them in action. That would be really neat.

I will obviously be available to help them in any way I can if they choose golf as their profession. I already get a kick out of passing along little tips and bits of wisdom I've picked up over the years. It is not so much in their swing that I take an interest – they have more knowledgeable people than I to help them there – but with how to actually play the game.

Every time we are out I'm asking them questions about what sort of shot they should be playing from whatever situation they are in. I love to help them think in the right way, just as I've helped young pros like David Law and Philip McLean with that sort of strategic advice. I look forward to doing more of that as I maybe ease down my own career in my late 40s.

Having said all that, of course, I have no idea what my sons will decide to do with their lives. At this point, I don't think they really know either. Nor should they; there is plenty of time for them to make those sorts of decisions. I'm very proud of them both though, especially in how well they have done at school and how well behaved they are every day of their lives.

Of course, as far as all that is concerned, the vast majority of the credit must go to Marian. She is a fantastic mother to both boys. Because I've been away so much she has had more than most parents to do and she has done a great job bringing them up. Their manners are good and so are their grades at school – which is more than their old man could ever say. I'm always pleased when people compliment me on how good they are and how polite they are.

That is important stuff in my mind. I like that my sons have been well brought up and know how to behave. I'm glad that they are well on the way to being good, proper people, even if, I'm sorry to say, I do spoil them more than a bit. I told them very early on that, as long as they behaved appropriately and do what they are told, they will pretty much get what they want from me. So if they want BOSS jumpers, I get them BOSS jumpers. But they have to behave. If they don't, the gravy train stops.

They laugh at me actually. I think they realise they are both a bit more academically minded than I ever was. Marian says they take after her in that respect…

But the core values I got from my parents are the same as those I'm trying to pass on to the boys. I lived out in the country when I was a kid. So even when I was a bit older than my sons are now, I never went to the pub. I would cycle home from school and practise my golf in the garden. I was always hitting balls into the field next to our house. I'm not sure if my Mum would agree, but I think I was pretty good at that stage, she certainly never had to wonder about where I was.

Ironically, the field where I used to practise is now an official driving range, The Pine Lodge Golf Centre. My old house is still there, but what surrounds it looks very different. In fact, the owners of the place, Jim Lees and his son, Mark, still tell the story about how they found maybe 3,000 balls when they came to landscape what is now the driving range. 'All of them hit by Paul Lawrie.'

As far as my future ambitions are concerned, I would like to rid myself of that 'top-three worst major winners ever' tag. I still read that more often than I would like. But I'm sure my form over the last couple of years has gone at least a little way to getting me more respect. Although I wonder about that. Even if I were to win maybe six more tournaments, I'm sure people would still hold that opinion.

The strange thing is, whenever people take a close look at my record, they are invariably surprised at how consistent it is over a long period.

That word 'respect' is important to me. I've been on the European Tour since 1992. I've never lost my card. I've won seven times, including one major championship. I've been in the top-20 of the Order of Merit numerous times. And I've played in two Ryder Cups. I actually think that's pretty good, even if others seem unimpressed. I'm proud of all that I've achieved.

Besides, at the end of my last round in my last tournament, I'll still be able to use what has to be the coolest phrase in golf. It's one I think I would like on my tombstone: 'Here lies Paul Lawrie. Champion Golfer of the Year 1999.'

Appendix

Paul Lawrie

1969 • Born 1st January, Aberdeen

1985 • T-1 North-east Golfers' Alliance, Royal Tarlair

1986 • Turned Professional (Assistant to Doug Smart, Banchory Golf Club)
     • 1st Moray Seafoods Pro-Am, Buckpool (first professional win – £300 – weeks after turning professional)

1987 • 1st Moray Seafoods Pro-Am, Buckpool

1988 • T-3 Peugeot PGA British Assistants' Championship, Coventry
     • 84th Tartan Tour Order of Merit and 72nd Money List (£937)

1989 • 3rd Bells Scottish Assistants' Championship
     • 10th RAM Classic, Royal Aberdeen
     • 1st North-east Golfers' Alliance Championship, Duff House Royal and Murcar
     • 1st Ballater, Peterhead, Balnagask, Huntly, Ballater, Huntly, Turriff (course record 64), Edzell, Deeside and 1T Royal Tarlair
     • 18th Tartan Tour Order of Merit and 27th Money List (£4,529)

1990 • 1st Krystal Klear Scottish Assistants' Championship, Cruden Bay
     • 1st Denis Lovell Assistants' Tournament, Royal Dornoch
     • 1st Livingston Deer Park PGA Open (Scottish Under 25 Championship)
     • 1st Clydesdale Bank Scottish Alliance Championship, Deeside and Banchory

- 1st North-east Golfers' Alliance at Ballater and Cruden Bay
- 1st Inverurie, Turriff, Ballater and T-1 Ballater
- 1st Moray Seafoods Open, Buckpool
- 1st Royal Aberdeen Pro-Am
- T-1 Torrance House Pro-Am
- 4th Northern Open, Nairn Dunbar
- T-4 Aberdeen Petroleum Club Pro-Am for SPARKS, Deeside
- 7th Scottish National Pro-Am Championship, Carnoustie
- 8th RAM Classic at Erskine
- 4th Scottish Assistants' Order of Merit
- 11th Tartan Tour Order of Merit and 6th Money List (£17,793)
- Failed to secure European Tour card for 1991 at qualifying event at Valencia

1991
- Married Marian
- 1st Daily Express Scottish National Pro-Am, Carnoustie
- 1st Moray Seafoods Open, Buckpool
- 1st Peterhead, Murcar, Deeside, Portlethen and Renfrew Pro-Ams
- T-1 Aberdeen Petroleum Club Pro-Am for SPARKS, Deeside
- T-2 Peugeot Cup PGA British Assistants' Championship, Wentworth
- 3rd Sunderland of Scotland Masters
- 4th Krystal Klear Soft Drinks Scottish Assistants' Championship, Kilmarnock Barassie
- SF Glenmuir Assistants' Matchplay, Torrance House
- SF Edinburgh Crystal Scottish Professional Matchplay, North Berwick
- 10th Scottish PGA Championship, Erskine (held halfway lead)
- 1st Scottish Assistants' Order of Merit
- 1st Tartan Tour Money List (£25,171)
- 2nd The Sun Order of Merit
- T-3 European Tour Qualifying, Bolton

- 12th European Tour Qualifying School at Montpellier (qualified for 1992 European Tour)
- Aberdeen Sports Council's Personality of the Year
- Green Final Golfer of the Year

1992
- MC Johnnie Walker Asian Classic, Bangkok (first European Tour event)
- Made cut in four out of first five tournaments on European tour (T-62 Dubai Desert Classic, T-44 Turespana Masters, Malaga, T-29 Open de Baleares, Majorca, T-50 Portuguese Open, Vilamoura)
- T-9 Volvo Open Di Firenze, Florence (first top 10 finish on European Tour)
- T-28 Volvo PGA Championship, Wentworth (guaranteed tour card for 1993 securing £30,136)
- T-6 Carroll's Irish Open, Killarney
- T-22 Open Championship, Muirfield (first Open, qualified at North Berwick)
- 1st Scottish Brewers' Scottish PGA Championship, Cardross
- 1st European Under-25 Championship, Le Prieure, France
- 83rd Order of Merit €78,022

1993
- T-6 Open Championship, Royal St George's
- 1st Scottish Golfer's Alliance Championship, Lossiemouth
- 57th Order of Merit €133,094

1994
- T-24 Open Championship, Turnberry
- T-4 Turespana Balearic Open, Majorca
- T-5 Honda Open, Gut Kaden
- 76th Order of Merit €100,766
- 1st Tenerife Open Pro-Am
- 1st North-east Golfer's Alliance, Turriff

1995
- Son, Craig born
- 1st Scottish PGA Masters, Downfield (played during a break from European Tour for Craig's christening)

- T-56 Open Championship, St Andrews
- 107th Order of Merit €74,985
- 1st Inchmarlo Golf Centre's Winter League title with Chippie's Gang!!!!

1996
- 1st Open Catalonia (€70,000)
- T-2 Volvo PGA Championship, Wentworth
- Broke into world top 100 golfers for first time (No. 98)
- 3rd World Cup, Cape Town, South Africa – represented Scotland with Andrew Coltart
- 21st Order of Merit €326,088

1997
- 52nd Order of Merit €165,087

1998
- Son, Michael born
- 62nd Order of Merit €149,939

1999
- 1st (play-off) 128th Open Golf Championship, Carnoustie (€490,000)
- 1st Qatar Masters €143,196
- T-34 US PGA Championship
- Ryder Cup, Brookline, USA (USA 14.5 Europe 13.5)
- Alfred Dunhill Cup
- 6th Order of Merit €901,453
- Honorary member of the European Tour
- The Tooting Bec Cup (lowest round in Open by a GB&I player)
- Braid Taylor Memorial Medal

2000
- T-5 WGC Accenture Matchplay
- World Cup
- Seve Trophy
- 26th Order of Merit €512,055
- 29th World Rankings (July – highest position)
- Awarded MBE in New Year Honours List
- Honorary Law Doctorate, Robert Gordon University

2001
- Founded Paul Lawrie Junior Golf

- 1st Dunhill Links Championship, St Andrews (€881,251, 63 (-9) – low round and course record)
- T-42 Open Championship, Royal Lytham and St Annes
- European Tour Shot of the Year
- 9th Order of Merit €1,428,831

2002
- 1st The Celtic Manor Resort Wales Open (€291,432) (course record 65 (-7))
- 2nd Italian Open Telecom Italia, Olgiata Golf Club (low round, 63 (-9))
- T-30 US Open
- T-59 Open Championship, Muirfield
- World Cup
- Seve Trophy (winners)
- 10th Order of Merit €1,151,434
- 1st Aberdeen Asset Management Scottish Matchplay Championship

2003
- T-15 Masters Tournament
- World Cup
- Seve Trophy (winners)
- 51st Order of Merit €477,248

2004
- 140th Order of Merit €98,122

2005
- T-52 Open Championship, St Andrews
- 1st Gleneagles Scottish PGA Championship
- 48th Order of Merit €468,680

2006
- Volvo China Open, Beijing Honghua International Golf Club (course record 67 (-5))
- 61st Order of Merit €394,034

2007
- Alfred Dunhill Links Championship, Carnoustie (course record 64 (-8))
- 72nd Order of Merit €422,510

2008
- 40th Order of Merit €679,530

2009
- T-47 Open Championship, Turnberry
- 82nd Order of Merit €379,258
- Royal Trophy, Thailand

2010
- T-6 BMW PGA Championship, Wentworth
- 69th Order of Merit €412,293

2011
- 1st Open de Andalucía de Golf by Turkish Airlines (€166,660)
- 2nd Dubai World Championship presented by DP World
- T-66 Open Championship, Royal St George's
- Barclays Scottish Open, Castle Stuart Golf Links (course record 64 (-8))
- 18th Order of Merit (€1,142,013)

2012
- 1st Commercialbank Qatar Masters presented by Dolphin Energy (€316,020)
- 9th – WGC Accenture World Match Play
- Semi-final Volvo World Matchplay Championship (my 500th European Tour Event)
- 2nd BMW PGA Championship
- T34 – Open Championship, Royal Lytham St Annes
- Tooting BEC Cup
- 1st Johnnie Walker Championship €296,119
- Ryder Cup, Medinah, USA (Europe 14.5 USA 13.5)